ETHNIC CONFLICT AND DEVELOPMENT:
THE CASE OF GUYANA

The United Nations Research Institute for Social Development (UNRISD) is an autonomous agency that engages in multi-disciplinary research on the social dimensions of contemporary problems affecting development. Its work is guided by the conviction that, for effective development policies to be formulated, an understanding of the social and political context is crucial. The Institute attempts to provide governments, development agencies, grassroots organisations and scholars with a better understanding of how development policies and processes of economic, social and environmental change affect different social groups. Working through an extensive network of national research centres, UNRISD aims to promote original research and strengthen research capacity in developing countries.

Its research themes include Crisis, Adjustment and Social Change; Socio-Economic and Political Consequences of the International Trade in Illicit Drugs; Environment, Sustainable Development and Social Change; Ethnic Conflict and Development; Integrating Gender into Development Policy; Participation and Changes in Property Relations in Communist and Post-Communist Societies; Refugees, Returnees and Local Society; and Political Violence and Social Movements. UNRISD research projects focused on the 1995 World Summit for Social Development included Rethinking Social Development in the 1990s; Economic Restructuring and New Social Policies; Ethnic Diversity and Public Policies; and The War-torn Societies Project.

A list of the Institute's free and priced publications can be obtained by writing: UNRISD, Reference Centre, Palais des Nations, CH-1211, Geneva 10, Switzerland.

This book forms part of a wider research project on Ethnic Conflict and Development sponsored by UNRISD. Covering 15 countries in Africa, South Asia, the Middle East, Central America and Eastern Europe, where ethnic conflicts have exploded with great intensity in recent years, the project is concerned with the nature of conflict among ethnic groups in the process of development, and with the implications of such conflict for the international relations of states. The origin and background of the conflicts are analysed, and the interests and motives of the major actors are explored; the relationship between particular conflicts and the broader development process is studied; and attention is given to the nature of external interests and to the internationalization of conflict. At same time, the project specifically attempts to provide comparative analysis of the solutions which have been set in place in different circumstances, including assessment of the procedures through which particular solutions have been found.

Ethnic Conflict and Development: The Case of Guyana

RALPH R. PREMDAS
Department of Government
The University of the West Indies
St Augustine, Trinidad and Tobago
and
Visiting Professor
Department of Political Science
University of Toronto
Toronto, Canada

Avebury

Aldershot • Brookfield USA • Hong Kong • Singapore • Sydney

Published by
Avebury
Ashgate Publishing Limited
Gower House
Croft Road
Aldershot
Hants GU11 3HR
England

Ashgate Publishing Company
Old Post Road
Brookfield
Vermont 05036
USA
Reprinted 1996

British Library Cataloguing in Publication Data

Premdas, Ralph R.
　　Ethnic Conflict and Development: Case of
　　Guyana – (Research in Ethnic Relations Series)
　　I. Title II. Series
　　305.8009881
ISBN 1 85628 995 8

Library of Congress Catalog Card Number: 95-78512

Printed in Great Britain by
Antony Rowe Ltd, Chippenham, Wiltshire

Contents

Figures and Tables

Abbreviations

AFL	American Federation of Labour
AIFLD	American Institute of Free Labour Development
ASCRIA	African Society for Cultural Relations with Independent Africa
BGLU	British Guyana Labour Union
BGTA	British Guyana Teachers Association
CSA	Civil Service Association
EIA	East Indian Association
FUGE	Federated Unions of Government Employees
GAWU	Guyana Agricultural Workers Union
GCC	Georgetown Chamber of Commerce
GIWU	Guyana Industrial Workers Union
ICFTU	International Confederation of Free Trade Unions
ICJ	International Commission of Jurists
LCP	League of Coloured Peoples
MAO	Movement Against Oppression
MPCA	Manpower Citizens' Association
MWU	Mine Workers Union
NPC	Negro Progress Convention
ORIT	Inter-American Regional Organisation of Workers
PAC	Political Affairs Committee
PNC	People's National Congress
PPP	People's Progressive Party
PYO	Progressive Youth Organisation
RPA	Rice Producers Association
SPA	Sugar Producers Association
TUC	Trade Union Council
TWG	The Weekly Gleaner

UF	United Force (Party)
WA	Women's Auxiliary
WFTU	World Federation of Trade Unions
WPA	Working Peoples Alliance
WPO	Women's Progressive Organisation
YSM	Young Socialist Movement

Preface

Guyana has become the classic case of an ethnic conflict which has degenerated to the point of pulverising and impoverishing the state. For some three decades, I have witnessed the steps and stages leading to this sad state of affairs and have written a series of essays on the evolution of the ethnic strife in Guyana. I was born in Guyana and came to know the conflict intimately. Even though I have left Guyana to conduct research on inter-ethnic relations in Fiji, Sri Lanka, Nigeria, Trinidad, and other places, I have stayed closely in touch with events in Guyana. My involvement was aimed not only at understanding the nature of the communal struggle and how it literally came to destroy what was once a relatively prosperous and peaceful country, but also in finding solutions. In this study, I have tried to document what factors and forces led to the ethnic explosion in Guyana. In the final chapter, I have attempted to identify the critical factors that seemed to have contributed most to the division of the two main communities into warring camps.

I have set forth what I call 'the Guyana anti-model' as a way to point out what not to do if almost total self-destruction is to be avoided in polyethnic states. The kinds of debilitating effects that tend to accompany intense ethnic strife are set forth in Part Two of the text. The Guyana case as portrayed in this work also shows what action must be taken if the fate of this small multi-ethnic Caribbean country is to be averted. For other countries bedevilled by communal divisions, the Guyana pathway must be eschewed at all costs.

Over the past three decades, I have benefited enormously from a large number of persons who have assisted me in many ways to understand the Guyana experience. Among these are Cynthia Enloe, R.S. Milne, Percy Hintzen, Paul Singh, Edward Dew, Raymond Gaskin, Lloyd Braithwaite, Ed Greene, Raymond Smith, M.G. Smith, P.K. Misra, Gregory Baum, Don Rothchild, Jeff Steeves, and Brinsley Samaroo. At the United Nations Institute for Social Development which convened a series of conferences to investigate the connection between ethnicity and development, I interacted with and benefited from the insights of several other scholars including Dharam Ghai, Rodolfo Stavenhagen, Crawford Young, Yusuf Bangura, Claude Ake, Valery Tishkov. Ashis Nandy, O. Nnoli, Y.V.Bromlei, and John Markakis. I must give special thanks to Anne Jayne who accompanied me on the first leg of field work on Guyana. To her and Justin, I have dedicated this effort.

For
Justin and Anne

Introduction: Ethnicity and Development

Julius Nyerere once remarked that ultimately, development is about what goes on in the head of the citizen, for it was under one's hat that exists the greatest under-developed part of the world (Nyerere, 1968). The social structure of the typical Third World is multi-ethnic. In the heads of citizens of this region are ethnic maps that are constituted of the many solidarity communities of the state, inter-group likes and dislikes, and scripts that guide the choice of friends and neighbours. These maps locate the identity of the citizen in the wider framework of the social order. They are critical, for they serve as the lenses through which not only friends and enemies are defined, but in the political world, they also serve to evaluate projects and programmes and the actions of governments in general. Indeed, the ethnic map also defines the very attitude that a citizen holds towards those who govern, imparting the government's legitimacy or illegitimacy and correspondingly, the citizens' willingness to co-operate or not with the ruling regime. The highest loyalty is to his solidarity group and not the state. Ethnic group consciousness, which suffuses the internalised map in the head, tends to emerge and manifest itself most acutely in the drive toward modernisation, bringing into contact and competition the diverse groups in the state, each seeking to claim its own rightful part of power and privileges. The ethnic map can be conducive either to inter-group trust or suspicion, thus positively or negatively affecting efforts aimed at the mobilisation of human and material resources for general welfare and development.

Because of the universal arousal of sectional consciousness, especially in the multi-ethnic states of the Third World, planned political change for development cannot succeed unless conceived through the prism of ethnicity (Enloe, 1973; Melson and Wolpe, 1970). Development change cannot follow a simple unilinear path driven by neutral factors such as capital and technology without being mediated through social processes, especially the recognition of

1

ethnic interests. The ethnic factor is a fundamental force in the Third World environment and must be incorporated into any strategy of development that is adopted. Ethnic pluralism cannot be ignored; it cannot be reduced to an epiphenomenon that will disappear when change transforms the environment. The ethnic factor is integral to the environment; it is at once both the subject and the object of change. If it is accepted that the ethnic variable is and must be an integral part of the process of planned change, then one would expect to find it occupying a central role in the many strategies of development that have been designed and implemented in the Third World. Yet, this is not the case. In the orthodox models of economic and political development from which strategies of change have been adopted for Third World transformation, the ethnic factor has generally been neglected. The obstacles that have been identified have come to define the nature of the development task. In the economic sphere, they are lack of capital, entrepreneurial and organisational expertise, infrastructure etc.; in the political realm, they are problems of participation, power, mobilisation, etc.; and in the social field, they focus on institutional structures, minimum standards of education, nutrition, maternity care, housing, etc. Different ideologies of development vary the salience and mixes of these factors in interpreting and facilitating change.

Regardless of whether it is founded on Marxist class analysis or capitalist *laissez-faire* market claims, interpretations of change for transformation tend to overlook or ignore the political-cultural claims of ethno-national groups, deeming these as residual factors which will in due course be assimilated or eliminated in the process of developmental change. The evidence against this de-emphasis of the ethno-cultural factor by the different ideologies is devastating. From Lebanon in the Middle East to Guyana on the South American continent, from Northern Ireland to Azerbaijan and Bosnia in Europe to Quebec in North America, from the Sudan and South Africa to Sri Lanka and Malaysia, the assertion of the ethnic factor has made a shambles of development objectives and social peace everywhere, on all continents, in both underdeveloped and industrialised societies. But particularly in the multi-ethnic states of the impoverished Third World, ethnic resurgence, like an unrestrained monster, has devastated all those promising plans for change, built on sophisticated economic and other models. The 'ethnic bomb', now exploded, has diverted enormous amounts of scarce resources from security and stability. From a neglected and peripheral factor, the ethnic variable has now emerged as one of the paramount forces of Third World change (Young, 1993; Stavenhagen, 1988; A.D. Smith, 1981).

The environment of cultural pluralism and ethnic diversity is now grudgingly, but generally, acknowledged as a critical variable that must be incorporated in designing new strategies for development. We know little about this factor, however, and only in a general way, not with the sort of sure-minded

2

confidence that goes with the manner in which an established body of knowledge is handled. The reason for this ambivalence is clear. Systematic knowledge of ethnicity in the operations of social structure and in particular, with reference to development, is desperately deficient. The ethnicity domain is a frontier which only recently received systematic exploration (Schermerhorn, 1970; Banton, 1967; Isaacs, 1975; Young, 1976; van den Berghe, 1967, 1978; Glaser, 1975; Barth, 1969; Esman, 1977; Enloe, 1973; Connor, 1972, 1973). Questions on the nature of this phenomenon are plentiful as settled answers are lacking. Many contemporary theorists and researchers are generating new insights into ethnic relations (Rex and Mason, 1986; Smith 1986; Hobsbawm, 1992; Young, 1993; Andersen, 1983; Breuilly, 1982; Hechter, 1985; Gellner, 1983; Armstrong, 1982; Banton, 1983; Keyes, 1981; Stone, 1977; Milne, 1982). There is urgent need to discuss the relationship between ethnicity and development in all its manifold political, economic, and social dimensions. The task is daunting; on its outcome may rest the fruitfulness of many designs of development involving billions of dollars and the fate of millions of poor people.

The aim of this work is to offer some empirical evidence and to generate some theoretical insights into the behaviour of the ethnic factor in the developmental experience of one Third World country. This effort has been undertaken in the belief that systematic data derived from individual case histories can offer important building blocks towards constructing a wider theory on the connection between ethnicity and development. The project was stimulated and sponsored by the United Nations Research Institute on Social Development which convened a group of scholars in the late 1980s and early 1990s to examine the issue. Each participant produced one or more works on the ethnicity factor in relation to development in the country of his/her expertise. This work is on Guyana. We must, however, begin with a discourse on and a definition of ethnicity.

Ethnicity refers to collective group consciousness, that is, a shared sense of identification with a larger community; it pertains to the perception that one shares a common identity with a particular group and is in turn so perceived by others. Ethnicity is akin to nationalism (Kohn, 1944; Hayes, 1948; Kedourie, 1960) and for this reason, ethnic consciousness may be referred to as ethno-nationalism so as to point to the fact that many states contain several sub-communities with a sense of consciousness distinct from other similar groups (Connor, 1972, 1973; Emerson, 1966; Premdas, 1977). The second component of ethnicity points to certain putative commonalities such as common language, religion, region, tradition, etc. or a multiple coincidence of several of these cleavages which together contribute to deep divisions in a state. Clifford Geertz referred to these factors as 'primordial' (Geertz, 1963:109). The primordial factors such as religion, race, language, custom, etc. may be

3

regarded as 'objective' features which underlie ethnic identity and facilitate collective consciousness (Premdas, 1993). It is not important that scientific evidence bear out the accuracy of group claims to these commonly apprehended bases of identity. Nor is it significant that the boundaries of these cleavages be consistently maintained. What is crucial, as Shibutani and Kwan noted, is that an ethnic group consists 'of those who conceive of themselves as being alike by virtue of their common ancestry, real or fictitious, and who are so regarded by others' (Shibutani and Kwan, 1965:47). Equally important to note is that ethnic boundaries are socially constructed and reproduced in relation to the symbolic and instrumental needs of a group. As Barth pointed out, they are almost entirely 'subjectively-held categories of ascription and identification by the actors themselves' (Barth, 1969). The maintenance of the boundaries is situationally determined, may shift over time and context, and generally serves to differentiate members dialectically and oppositionally from other groups in terms of 'we-they' antipathies.

The third feature of ethnicity refers the behavioural effects of this variant of group membership. Specifically, ethnic group membership, as a politically self-aware entity, confers symbolic solidarity satisfactions as well as instrumental and material advantages (Rothschild, 1981). The important point here is that ethnicity is a politically charged phenomenon whose consciousness is stimulated into existence by certain 'triggers' such as group contact, decolonisation, modernisation, and policy choices by the state which in turn precipitate defensive group quest as well as initiatives for symbolic and material gains. Consequently, ethnic group formation is expressed behaviourally as rival claims to those of other groups. Ethnic group identity is relational and conflictual. It is often marked in the pursuit of an objective by an intensity of emotion that is at once community-building when moderately expressed, and self-annihilating when fanatically followed (Young, 1993). Ethnic solidarity sentiments bear their own internal logic and are compelled by their own formative needs, but once they pick up momentum, they can rarely be denied. To some, they are is a marauding monster, while to others they embody the finest creative spirit of a community. Such sentiments can easily ignite into uncontrollable violence, completely out of proportion to the rational goals that impelled them to act in the first place. Critical to this phenomenon from a behavioural perspective, is the element of comparison and competition that is found in the irrational behaviour of ethnic groups. Social psychologist Henry Tajfel pointed to the propensity for group loyalty to be sustained intensely and irrationally not for 'greater profit in absolute terms' but in order 'to achieve relatively higher profit for members of their in-group as compared with members of the out-group' (Tajfel, 1970). Ethnic groups are, however, not always negative social entities, as their well-reported outbursts suggest. They are more frequently very rational bodies which act as pressure groups in pursuit of the programmatic interests of their members. They may seek limited ends following legal procedures and provide a host of solidarity services for their members (Horowitz, 1985).

This book consists of two parts. Part I deals with the evolution of ethnic politics in Guyana. It commences by tracing the origins of Guyana's multi-ethnic structure from colonial conquest, when the indigenous population was subdued, to resettlement by an influx of Europeans, Africans, and Asians. In the creation of the state, the different ethnic components were separated residentially, occupationally, and culturally. The multiple cleavages of race, religion, residence, and culture reinforced each other and, in the context of a colonial policy of divide and rule, the divisions became deep and persistent. The colonial state was ethnically riven and, with the communal clusters deeply distrustful of each other and sharing few institutions, a legacy was bequeathed which would come to bedevil efforts at nation-building in the post-colonial era. Following World War II, in the wake of a world-wide movement towards decolonisation, democratic politics on a mass scale were introduced to Guyana. Except for a brief period, this led to the formation of ethnically-based parties which competitively mobilised the mutually distrustful communal segments against each other. Organised down to the grassroots, the communally-bound parties appealed to ethnic fears and exacerbated the divisions, bringing the state to the brink of civil war.

Ethnic politics became embedded, defining the direction of political change from the promise of democracy to the seizure of power by one of the ethnic communities. How communal politics would evolve was not entirely predictable. When universal adult suffrage was conceded and mass parties emerged, there first appeared a multi-ethnic independence movement that successfully mobilised majority support from the main ethnic sections in the population. Under a collaborative communal leadership, the state seemed safely launched in the direction of development, without much worry about the assertion of divisive ethnic sectionalism to distract it from its purpose. This optimistic prospect was torpedoed however, when the two main communal leaders, jockeying for leadership of the independence movement, parted company and created rival parties which appealed to primordial passions for support. This unleashed collective communal forces which dictated the direction of politics thereafter. How this occurred is traced out in the first part of this work, underscoring the role of the zero-sum aspects of the inherited electoral and parliamentary system; the pursuit of private ambition by the communal leaders; partisan organisation and appeals for votes at the grassroots; and the role of foreign intervention. In the end, a rigid, ethnically bipolar state became a reality, eventuating in virtual civil war, the rigging of elections and the seizure of the state by one of the two communally-bound parties. Divided, the state could hardly undertake effective programs for

5

development. The economy was organised so that there was a ethnic division of labour, with each of the major communal groups in virtual control of one or the other vital components in the productive process. Inter-ethnic co-operation was dictated by this economic organisation of complementary parts; this meant that each section had the capability to wreak havoc on the whole economy by withdrawing its support. This, in fact, occurred. The public will was crippled and those who governed lacked cross-sectional legitimacy. Those who were defeated in elections, which were conducted as total communal wars, tended to withdraw from national efforts aimed at development and instead resorted to strikes, boycotts, and even sabotage. The pattern is a familiar one in multi-ethnic states which inherited a form of institutional politics based on zero-sum competition for control of the state. The Guyana case offers a detailed picture of how this occurred.

Additionally, the Guyana case illustrates the phenomenon of the partial transmutation of ethnic politics to an interesting admixture of ethnic and class politics, as the state became steeply impoverished and the ruling regime victimised all overtly dissenting sections of the society, including its own erstwhile communal supporters. The ethnically-based ruling party, the Peoples' National Congress under Forbes Burnham, by seizing power and regularly rigging elections, was no longer accountable to anyone but itself and a small strategic elite that was in part inter-ethnic in composition. Did in fact a new class-oriented regime emerge from the foundation of an ethnically-mobilised base? At one level, this did occur but at another level the regime, invoking the fear of ethnic domination, continued to rely overwhelmingly on its own communal section for continued mass support. It ruthlessly dealt with challengers such as Walter Rodney, who had sought to re-align the ethnic bases of partisan support towards class mobilisation. Did Rodney actually succeed in shifting the axis of politics away from ethnic sentiment? The evidence showed that even his own growing support erected around the Working People's Alliance relied on the ethnic endorsement of the Indian-based Peoples' Progressive Party, so that there was no melting away of primordial sentiments into a new mode of rational political organisation. The Guyanese were caught under two motivations, ethnic identity and class, and responded to each circumstantially, seeming at times more inclined to yield to class interests but more frequently to ethnic bonds. This dissonant tension was put to a test in the early 1990s with the return of open competitive elections. After two decades of intense suffering from the ravages of polarised ethnic politics, it could have been reasonably expected that the Guyanese people would disengage from the politics of ethnic affiliation and mobilisation. Ethnic solidarity however, dies hard if ever. The old, discredited, communal monster had returned in a new flowering of party formations, and attempts to restrain it did not succeed.

In the final chapter of Part I, the 1992 elections are examined and the initial days of the new regime are compared with the antecedent regime for the role of ethnic appeals in the attempt to restore national unity. For this to succeed, the new rulers acceding to power needed to operate a cross-communal reconciliation system based on the accommodation of rival ethnic claims. Assimilation and integration are not realistic policies or options. The ethnic factor does not lose the identity spots of its leopard skin. New viable political orders, the Guyana case suggests, must be ethnically multi-layered reconciliation systems if they are to succeed.

Part II consists of critical reflection and systematic analysis of the Guyana data in relation to the issue of development. In general, a plethora of inter-related problems is directly and indirectly probed, especially issues related to ethnic formation, ethno-nationalist politics, and modes of ethnic resolution. In particular, the pivotal problem of development and its connection to ethno-nationalist politics is emphasised. The social, economic, cultural, psychological, and political ramifications of persistent ethnic conflict are probed. The development aspects of ethnic conflict will, however, require greater systemic treatment as this dimension of sectional strife is placed under more minute screening from case to case around the world. As other scholars probe more comprehensively into the development dimension, the data from several case histories should provide a rich load of materials that could yield important and more precise insights into the enigma of development in this context of the multi-ethnic milieu. The final chapter not only recapitulates the central arguments of the book, but looks at the options available for the resolution of the ethnic conflict, not only in Guyana but in other multi-ethnic societies caught in the vice of ethnic strife.

Part I
THE GUYANA CASE

I   The Making of a Multi-Ethnic State

The Ethnic Segments

Guyana is a multi-ethnic Third World state situated on the north-coast shoulder of South America. Although geographically part of the South American land mass, culturally it falls within the Caribbean insular sphere marked by plantations, monocrop economies, immigrant settlers, and a colour-class system of stratification (Wagley, 1960). The country is populated by six ethnic solidarity clusters – Africans, East Indians, Amerindians, Portuguese, Chinese and Europeans. A significant 'mixed' category also exists, consisting of persons who have any combination of the major groups. Racial and ethnic categories are apprehended in a rather peculiar way among Guyanese. In the popular imagination, everyone is placed within a communal category which, as anthropologist Raymond Smith has noted, 'is believed to be a distinct physical type, an entity symbolised by a particular kind of "blood"' (R.T. Smith, 1976:205).

Table 1.1: Ethnic Distribution of the Guyanese Population

Ethnic Group	Per Cent of Total
Indians	51.4
Africans	30.5
Mixed Races	11.0
Portuguese and Europeans	1.2
Chinese	0.2
Amerindians	5.3

Source: Ministry of Information: *1980 Census*, Georgetown.

11

Hence, even though objectively there exists a wide array of racial mixtures, a person is soon stereotyped into one of the existing social categories to which both 'blood' and 'culture' are assigned a defining role. From this, a society of ethno-cultural compartments has emerged with various forms of inter-communal antagonisms of which the African-Indian dichotomy dominates all dimensions of daily life (Premdas, 1994).

Nearly all of Guyana's 850,000 people are concentrated on a 5 to 10 mile belt along the country's 270-mile Atlantic coast. The multi-ethnic population is loosely integrated through an indigenous Creole culture which has evolved from the admixture of experiences of the immigrant population during the last two hundred and fifty years of Guyanese history. Sub-cultural patterns of consciousness are dominant in identity formation, even while social integrative institutions are not entirely non-existent. In moments of inter-ethnic confrontation and conflict, the strong sub-cultural patterns threaten to burst the society asunder at its ethnic seems. The inter-play of integrative centripetal institutions such as commonly shared schools, along with the fissiparious ethnic cultural features such as different religious faiths, have created a split national personality.

The origin of the Guyanese immigrant people can be traced to the first efforts at New World colonisation by European explorers. Columbus reportedly sailed past the Guyana coast in 1498. More interestingly, the Pilgrim Fathers 'decided after some discussion of Guyana as an alternative, to sail for New England' (Smith, 1962:13). The entire area stretching from the Orinoco River to the Amason, called the 'wild coast' which includes the Guyanas, came at one time or another under the purview of the French, Dutch, and British explorers. All three states represented by the explorers claimed the area, but none could settle or control more than a small part at a time. In the early seventeenth century, the British started a settlement in Surinam, the French established two settlements in French Guyana and, most importantly in the context of our discussion, the Dutch planted settlements at various points of what is today called Guyana.

The Dutch were the first European settlers; they established a network of trading depots in Guyana's interior. They bartered with the Amerindians, the indigenous inhabitants of Guyana, exchanging trinkets and other trading goods for cotton, dyes, and wood. 'As the importance of this trade declined, increasing attention was paid to the production on small plantations, of tobacco, coffee, and indigo, and lastly on a large scale, of sugar' (Report, 1950:3). As a consequence, the Dutch moved away from the country's sandy interior to the rich alluvial coastland where plantation production of coffee, cotton, and sugar was inaugurated.

Importation of Africans, East Indians, Portuguese, Chinese, and 'poor Whites' into Guyana resulted from the nature of the plantation system. Trading and

12

peasant farming, in which the early Dutch settlers engaged, did not require substantial numbers of labourers. With the introduction of tobacco, cotton, and sugar cultivation on a plantation scale however, massive amounts of cheap labour became necessary. The Dutch began plantation production in the seventeenth century. When they were finally evicted by the British in 1803, the dominant economic organisation of the colony was the plantation. By 1829, 230 sugar plantations, and 174 coffee and cotton estates existed in Guyana (Despres, 1967). Under the British, cotton and coffee did not enjoy preferential prices, so they quickly succumbed to North American competition. By 1849, only 16 coffee and cotton plantations remained of the 174. Sugar production became the dominant economic activity in Guyana. Indeed, Guyana was little more than a huge sugar plantation.

In the Caribbean, including Guyana, the establishment of plantations corresponded to the introduction of massive numbers of African slaves. Slavery was an economic phenomenon. 'A change in the economic structure produced a corresponding change in the labour supply' (Williams, 1964). Africans were not the first, nor the only people to be enslaved, for the Amerindians and 'Poor Whites' had been experimented with earlier. Because Europeans often engaged in the Amerindian slave trade throughout the new world in general, aboriginal Indian populations dwindled, succumbing to the excessive labour demanded of them (Saunders, 1969). The immediate successors to the Amerindians were the 'Poor Whites' (Rodway, 1912). However, these were not numerous, nor were they as robust in enduring plantation life as Africans. Besides, they came on short indentures, while slaves were permanent chattels. The inadequacy of Amerindian and 'Poor White' labour for the rigorous tasks of plantation life led to the recruitment of African slaves.

When Africans came to Guyana, therefore, two principal 'ethnic' groups were already in the country, the Amerindians and the Europeans. The Europeans, who were predominantly planters and settlers, controlled nearly all of the colony's wealth and power which centred in sugar production. They owned and controlled all the sugar plantations on which both slaves and indentured labourers worked. In the political sphere, the Europeans sat in the existing colonial decision-making body, the Court of Policy, and controlled the finances of the colony through their permanent majority in the Combined Court. Not surprisingly, through the nineteenth century, colonial policy was formulated and instituted almost invariably to promote the interest of sugar producers.

European economic and political influence was not challenged until the twentieth century. When sugar was King and ruled an exclusive plantation empire, the power and prestige of the white planters were at their highest. During and after World War I, the growth and development of rice production and the bauxite industries contributed to a gradual erosion of the sugar industry's importance in the colony, as did the appearance of alternative sources of sugar, such as beet. The number of sugar estates declined from 157 in 1870, to 16 in the 1960s (Jayawardena, 1963). While the sugar industry monopolised nearly all of the labour market in the nineteenth century, by 1968 only 16, 925 labourers from a population of over half a million people were directly employed on sugar estates (Report, 1968a).

During the nineteenth century, the planters paid most of the colony's tax revenues; for the period from 1960 to 1966, the sugar industry contributed an average of only 7.4 per cent of government revenue (Ibid.). Until 1891, the planters were the only representatives of local interest in the colonial policy-making bodies, the Court of Policy and the Combined Court. In the 1950s and 1960s, with the introduction of universal adult suffrage and the granting of national independence, political power passed into the hands of representatives of the majority of the people.

The decline of the sugar industry's relative strength has decreased but not eliminated the overwhelming powerful role that the Europeans once played in Guyanese society. The sugar industry is still considered a mainstay of the country's economy; it accounts for 50 per cent of all exports, and employs more people weekly than any other industry (Ibid.). Accordingly, in Guyana the influence of persons of European stock is still strong, although not as visible and ubiquitous as in colonial days. Nearly all of the Europeans (about 0.57 per cent of the total population) in and out of the sugar industry-held top echelon, high-paying executive positions. They live mainly in exclusive residential areas, and in guarded enclaves on sugar estates (Report, 1965a). Strict adherence to traditional European living patterns characterises these settlements.

The persistence of European economic and political power for over three centuries has left permanent marks on Guyanese social structure. A pervasive colour-class stratification has evolved and permeates every stratum of Guyanese society:

> Things English and 'white' were valued highly whilst things African and 'black' were valued lowly ... the ability to speak properly, to dress properly, and to be able to read and write were all marks of prestige defined with reference to 'English' culture (Smith, 1956:191-263).

Partly because the various kinds of skills were bound up in status situations, and partly on a racial basis, the colour-class continuum of differentiation established the basis for the allocation of jobs, offices and prestige. As late as the 1950s this stratification system was virtually unaltered (Braithwaite, 1953). The nationalist movement, which gathered force in the early 1950s, and subsequent independence in 1966, witnessed a gradual replacement of the colour ascriptive norm by achievement criteria in the general allocation of values. The colour-class system has not been completely eradicated, so that in contemporary Guyana a dual system of values distribution now operates, with colour-class ascriptive values operating side-by-side with emerging achievement norms.

The Amerindians, who also preceded the arrival of Africans, are the descendants of the original people of Guyana. When the first colonist arrived, there were 19 tribes with about 700,000 Amerindians (Saunders, 1969). In 1969, the Amerindian Land Commission estimated the number of Amerindians as 32,203 living in 138 communities. They have been classified into two residential groups, coastal and interior, of almost equal numbers. On the Atlantic coast live the Arawaks, Waraos, and Caribs; in the interior, along the border with Venezuela and Brazil in the Rupnuni Savannahs live seven tribes : the Akawaio, Arakuna, Macusi, Wapisiana, and Waiwai. Amerindians for the most part still live in small villages with populations ranging from 100 to 1000. The life-style for many of them is still semi-nomadic, with an economy based on shifting slash-and-burn agriculture (Ibid.; Cullen, 1948). Most however, live in stable villages and communities and a small number have intermarried with descendants of the immigrants.

Prior to the emancipation of slaves in 1833, the Dutch and British colonists traded with the Amerindians, enslaved some, and utilised others for the capture of runaway slaves and the suppression of slave rebellions. In 1793, the Dutch prohibited Amerindian slavery. However, the Amerindians continued to live mainly outside the framework of the plantation society that was being erected by the Europeans, and were paid to capture run-away slaves and suppress slave rebellions. After slavery was abolished in 1807 and the fear of slave revolts had been removed, the Amerindians were neglected (Daly, 1966; Menezes, 1973; Saunders, 1987). Subsequently, they played only a peripheral role in directing and developing Guyanese society. In 1910, the colonial government promulgated an 'Aboriginal Indian Protection Ordinance' under which Amerindians were assigned to twelve reservations. This physical isolation contributed immensely to the retarded integration of Amerindians into Guyanese Creole culture. Missionary activities, the major remaining external force that impinged on the Amerindians, were the main contact that the Amerindians maintained with the coast. The Christian missionaries, who were brought from England, partly acculturated the Amerindians to British norms and behaviour.

In 1902, the Amerindians Protection Ordinance created exclusive reserves for Amerindian residence. A 1951 revision of the 'Aboriginal Indians Protection Ordinance' officially established ten reservations and incorporated the reservations into the country-wide local government mainstream of coastal living-patterns. Assimilation became the official policy under the Peberdy Commission of 1948. The measure failed to achieve its aim, however, since the Amerindian tribes had already developed their own identities and living patterns. Anglicisation of the Amerindians by the British missionaries did not prevent the rest of the population from regarding Amerindians as a separate group. In fact this served partly to isolate the reservations from the coastal multi-racial population. About half of Guyana's 32,000 Amerindians are literate and many speak a British form of English. Many of these Amerindians consider themselves as and identify with 'Whites' however, and nearly all of them regard themselves as separate from the coastal peoples. There is strong evidence that the Amerindians' consciousness of themselves as separate groups led to the development of a form of 'Amerindian ethno-nationalism' (Saunders, 1987). The most dramatic expression of this consciousness of a separate identity occurred in January 1969, when certain Amerindian tribes in the southern Rupununi Savannahs unsuccessfully attempted to secede from Guyana and join Venezuela. Generally, Amerindians remain outside the mainstream of Guyanese life.

Africans were carried to Guyana to meet the heavy demands for labour created by the establishment of plantations. African slaves, relatively inexpensive and well-adjusted to the rigors of plantation life, were brought as chattel and allotted to the plantations along the 270-mile coast of Guyana. For centuries, the planters prospered by virtue of the continued supply of African slave labour. In 1807, the British slave trade with Africa was halted. Agitation by anti-slavery groups in England succeeded not only in terminating the slave trade, but also set in motion a series of events which culminated in the abolition of slavery in the colonies in 1833. The 'Imperial Abolition Act of 1833' released the slaves from compulsory labour in phases. Only slaves who were six years of age or younger in August, 1834, were freed immediately. All others were 'apprenticed' until August, 1838, when they were completely emancipated. The planters secured this concession, plus a compensation of £4,297,117, 10 shillings, 6½ pence for the loss of 84,915 slaves, as a means of preparing for the anticipated loss of labour to occur after 1838 (Smith, 1962).

The planters feared an economic collapse of the entire colony since 'in 1838 ... sugar production was much more the backbone of British Guyana than it is today' (Young, 1958:7). After the expiration of the apprenticeship period, 'the first thought of the Negro ... was to desert the plantation' and set himself up independently 'where land was available' (Williams, 1964:28). In Guyana, land was abundant, so most emancipated Africans who left the plantations either squatted on the open spaces or bought their own land. The majority of the planters, with the aid of the Government, attempted to keep the Africans on the plantations by raising the price of land and by initiating legislation that prohibited squatting (Young, 1958:10). The administration of the anti-squatting laws was hopelessly ineffective because of 'the boundless extent of the colony' (Farley, 1954:95). Some planters went so desperately far as to cut down fruit trees which contributed to the livelihood of the emancipated Africans, in order to encourage their return to the plantations. Not all planters, however, resorted to such extreme actions to coerce the Africans back to the plantations. The more far-sighted of them made plots of farm land contiguous to the plantations available to the ex-slaves. By this strategy, they successfully retained the labour of the many Africans who ordinarily would have deserted the plantation altogether (Young, 1958).

While the end of the apprenticeship period did not immediately produce a complete exodus of Africans from the plantations, it did trigger 'the most spectacular and aggressive land settlement movement in the history of the people of the Caribbean' (Farley, 1954:98). Many ex-slaves banded together and purchased abandoned coffee and cotton estates. At the end of the 'Free Village Movement,' which lasted for a decade (1838-1848), twenty-five communal villages had been established (Young, 1958). Individual plots of about half to a third of an acre also were purchased in large quantities. In 1848, for example, over 7,000 small proprietary plots were purchased by individual Africans (Ibid.).

The 'Free Village Movement' culminated in 1848 with the establishment of over one hundred villages along the coast of Guyana where, in 1838, only two such villages had existed (Despres, 1967). Africans who remained on the sugar plantations in 1848 totalled 19,939; at the same time, their population in villages and various settlements stood at 44,456 (Young, 1958).

Part of the continued exodus of Africans from the sugar estates was accelerated by labour strikes in 1841 and 1846-1847, which were caused by the reduction of plantation wages. Africans did not remain long in the villages; more than half of them moved to urban centres by the end of the nineteenth century. Several factors contributed to this new migration. The peculiar problems of drainage and irrigation of Guyana's sub-sea level coastland required large capital outlays to cultivate successfully. The ex-slaves literally had expended all their savings to purchase lands and were left with little for capital improvements and maintenance. To compound this difficulty, the Africans, after centuries of plantation life, had 'no tradition of village organisation or local government to solve the problems of land management' (Despres, 1967:49).

As villages fell into disrepair, few Africans returned to the sugar plantations, for their place was taken gradually by the arrival of indentured labourers. Government activities in urban centres were proliferating to cope with the administrative complexity of post-emancipation Guyana, however. Employment in urban centres attracted many Africans who, at this time, were the non-European group most capable of filling the government vacancies.

Migration to the cities proceeded apace; by 1891 Africans constituted about 47.19 per cent of the colony's urban population. Between 1900 and 1965, the African population as a percentage of urban dwellers stabilised at roughly 50 per cent (Report, 1965a). Africans who have remained in villages constituted about 20 per cent of the total village population; most live in predominantly African villages. African plantation population declined from 11.3 per cent in 1891 to 6.8 per cent in 1960 (Ibid., p.165). In 1960 the totally African sector amounted to 183,950 persons, or 32.83 per cent of the total population (Ibid., p.174). Paralleling their concentration in urban centres, Africans increasingly provided the staff for government service. 'By 1950, the Africans dominated every department of the Civil Service' (Despres, 1967:52). In 1960, some 73.5 per cent of the Security Forces, 53.05 per cent of the Civil Service, 62.29 per cent of the Government Agencies and Undertakings, and 58.87 per cent of teachers in primary education were Africans (Report, 1965a).

The ascendancy of Africans to positions of dominance in the Guyanese governmental bureaucracy was substantially due to their adoption of British cultural patterns. Centuries of close contact with Europeans, urban dwellings, ready attendance at British schools, all contributed to make this possible. The absorption of British values and norms by Africans generally have ensured their relatively high prestige among the non-white population in Guyana. While the Africans have not become 'cultured' of 'Fine English men and women', they have evolved a Creole variant of British ways which is adequate to maintain their 'English' status. 'Creole Culture,' as the local English variant was called, is an intermixture of indigenous experiences with British ways. It is characterised overtly by 'broken English', Western clothes, and attendance at English-type schools and churches. In the eyes of most non-white native Guyanese, it is at best a corruption of British ways (Singer and Araneta, 1967).

Contemporary Guyanese nationalism has tried to elevate Creole culture to a position of dignity by stressing its indigenous creation, but neither nationalism nor post-Independence pride has eradicated the British-oriented biases which Creole culture implicitly accepts. This includes the acceptance of the colour-class stratification system which relegates blackness to a position of inferiority.

No group more effectively demonstrates the operating nuances of the colour-class stratification system than the 'Coloureds'. This mixed category is mainly the product of European-African miscegenation, although mixes of any light skinned group with persons of African descent could produce a person of 'colour'. Unlike the United States, in Guyana 'Coloureds' are not considered Negroes, but are perceived as and treated as a separate group. Their relatively light skin has placed them in an intermediate position in the social status system, provide them with greater educational opportunities, and has generally accorded them intermediate white collar and administrative jobs. The very

18

light skinned 'Coloured' is likely to occupy a position of greater responsibility and pay than a 'Coloured of medium light pigmentation. Nearly all 'Coloureds' are privileged, English-speaking, and enjoy middle to upper middle class socio-economic status. 'Coloureds' act and behave as a separate group, although many still identify with the Europeans in economic and political matters. 'Coloureds' constitute about 11.99 per cent of the total population, live mainly in urban centres, and are dispersed occupationally in the Civil Service, the professions, and businesses (Report, 1965a).

Labour shortages following emancipation of the Africans explain the addition, after 1833, of Chinese, Portuguese and Indians (from the Indian subcontinent, including Hindus and some Muslims) to the already existing ethnic groups in Guyana. The anticipated dearth of labour after the freeing of the slaves prompted the planters to seek new sources of manpower. Once again, the Old World was tapped. Between 1835 and 1840, experiments were made with small batches of German, Portuguese, Irish, English, Indian and Maltese labourers (Smith, 1962). During 1853, even Chinese were tried. In the end, Indians proved most adaptable, economical, and available, although Chinese and Portuguese immigrants trickled in for over half a century. Nearly all the Indians, Portuguese, and Chinese who were imported to replace African slaves came under contract indentures that required their labour for a five year period.

The first batch (396) of Indians arrived in the colony during May, 1838. With the exception of a brief interruption in the early 1840s, Indian immigration continued at the average pace of two or three shiploads annually, until the indentureship system was abolished in 1917 (Jayawardena, 1966). Between 1838 and 1917, approximately 238,960 Indian indentured labourers arrived in Guyana (Nath, 1950). An additional 707 Indians were imported as free settlers between 1917 and 1926 (R.T. Smith, 1959). At the expiration of their indentures, nearly two-thirds of the colony's Indian population opted to remain as permanent residents.

Under the indentureship system, the Indians endured great hardship, for 'coolie' labour suffered as much as 'slave labour.' There was one notable difference however. The indenture was for five years, while the condition of slavery was permanent. When their indentures were over, Indians could opt to return home. Between 1843 and 1845 alone, more than 75,700 Indians returned to India on official repatriation schemes (Smith, 1962). A majority of the Indians remained. However, most of these reindentured themselves. Reindentured labourers were offered an incentive of G$50 plus half the cost of their return passage to India at the end of their second indenture (Jayawardena, 1963).

Indians who remained in Guyana at first continued some sort of association with the sugar plantations. Many acquired farm land contiguous to the estates in exchange for giving up their contractual right to return to India. Gradually, however, many Indians moved away from the sugar estates, first sharing their labour between their farm plots and the plantation, then turning completely to peasant farming, often on lands separate from the plantations. By 1881, out of a total Indian population of 79,929, 34 per cent lived outside the plantations. A series of Indian villages sprang up, mainly within a radius of ten to fifteen miles of plantation lands. By 1911, the gradual but steady movement of Indians away from the plantations resulted in less than half of them remaining on the sugar estates but, significantly for this study, only 5.7 per cent gravitated to urban centres. To put it differently, in 1911, about 94 per cent of all Indians were rural dwellers and this residential pattern continued without much change right up to the 1960s. By 1946, the Indian outflow from the sugar estates left only a third of this population sector as plantation residents, but the Indian urban percentage had increased only to 9.9 per cent. In the 1960s, 25.5 per cent of the Indian population was on the sugar plantations, 13.4 per cent in urban centres, with the remaining 61.1 per cent found in villages. Guyana's Indians are therefore predominantly rural dwellers, living mainly in Indian villages and on-land adjacent to the sugar plantations.

The Indian peasantry residing in villages developed the colony's rice industry. Throughout the nineteenth century, Guyana relied on a one-crop sugar economy for survival. The fortunes of the colony fluctuated with the varying prices for sugar on the world market. Indian farmers had cultivated rice in the nineteenth century, but in small quantities and on small plots. But 'it was during the depression of the late eighties and nineties, when the sugar estates' demand for labour was not so pressing, that rice began to assume its importance as a cash crop' (Newman, 1964:31). Rapid growth of commercial rice production resulted in the attainment of domestic self-sufficiency by 1905 (Ibid.). World War I created new international demands for Guyana's rice, so that exports grew steadily. In the early twentieth century the rice production expanded to such proportions that by the 1960s it occupied most of the arable land on the coast and provided a livelihood directly for 45,000 families, and for 200,000 persons indirectly (*Rice Review*, 1965:11). Commercial rice growing for some time was the only major privately managed enterprise in Guyana that was locally owned.

The domination of the prosperous rice trade by Indians established the main economic basis for their upward mobility and improved status. Indians, known for their thrift, invested their savings in small businesses and in the education of their children. Increasingly after the First World War, they began to compete for places in the civil service and the teaching profession, but prior to World War II Indian participation in the governmental bureaucracies was negligible. According to the 1931 census, Indians 'constituted 8.08 per cent of all persons in the public service and nearly half of them were in the lower grades such as messengers. Out of 1,397 teachers only 100 were Indians ...'

(Smith, 1962:112). By 1964, when Indians constituted slightly over half the country's population, their social, political and economic condition had improved so dramatically that they constituted 33.16 per cent of the Civil Service, 27.17 per cent of government agencies and undertakings, and 41.49 per cent of teachers in primary education (Report, 1962b:33).

The involvement of many Indians in the governmental bureaucracy points to their assimilation of at least some British values. Generally Indians speak a broken form of English and wear Western-type clothes; they have been partly 'creolised' (Skinner, 1960:904-912). But this should not distract attention from the persistence of a sub-culture of Indian norms in Guyana (Despres, 1967:58). The overwhelming majority of Indians dwell in rural areas and display certain distinctive patterns of living that set them apart in significant ways from their non-Indian compatriots. Most Indians worship in Hindu temples and Muslim mosques, marry according to Hindu and Muslim rites, celebrate Hindu and Muslim festivals, and practise their respective religious rituals. Besides, Indian family practices require Indians to marry Indians, thus perpetuating existing Indian traditional patterns. Indians not only regard themselves as a separate community in Guyana, but are perceived by other Guyanese as a distinct entity.

Portuguese were also imported as indentured labourers to serve on plantations. Between 1834 and 1890, the period of Portuguese immigration, over 32,000 Portuguese from Madeira arrived in Guyana. Many Portuguese returned home with savings after serving their indentures, but most stayed in the colony. Those who remained immediately abandoned the estates and entered the retail trades. Within a few years following the termination of their indenture, the Portuguese literally dominated the retail trades (Smith, 1962:45). By 1851, out of 296 shops licensed to Georgetown, 173 belonged to Portuguese; in New Amsterdam 28 out of 52; in the rural areas, 283 out of 432 (Ibid.:43-44). Part of the Portuguese success was attributed to the preferential treatment they received. Portuguese obtained credit from Europeans, but Africans did not. As a result, many Africans were driven out of the retail business, and Afro-Portuguese hostilities naturally ensued. In 1856, 'practically every Portuguese shop in the country was destroyed' by rioting Africans (Young, 1958:51-53). The Portuguese were compensated by a Registration Tax which was designed to fall primarily on African peasants (Ibid.). Similar Afro-Portuguese hostilities occurred in 1889 and 1905.

The Portuguese did not remain in the petty retail business, which in the twentieth century was taken over by Indians and Chinese. They gradually moved to urban centres, where they diversely engaged in pawnbroking, the professions and big business. From the status of indentured labourers, they have moved to occupy upper-middle to upper-class positions in Guyanese society. This despite the fact that Portuguese constitute a very small part of the population after large numbers migrated from Guyana in the 1960s and 1970s. The Portuguese immigrant came to Guyana with a culture different from the prevailing one. Although he was white, his alien ways, Catholic religion, indentured condition, and subsequent petty shop-keeping activities denied him the high status that most other Europeans were accorded. He was generally despised partly because he 'lived in such a different manner to the "white" gentleman' (Smith, 1962:45).

Low status was the condition of every recently-arrived immigrant group and the Portuguese was no exception. The main difference was that the Portuguese caucasoid phenotypic features potentially prepared him to occupy a high position in the existing class-colour system. The Portuguese eventually acquired English culture, education and wealth, and entered 'the higher status group with relative ease' (Ibid.). In contemporary Guyana, the Portuguese section of the population enjoys social status next to the Europeans. Nearly all Guyanese, however, differentiate between the Portuguese (derisively pronounced 'Potagee') and his European counterpart, partly because of the stigma of the indentured past. Moreover, the Portuguese do not enjoy the same measure of isolation as the Europeans. They interact daily with ordinary non-white Guyanese and have absorbed many Creole norms. Nevertheless, the Portuguese community in Guyana regards itself and conducts most of its social life as a separate group.

Chinese were the last of the indentured labourers brought to Guyana. The first Chinese immigrants landed in 1853; by 1880, a total of only 13,533 had arrived (Fried, 1956:57). The largest number of Chinese to live in Guyana at any one time was in 1866, when there were about 10,000 in the colony (Ibid.:58). The Chinese population declined to its lowest level, 2,118, in 1910; slow gains increased their numbers to 3,528 in 1947, and to 4,074 in 1960. The marked decline of Chinese numbers immediately after their arrival underlined the extent to which they suffered in plantation Guyana. Following their indenture, the Chinese attempted in 1865 to establish an exclusive Chinese ethnic settlement in Hopetown. The effort failed, mainly because of soil exhaustion and the scarcity of women. By 1902, Hopetown disappeared as a Chinese settlement (Young, 1958:51-53).

The Chinese did not choose to stay with agriculture; most entered the petty retail business as shopkeepers. By 1960, about 72.2 per cent of them had moved to urban centres where they engaged mainly in the restaurant, laundry and supermarket businesses. A few Chinese also are found in the professions and the governmental bureaucracy. In fact, in the immediate post-independence period the Chinese were the only ethnic group in Guyana that had proportional representation in the governmental bureaucracy. They constituted 0.75 per cent of the total population and held 0.75 per cent of governmental positions (Report, 1965a:33).

Culturally, most Chinese in Guyana have only 'the skimpiest appreciation for the history and culture of China' (Fried, 1956:33). They speak English, wear Western clothes and are losing their Chinese names. Although their numbers have been replenished in recent years by immigrants from mainland China, their living patterns and economic activities appear comparable to urban Guyanese of similar socio-economic status. 'However, there remains a certain residuum of institutions, behaviour and values that mark them, perhaps not as Chinese in terms of Chinese culture, but as distinct from people who surround them. Perhaps the most important element of distinction is their self-recognition as a group and their action upon this recognition, a certain withdrawal from the total society and an explicit tendency to marry among themselves' (Ibid.). Most Chinese accept the colour-class system. They benefit from it on account of their clear skin and straight hair. The members of the Chinese community enjoy relatively high social prestige among other Guyanese as a result of their assiduous work habits, internal cohesion and high level of economic well-being.

Thus, then, would a multi-ethnic plural society be formed constituted of East Indians, Africans, Amerindians, 'Coloureds' (Mixed Races), Portuguese, Europeans and Chinese. (Table 1.1 gives the ethnic population distribution.) Slavery and indenture were the twin bases on which successful colonisation of the climatically harsh tropical coasts occurred. A workforce of culturally divergent immigrants was recruited to labour on plantations in the New World. The different patterns of residence, occupation and political orientations by the imported groups reinforced the original differences of the settlers laying from the inception of colonisation the foundations of Guyana's multi-ethnic politics. By the beginning of the twentieth century, certain features were clearly embedded in the social system. A communally-oriented multi-ethnic society was being fashioned and institutionalised. Several layers of cleavage appeared and reinforced each other. Hence, separating East Indians and Africans were religion, race, culture, residence and occupation. Multiple coinciding divergencies deepened the divisions without the benefit of a sufficiently strong set of countervailing integrative forces. To be sure, most immigrants participated in varying degrees in a commonly shared school system, national laws, colour-class stratification system and experiences in suffering. At an elementary level there was even a measure of shared cross-communal class unity at places where Indians and Africans worked such as certain factories or labour gangs. But these were few and far between. The trajectory of social organisation was firmly launched from the multi-layered foundations set in the colonial period. These patterns would be sustained by voluntary associations that were formed.

As the immigrants took roots in Guyana, they gradually developed voluntary associations to serve their specific interests. Prior to 1910, few voluntary associations existed; as the freed slaves and indentured immigrants stabilised around specific occupations and residential areas, they started to build community organisations to institutionalise their separate ways of life. By the 1920s, cultural organisations such as the League of Coloured Peoples, the East Indian Association, the Chinese Association and the Portuguese Club sprung up to cater to the social, cultural and religious needs of the several ethnic communities. This uni-ethnic pattern in the composition of voluntary associations has persisted to the present, extending to practically all kinds of clubs and groupings. The large economic organisations such as trade unions also became preponderantly uni-ethnic, like the cultural and religious organisations, so that they were individually identified by the public as belonging to the "Blackman", the 'Coolie', or the 'Potagee'. It is our contention here, that while it was almost inevitable that voluntary associations historically emerged predominantly uni-ethnic bodies, this very fact in turn reinforced ethnic exclusivism and exacerbated sectional divisions and fears. As mass political parties emerged after World War II, especially after 1955 when separate *de facto* Indian and African mass parties were launched, the voluntary associations would support and develop interlocking relationships with their *de facto* ethnically-based parties. Mainly because of this interlocking ethnic relationship between party and voluntary associations, race relations were intensified and the segregation in the polity deepened.

In addition to voluntary associations, the role of stereotypes accentuated inter-ethnic divisions between Indians and Africans. Typically, an Indian conceives of an African as (1) physically strong and powerful (most Indians being relatively small in stature as compared with most Africans). While this appears to be a positive stereotype with regard to the African's physical endowment, most Indians view the physical power of the African as a threat to their security. (2) The Indian sees the African as economically undisciplined. Indians view the high consumption habits of the African as irresponsible behaviour. Instead of saving some of the high earnings which come from good civil service and teaching jobs, as well as cane-cutting on the sugar estates, the African, as seen by the Indian, spends all his money on liquor, dances and good clothes. For the Indian, the 'economic extravagance' of the African accounts for the shabby houses in which many Africans live and the paucity of African businesses. In holding this economic stereotype of the Africans, Indians have failed to consider the numerous cases in their own villages and towns which attest to the economically conservative behaviour of many Africans. For Indians, the 'economic irresponsibility' stereotype is not peculiar to a segment of the African population, but is true of all Africans generally. (3) Indians view Africans as culturally inferior. Most Indians regard the wholesale adoption of 'British' ways by Africans as a mark of African inferiority. Although partly bastardised as Africans by British norms, Indians consider the

24

African inferior for not retaining any traits of his cultural heritage. Some cultural traits which obviously have been retained are not recognised by Indians or are condemned as 'juju' culture.

On the other hand, typically, Africans conceive of Indians as (1) physically weak and inferior. African disrespect of Indians substantially stems from the rather frail physical features of the Indian. Indians are 'dhal and rice coolies', a slur phrase which points to the frugal dietary habits of Indians, who generally eat split-peas, rice, vegetables and fish, but little meat. (Most Hindu Indians do not consume beef and Muslim Indians similarly do not consume pork; the African eats both.) (2) The African considers the Indians as miserly, that is, Africans view the Indian as a miserly person who sacrifices his dietary well-being and clothing habits for saving a few cents from every pay package. While this appears as a positive stereotype, most Africans view this (exaggerated) behaviour trait as a threat in the long run to the superior status of the African derived from the colonial social hierarchy which has accorded the lowest rung to the Indian. (3) The African holds the Indian culturally inferior quite as much as the Indian holds the African culturally inferior. Most Africans pride themselves on having acquired the English language and English norms (which in colonial British Guyana were the criteria for status and jobs), and regard the 'retarded' acquisition of English ways by Indians as a mark of the Indian's inferiority. Hence, Indians are frequently called, in a derogatory way, 'coolie babu' and Indians ways are called 'coolie custom'.

Thus would a deeply divided society emerge. The foundations of inter-ethnic rivalry were forged on the anvil of the colonial policy of immigration and 'divide and rule'. There was no evidence of any sort of inherent antipathy among the imported immigrants. It was, however, the manner in which colonial society was organised, stratified and exploited that triggered and sustained inter-communal fears and rivalries. There were few cross-communal integrative institutions. One observer noted that from the colonial authorities 'no serious effort was directed towards building institutions which could give cohesion and some measure of unity to the plantation mosaic' (Glasgow, 1970:35).

In an interdependent communal order, the political balance was held at the beginning of the twentieth century by a colonial government originating in conquest, maintained by coercion and perpetuated by a colour-class stratified order. The type of politics that was practised was distinguished by a repressive state apparatus that staffed the police mainly from one ethnic group (the African section) and thus by a policy of 'divide and rule' prevented inter-communal collaboration between the two largest ethnic sections from evolving. Representation in the colonial councils left most Guyanese disenfranchised. The only method of influence left open was 'representation by riot' (Bendix, 1969:77). To that we turn next to see how the ethnic groups organised to evict the colonial power and its implications for a just communal order.

II   The Structuring of Communal Identities

The logic of the communal society implanted in Guyana pointed to a future of inevitable sectional strife. Not only were many layers of fairly distinct communal divisions erected but, in the absence of equally strong, rival, overarching integrative institutions, the immigrant groups viewed each other from the perspective of their respective compartments with misinformed fear and much hostility. The colonial pie was small, most of it allocated to the governing European coloniser element occupying the top echelon of the colour-class- stratified system. Of the remaining jobs and other opportunities, the non-white segments fought among themselves for a share. African-Indian rivalry for the few scarce values of the colonial order would feature as a fundamental source of inter-communal conflict from the outset of the creation of the multi-tiered communal society. It would be sustained by a deliberate policy of divide and rule, but would be mitigated by the urban-rural pattern of residence, especially of Africans and Indians. What had evolved and assumed the pretensions of a society was, in reality, an order based on sustained and manipulated communal conflict without any prospect of overcoming these basic divisions in the foreseeable future. Institutionalised division and embedded conflict were the defining features of the system in perpetuity. Or so it seemed, even at the end of the nineteenth century.

The twentieth century would witness the unleashing of new forces which would erode and eliminate the seemingly permanently set colonial structures of dominance in Guyana. The mutual antagonisms shared among the subjugated ethnic elements would be diverted towards a unique opportunity to unite against the plantation society and its rulers. In particular, Indians and Africans, under the leadership of sectional charismatic leaders acting in unison under the umbrella of the same political party, would commence a shared struggle to uproot the colonial oppressors. Against the trajectory of a divided society consigned to perpetual internal strife dominated by a manipulative

27

coloniser, a new tidal force of unity was unleashed in the independence movement. A common enemy in colonialism impelled the emergence of cross-communal leadership which mobilised non-white workers and others to challenge the plantocracy, the colour-class value system, the unjust distribution of jobs and privileges and all the other iniquitous aspects of the multi-ethnic immigrant society. How this was achieved and how this new opportunity to re-build and restructure the society was utilised will be the concern of this and the next chapter. In this chapter, we look at the emergence and role of the first important movements and associations in Guyana in paving the way towards a new type of mass politics.

A.   Forerunners of the People's Progressive Party (PPP)

a) The Ethnically-Based Voluntary Associations

Prior to 1950, the historic year when the PPP was launched, certain voluntary associations such as the League of Coloured Peoples (LCP), the East Indian Association (EIA), the British Guyana Labour Union (BGLU) and the Manpower Citizens' Association (MPCA) among others, constituted the stable building blocks from which a wider political consciousness would evolve to challenge the colonial system. The first efforts by the various communal sections to organise voluntary associations for cultural, social and economic ends followed the basic ethnic patterns that were embedded in the Guyanese social structure. While such associations almost inevitably served to accentuate sectional divisions and exacerbated inter-ethnic suspicion by structuring communal competition for the limited advantages available, they also provided an organisational infra-structure responsible for arousing and orienting political consciousness generally. Initially, as these associations were formed, they offered some measure of stability to the disarrayed lives of the immigrant population.

Communal organisations of major consequence did not emerge until after about 1900. For a period of approximately seventy-five years, beginning with the Emancipation Act of 1833 and ending with the termination of the indentureship system in 1917, the various ethnic sections gradually but steadily established their ways of life. These years were a period of relative instability for the labouring immigrant groups. Since the end of the Village Movement in 1848, Africans had gradually been moving to urban centres. Until the end of the indenture system in 1917, many Indians were in a somewhat similar unstable state, moving off the plantations and taking up residence in contiguous areas. Portuguese and Chinese were busily engaged in entrenching themselves into a mercantile pattern of urban living. In 1910,

28

Amerindians were put on reservations. Between 1900 and 1920, occupational and geographical living patterns practically solidified, and each community carved out its own occupational and residential 'preserve' with which it identified and was identified. The stabilisation of each section's living patterns established the basis for the development of exclusive ethnic organisations.

Indians and Africans formed the most active voluntary organisations during the early twentieth century. To be sure, the Portuguese and Chinese did constitute their own associations; the Portuguese Benevolent Society was formed in 1917 and the Chinese Association was formed in 1916. The British had their own segregated clubs and associations. The Amerindians had no choice as to political organisation. Isolated in reservations, they appeared to have accepted their economic lot contentedly. Their interests were 'represented' by the Catholic and Anglican Churches.

African and Indian organisations which emerged between 1915 and 1940 were the main bodies that agitated for colonial reforms. These organisations advocated programmes which were concerned with both economic and political changes. They recognised that economic conditions were inextricably bound up with the colonial political order. They insisted, therefore, that the restrictive voting requirements which, in 1850, had witnessed the registration of only 916 voters in a total population of 127,695 (Clementi, 1937) and in 1908 only 3,628 voters in a population of a quarter million people, (Report, 1953) be liberalised. The franchise, which before the emancipation of slaves in 1833 was the right of only those who possessed 25 or more slaves, restricted the electorate to the European elite. Immediately after the abolition of slavery, high property and income requirements were substituted for slave ownership, but predictably this still resulted in 'an electorate . . . almost exclusively of adult males of European race . . .' (Clementi, 1937:36).

In 1891, a constitutional revision substantially lowered the franchise requirement, granting the vote to persons with an income of at least G$480 a year. The sum was decreased to G$300 in 1905, and remained unchanged for three decades. The liberalisation of the franchise did little to increase the number of lower-class members of the electorate. The property and income qualifications for voting effectively excluded the preponderant majority of the population from participating in the decision-making bodies of the colony. The planters, who controlled the Board of Financial Representatives and the Combined Courts through their virtual monopoly of the franchise, were able to dictate economic policy that promoted their own sugar interests. Consequently, through their voluntary organisations, Africans and Indians sought to reform the colonial constitution to facilitate their increased participation in the political direction of the colony.

In Guyana, demands for political reforms were initiated mainly through the efforts of middle class individuals acting within the African and Indian voluntary associations. These middle-class elements were the most educated and culturally advanced persons in their respective sections. They were impelled to participate on an equal basis with the British and Portuguese in obtaining access to the bounties and privileges of colonial society. To realise their demands for improved social and political status in the early part of the twentieth century, middle-class Africans and Indians organised the Negro Progress Convention (NPC) and the East Indian Association (EIA) respectively. These organisations purported to act on behalf of all the members of their respective communities as a means of pressuring the colonial decision-making bodies to grant them political and constitutional concessions. Almost invariably however, the EIA and NPC pursued the narrow interests of their middle-class supporters, but did so by invoking the collective interests of their communal sections.

Between 1910 and 1921, several African associations appeared on the Guyanese scene. These included the Universal Negro Improvement Association, the African Communities League, and the Negro Progress Convention, all of which were urban-based organisations with relatively small memberships. The Negro Progress Convention (NPC), which was formed sometime before World War I, persisted longest and evolved into the League of Coloured Peoples (LCP) in the late 1930s. The NPC aimed 'to provide means ... and build institutions...to assist persons of African descent to develop self-help, self-respect, and self-determination' (GIIA, 1968:13).

The NPC operated intermittently until 1939, when it was reconstituted into the LCP. Headed by Dr. Claude Denbow, an American-trained dentist, the LCP originally sought to represent the interests of all non-white persons. But, given its African leadership, urban base, evolution from the Negro Progress Convention, and the existence of an East Indian Association, the LCP became an exclusively African group. From an organisation with a formal multi-racial front, it changed formally 'to promote the social, economic, educational and political interests of the people of African descent' (Despres, 1967:166).

Partly because of its representation of one ethnic group, the LCP evinced views with strong racial overtones. It strongly favoured a British West Indian Federation which would include Guyana. The implication of a pro-Federation stand at this time was tantamount to elevating an African minority in Guyana to one of an African majority. On the matter of liberalising the franchise, the LCP opposed universal adult suffrage without a literacy test. According to one view, in the evolving rivalry between Africans and Indians, this stand was meant to deny the franchise to the significant segment of the mostly illiterate Indian population in favour of the much more literate African population.

The LCP entered the political contest in the 1947 general elections when the total electorate was composed of only 59,193 persons, most of whom were middle class persons. Two LCP members, Dr. Nicholson, a surgeon, and Rudy

Kendall, a businessman, were elected to the House of Assembly. Nicholson and Kendall won in the two major urban centres, Georgetown and New Amsterdam, where the LCP was very powerful. Campaigning methods by the LCP candidates, especially Nicholson's, were marked by an uninhibited appeal for the political expression of African racial solidarity.

The East Indian Association (EIA) was organised in 1916 by Joseph Ruhomon, a middle class Indian merchant and writer. Most of the officials of the EIA were professionals, businessmen, landlords and rice millers. The exclusive Indian organisation aimed 'to unite the members of the East Indian race in all parts of the colony for representation purposes' and 'to advocate and promote, by all possible legitimate means ... the general public interest and welfare of the East Indian community at large' (Ruhoman, 1946:228-229). The membership of the EIA was small and economically well above average but, like the Negro Progress Convention and the League of Coloured Peoples, it purported to represent the interests and views of its entire ethnic sector.

The appearance of the EIA occurred at a time when Indian community life was beginning to stabilise. An Indian middle class had emerged and had begun to clamour for social recognition and jobs in the civil service. Although a small number of these Indians became Christians and 'adapted the prevailing middle class Creole culture, ' they 'no doubt found a certain amount of social discrimination particularly in the matter of admission to clubs and social cliques' (Smith, 1962:108). It therefore became necessary for middle- class Indians to form their own parallel organisations, of which the EIA was the first, and to extol, in reaction to their social exclusion from English and Creole society, 'the glories of Mother India' and the worthiness of Indian values and culture. The EIA embarked upon a programme to stimulate Indian religious activities by importing missionaries from India. Simultaneously, it demanded 'the establishment of special Government schools under the East Indian masters for the teaching of both Hindi and English to children of East Indian parents' (Ruhoman, 1946:228-229). The EIA, in these respects, served to integrate the Indian cultural community and forge a coherent identity.

Indian representation in the governmental services was negligible during the early twentieth century. According to the 1931 census, the occupational tables indicated that only 8.08 per cent of the governmental bureaucracy was staffed by Indians, although the Indian section constituted about 42 per cent of the population. In the teaching professions, Indian personnel constituted about 0.7 per cent of all teachers in the colony. The EIA believed that lack of access for its members into the Civil Service and teaching professions was due to discrimination against Indian generally. Consequently, one of the aims of the EIA was to encourage 'the employment of East Indians at a much greater extent in public offices with which immigrants transact business or where they apply for various places' (Jagan, 1966:340). In this respect, 'like the LCP, the

EIA also saw its function in middle class terms, competition with the Negro middle class for positions and places' (Clementi, 1937:367). The EIA's political activities were as ethnically related as the LCP's. In 1916, Indian participation in the decision-making bodies of the colony was minimal, as illustrated by the Table 2.1.

Table 2.1: Sectional Political Participation in 1916

Section	% of each group in adult male population	% of each group in total electorate	% of adult males of each race registered as voters
East Indian	51.8	6.4	0.6
African	42.3	62.7	6.8
Portuguese	2.9	11.4	17.7
British	1.7	17.0	46.1
Chinese	0.9	2.4	12.3

Source: C. Clementi, *A Constitutional History of British Guyana*, Macmillan, London, 1937:367.

It can be observed that, although Indians constituted the largest segment of the adult male population (52.8 per cent), only 6.4 per cent of the electorate was Indian, and only 0.6 per cent of Indian adult males were registered to vote. The EIA undertook to arouse Indian political consciousness therefore and 'succeeded in lighting the flame of Indian nationalism in Guyana' (Despres, 1967:168). One of the proclaimed aims of the middle class Indian community was to establish a 'New India' in Guyana under Indian domination. Accordingly, the EIA advocated universal adult suffrage to enable Indians to increase their political influence in the colony. It even initiated a scheme to continue the influx of Indians into Guyana when the indentureship system was terminated in 1917.

The Negro Progress Convention co-operated with the EIA in this project on the condition that Indian immigration be equally matched by Negro immigration from Africa. After extensive negotiation with the Government of India, the EIA immigration plan was finally approved in 1926, but failed to be implemented because of the exorbitant costs which were now required to facilitate entry of non-indentured immigrants into the country. On the matter concerning Guyana's prospective entry into the federation with the West Indies, given its 'New India' aims, the EIA naturally opposed any plan that would involve the movement of Africans from the British Caribbean islands into Guyana, or lump the populations of the several units together for voting or other political purposes. In this regard, the EIA was as racial as the LCP.

b) The First Politico-Economic Associations

While the cultural and social associations such as the LCP, EIA, the Portuguese Benevolent Association, the Chinese Club etc. conferred communal solidarity and identity to their respective ethnic communities, this did not prevent attempts at forming cross-communal organisations aimed at economic and political amelioration. Strong cross-communal voluntary associations would nevertheless be difficult to forge into existence since the pattern of settlement had already prejudiced participation in employment and residence into virtual communalised compartments. Nevertheless, it will be useful to examine two attempts to form cross-communal economic associations. Even though in practice they tended to become preponderantly uni-sectional groupings, they laid the foundations for a commonly shared political experience and consciousness in confronting the colonial order.

The British Guyana Labour Union (BGLU) was formed on June 11, 1919, primarily through the initiative of Hubert Nathaniel Critchlow. Initially, the BGLU was a multi-racial labour organisation whose immediate objective was to improve the wages and working conditions of its members. Its long term objectives were inspired by the socialist British Labour Party of the early 1920's. The BGLU aspired to achieve 'the realisation of a collectivist state,' and to institute 'a glorious time when all children, all women and men, shall have an abundance of life essentials' (BGLU n.d.:1). These objectives were not to be attained by violence, but by utilising constitutional procedures and strikes. Although the BGLU represented lower-income workers, most of its important offices were held by middle-class professionals (Smith, 1962:166). From its inception, the organisation was 'advised and supported . . . by Negro professional men of liberal national beliefs' (Mark, 1964:14-15). This did not hinder the rapid growth of the union, which entered the national scene 'at a time when the working class was not organised in any mass movement' (Chase, 1964:14-15).

The immediate precipitating cause that prompted the formation of the BGLU was the steep rise in the prices of essential food articles following World War I. By 1916, the undercurrent of dissatisfaction had erupted in sporadic strikes on the sugar estates and in Georgetown. This was but a prelude to the explosion that took place in the following year in widespread strikes and agitation (Ibid.).

The BGLU was organised to provide the workers with machinery by which they could negotiate collectively with management. Membership enrolment in the union rose from 12 in April, 1919, to 100 by June 3, 250 by July, and more than 10,000 by the end of the same year. The rapid growth of the union was due mainly to its initial success as a bargaining agent of the workers. At this time, the BGLU represented not only Negro industrial employees in the urban centres, but also Indian sugar estate workers. Out of 10,000 members in 1921, over 2,000 were reportedly East Indians. The union established several subsidiary regional branches, but maintained its headquarters in Georgetown.

The BGLU dominated the labour scene in Guyana for over a decade and a half. At its formation, 'employers welcomed the union as an influential and disciplined agent with which they could deal' (Ibid.). By 1922 however, an economic depression had cut the price of sugar on the world market, adversely affecting wages and employment in Guyana. The BGLU called many strikes, but the employers no longer responded to its demands. The depressed price of sugar continued until late in the 1930's, and the BGLU, consistently rebuffed by the employers, consequently lost prestige and membership. Several new unions were formed in the 1930s as a result of the workers' frustrations with the BGLU. The dominance of the BGLU over the labour movement did not, however, come to an end until 1939 when the East Indian-oriented Man Power Citizens Association (MPCA) was recognised by the sugar planters as the bargaining agent for sugar workers. Of the 2,000 sugar estate employees the BGLU represented in 1921, most were Indians, but these constituted only a small percentage of the 100,000 Indian who derived their living from the sugar plantations. Indian reluctance to join the BGLU was mainly due to the urban focus of the union's activities, its preponderantly African leadership, and to Critchlow's and other union officials' association with the Negro Progress Convention. The fact that the BGLU's headquarters were located in Georgetown, where nearly all the union's officials also resided, added to the Indian sugar worker's reluctance to join or identify with the union. In 1934, when the Indian MPCA was formed to represent sugar workers, the BGLU was left almost completely and uniformly with an African membership.

The emergence of the Man Power Citizens' Association (MPCA) must be viewed in relation to the working conditions of the Indian indentured labourers. When Indian indentured immigrants arrived in Guyana in 1838, they were placed under a special and separate set of laws which governed their relations, including their labour relations, with their employers. A specific governmental institution, the Immigration-Agents General, was established in 1838 to administer the Immigration Laws with regard to the distribution, supervision and welfare of all indentured labourers. The Immigration-Agents General was also charged with the specific responsibility of ensuring that the immigrants 'were treated properly and not denied such rights as they might possess' (Smith, 1962:166). In the numerous and frequent disputes that occurred between estate labourers and management, the Immigration Agents General was required to intervene on behalf of the indentured workers and serve as 'a sort of conciliation officer in labour disputes between the indentured labourers and their employers' (Chase, 1964:31).

The sugar plantation workers had no voluntary labour organisation of their own. One of the stipulations of the labour indenture contract prohibited sugar workers from persuading or encouraging other sugar workers from going to work. It was a crime to infringe the labour laws of the sugar estates; exorbitant fines and/or imprisonment followed infractions of the labour laws. For this reason, no voluntarily organised labour group designed to express the views and grievances of the plantation labourers emerged until after 1917, when the indentureship system of labour recruitment was terminated and the estate labour laws were modified. After 1917, the infringement of estate labour laws resulted in civil complaints for which civil suits had to be filed. In 1917 also, the Immigration-Agents General's labour functions were transferred to the Labour Section of the Local Government Department. Labour mediation functions were moved thereby from one governmental agency to another, but the sugar workers were still left without their own bargaining machinery. With the formation of the BGLU, not only were sugar workers represented by a union for the first time but, more importantly, the principle of direct collective bargaining between employers and employee organisations was established.

Disenchantment with the BGLU led to the formation of the MPCA in 1934. The MPCA did not easily gain recognition from the sugar producers. The union was registered on November 5, 1937, but it took the bloody Leonora Estate riots of February, 1937, and the subsequent appointment of a Commission of Inquiry to win acceptance of the MPCA as the competent negotiator of sugar workers' interests. The MPCA, which was founded by Ayube Edun and C. R. Jacobs, both prominent members of the East Indian Association, was recognised as the bargaining agent of field workers on the sugar estates. In its first year, the membership of the MPCA grew as fast as the BGLU. 'Between 1938 and 1943 its membership rallied at over the 20,000 mark. In comparison with other unions, it was a giant among pygmies' (Ibid., p.21). By 1939, the MPCA had 41, branches mainly on the sugar estates. As in the case of the BGLU, the overwhelming Indian membership of the MPCA led to criticisms that the union was an ethnic organisation.

B.   The Independence Movement Emerges

The occasion for the dramatic and unified effort in challenging the colonial order came with the impact of the Great Depression. All of the major voluntary associations that had appeared up to this point had advocated and demanded some sort of reform of the colonial system. When the effects of the Great Depression began to register its toll on the economic life of the colony, the methods adopted to articulate demands, especially by the BGLU and the MPCA, were agitational. The sugar industry was depressed and the disastrous toll was imprinted in the widespread increase in unemployment, while at the same time wages plummeted (Ayearst, 1969). From their organisations – particularly the MPCA, and the BGLU – African and Indian workers learned their first lessons concerning the need for applying political pressure for the satisfaction of their demands. Strike action, exposure to street-corner political oratory, and picketing of government buildings not only instructed the workers on agitational methods of persuading authorities to negotiate, but showed them the connection between the economic and political orders in Guyana. More particularly, workers were persuaded that their economic ills were attributable to the colonial constitutional system that denied them representation in the Government. As then constituted, however, the unions were not ethnically, regionally and industrially comprehensive enough in membership and organisation to initiate a full-scale programme to agitate for the reform of the entire political and constitutional order. In this inadequacy, the need for a more broadly-based political organisation arose. In most modern political systems, political parties generally tend to fill this need. To be sure, a few political parties did, in fact, exist before the Great Depression in Guyana. However, they were invariably ephemeral groups organised at election time to promote a limited number of specific issues. It was the voluntary non-governmental organisations such as the BGLU, MPCA, EIA and LCP which functioned within their limited interests and perspectives to pressure the colonial regime into according increasing benefits to Guyanese. However, these organisations demanded what may be correctly be called 'patch-work' reforms in colonial Guyana, when the situation in fact called for a comprehensive political and economic overhaul and overthrow of the entire colonial system.

The strikes and other forms of agitation carried out primarily by the BGLU and the MPCA in the 1930s culminated in the appointment of the West Indian Royal Commission of 1939 (hereafter referred to as 'The Moyne Commission') to investigate the social and economic conditions throughout the Caribbean and British Guyana. The report of the Moyne Commission was not, however, published until after World War II, and was only presented to the British Parliament in July, 1945. This delay, justified on the basis of the war, gave the British colonial authorities some time to study the report and prepare suggestions for the political and economic changes which were necessary if stability in the Caribbean and Guyana were to be attained. In fact, the Colonial Office commenced action on the Commission's recommendations even before the report was submitted to Parliament. In 1941, a Franchise Commission was appointed to examine the franchise in Guyana and 'to recommend measures for widening the democratic base of the government' (Blanshard, 1947:126).

The Franchise Commission rejected demands by the EIA, MPCA and

BGLU for universal adult suffrage and instead introduced a literacy test, but reduced the income requirement for the franchise from G$300 to G$120. The number of enfranchised voters increased from 9,513 in 1937 to 11,000 in 1944. The change in the franchise requirement was not significant, and clearly indicated to the BGLU and MPCA that the colonial office did not intend to support the wide-ranging social and economic changes for which they had agitated during the depression years.

Strikes and agitation continued despite the war, yet no comprehensive political party emerged to fill the political vacuum created by the limited political effectiveness of the BGLU and MPCA. It was not until after World War II that this need was filled. Also at this time, a world-wide movement aimed at gaining self-determination for the colonies was beginning to gather momentum. Elites in many of the colonial countries of the world were insisting that the principles of self-determination enunciated in the Atlantic Charter applied to them as well. The demands for independence and, more importantly, the colonial struggles that accompanied them, notably in India, provided immense morale to the pioneers who were to organise a broadly-based political party in Guyana to agitate for independence.

In 1946, the Political Affairs Committee (PAC), the nucleus and forerunner of the broadly-based People's Progressive Party (PPP), was formed. Led by Cheddi Jagan, Janet Jagan, Ashton Chase and Jocelyn Hubbard, the PAC's immediate aim was 'to assist the growth and development of Labour and Progressive Movements of British Guyana to the end of establishing a strong, disciplined and enlightened Party, equipped with the theory of Scientific Socialism' (PACB, 1946a:1). The PAC's leadership realised that it could not achieve its aim without a systematic programme to 'educate' Guyanese about the basic political and economic issues in colonial Guyana. The Guyanese masses were already aroused, but their appreciation for the economic and political bases of colonialism was as sketchy as their reactions to colonial conditions were sporadic and momentary. The PAC therefore embarked upon a public programme 'to provide information and to present scientific political analyses on current affairs both local and international' (Ibid.). A newsletter called the PAC Bulletin was issued and efforts were made to 'foster and assist discussion groups through the circulation of bulletins, booklets, and other printed matter' (Ibid.).

Originally, the PAC was a small and obscure group which, upon its publication of the *PAC Bulletin* with its bold radical line, attracted many foreign-educated Guyanese intellectuals to its fold. The *PAC Bulletin* fully utilised the British-inspired Moyne Commission Report as a legitimating basis for its attack on living conditions in Guyana. But while the Moyne Report provided a vivid description of the miserable living conditions in the colony, it lacked a programme of redemption by which these conditions could be ameliorated. The PAC filled this gap. It propounded a Marxist-Leninist interpretation of society which analysed the Guyanese economic and political system in terms of property and class relations, pointing invariably to colonial exploitation and capitalism as the fountain from which the depredations and evils of colonialism flowed.

In addition to its criticisms of specific colonial conditions, the PAC advocated a programme based on 'Scientific Socialism.' 'The establishment of a well-planned collective industrial economy' was to replace the capitalist economy 'which yielded a very low standard of living to the majority of inhabitants in British Guyana' (PACB, 1946a:2). The political objectives of the PAC included universal adult suffrage, self-government, and a collective state run by workers. The PAC was the first organisation in Guyana to set forth an interpretation of the country's living conditions that was potentially attractive to a cross-section of workers of all races. Unlike the EIA and LCP which made open ethnic appeals in their cultural and political programmes, the PAC advocated the establishment of a new value system which was free from sectional appeals (that is, a classless society). On the economic level, unlike the BGLU and MPCA, which fought for limited economic reforms, the PAC advocated a radical restructuring of the economic system which would abolish private capital and institute collective control of the 'commanding heights of the economy.' The PAC provided a comprehensive survey of colonialism, including Guyana's case, covering and explaining all political, social and economic issues through the application of a single integrated ideology. The *PAC Bulletin* took concrete local issues and systematically analysed them in simple Marxist terms, mainly for the consumption of city and rural workers. When the *PAC Bulletin* was first published in 1946, however, the ideas and ideals of the PAC members were too novel to immediately galvanise the workers into action outside the framework of their sectoral loyalties and unite them under the banner of a single organisation. The PAC members realised this; hence they initiated a programme of intensive public 'education.' Between 1946 and 1952, over half a million publications were distributed in Guyana by the PAC and its successor the PPP (PPP, 1961).

Between 1946 and 1950, the PAC was mainly an agitational and propaganda organisation. It grew in membership, continued its publication of the *PAC Bulletin* which became increasingly popular and, most importantly, it recruited many of the most outstanding intellectuals in the colony to its cause. Concomitantly, the name 'Jagan' became closely associated and identified with the *PAC Bulletin*. In 1947, new general elections were scheduled for the colony and certain PAC members decided to join the contest in a limited number of constituencies to ascertain the PAC's strength and popularity. At this time, the PAC was only about a year old and had not yet converted itself into a political party, which was its next goal.

The 1947 elections were contested by two electoral parties (of a personalistic, *ad hoc* type,) and 31 Independents, for 14 seats in the lower house of the colonial legislature. The MPCA formed its own political party, the MPCA Party, and contested in 7 of the 14 constituencies in the colony. The other party, the Labour Party, was put together by several trade union leaders, excepting MPCA personnel, to contest 13 of the 14 constituencies.

The presence of two labour-oriented parties in the 1947 elections clearly indicated that the trade union movement in Guyana was divided. In fact, the Labour Party put up an opposing candidate in every constituency that the MPCA Party contested. Competing with the two parties in the electoral race were the 31 Independents, who included the PAC candidates Cheddi Jagan, Janet Jagan, and Jocelyn Hubbard. The election results gave victory to five candidates of the Labour Party, one MPCA candidate, and eight independents including Cheddi Jagan of the PAC. Janet Jagan of the PAC ran second in a keen five-way contest for the Georgetown Central constituency and Jocelyn Hubbard, the last PAC candidate, polled third in a three-way contest for the Georgetown North constituency (Chronicle, 1947).

The immediate implication of these results were clear: candidates who appealed primarily to labour sympathies won their seats. The Labour Party and MPCA Party together won six seats. Most of the eight victorious independent candidates, including Cheddi Jagan, who refused to fight either under the banner of the Labour Party or the MPCA Party, appealed mainly to workers in their campaigns.

The heavy impact that labour votes had on the electoral outcome was due to the sudden expansion of the electorate from its 1944 level of 11,000 to the 1947 total of over 59,000. Evidently, most of the new 48,000 voters were wage earners. Increased political agitation by the PAC, the unprecedented number of candidates running for electoral office and, finally, the efforts of independent candidates to register voters were, also factors that contributed to the large number of persons in the electorate. The labour candidates who were elected to the Legislature did not stand together as a coherent voting block. In fact, not long after the Legislature was convened, the Labour Party, which began as a loose association of candidates with trade union sympathies, fell apart, so that a Legislature of uncommitted individuals prevailed thereafter until the 1953 elections (Blackman, 1947).

From their limited participation in the 1947 elections, the PAC learned several valuable lessons which inspired a practical strategy for political success. First, the elections underscored the fact that liberalisation of the suffrage resulted in proportionately greater inclusion of lower-income groups in the electorate. The significance of this point was that lower income individuals tended to be wage workers who were like to support a labour-oriented party. Victory for labour candidates in the 1947 elections was traceable to the 48,000 new voters on the electoral list, most of whom were labourers. The important lesson taught by these post-election facts was that persons aspiring for political office ideally ought to be activists in trade unions. A trade union basis for successful political action was now convincingly demonstrated in Guyana, but had already been established in the British Caribbean islands, notably in Barbados and Jamaica.

For the PAC, which acclaimed itself as a working class group, involvement in the trade union movement, preferably at the leadership level, was vital to its success in achieving its political objectives. Hence, with the defeat of the MPCA, which convincingly signalled that the sugar workers' confidence in that organisation was negligible, Dr. Jagan, along with a popular sugar estate Indian leader, Dr. Latchmansingh, formed the Guyana Industrial Workers Union (GIWU) in 1947, to replace the MPCA. The GIWU began uncertainly at first, but after the bloody Enmore Estate Strike in 1949, in which the lives of workers were lost, it became the officially unrecognised but unequivocal representative of the sugar workers. Subsequent to the Enmore incident, Dr. Jagan appeared to represent the interests of sugar workers before the Venn Commission of Inquiry. Recommendations of the Venn Commission resulted in 'the vast improvement in housing on sugar estates and other social amenities and certain changes in working conditions...' (Chase, 1964:41). The PAC founder members, especially Dr. and Mrs. Jagan, were thereafter idolised by sugar workers, the first major group of wage earners to come under the control of the PAC.

Trade Union 'infiltration' had become a corner-stone of the new PAC strategy. Ashton Chase, a PAC founder, became Secretary-General of the BGLU and Jocelyn Hubbard, another PAC founder, was an ex-Secretary General of the Trades' Union Council, which was a loose federation of the most important trade unions in Guyana at the time. By 1950, when the PPP was formed, the PAC strategy had succeeded in capturing the leadership of the most important unions in Guyana.

The second significant lesson that the PAC learned from the 1947 elections was that, notwithstanding its integrated ideological appeal to the common man, ethnic identification was still a major determinant of voting behaviour in Guyana. Dr. Jagan won the Central Demerara Constituency in the 1947 elections, partly because of his personal popularity and partly because his constituency was predominantly Indian. The other two PAC candidates, Mrs. Jagan and Mr. Hubbard, who were both Europeans, lost in constituencies which were predominantly African. All these PAC candidates appeared to make inroads upon the sectional voting patterns because of their ideological programmes, but not enough to win a victory on this basis. Mrs. Jagan in particular, succeeded most impressively in gaining African and Indian votes; she would later return to contest and win another predominantly African

Georgetown constituency in 1950, during municipal elections for the town council. Mr. Hubbard, the European founder member of the PAC, contested the Georgetown North Constituency and encountered uninhibited racism in the election campaign; nevertheless, he did succeed in obtaining a considerable number of votes. In other constituencies, independent Indian candidates appealed for votes by telling 'Indian workers that only they could get the workers Government jobs which were now being denied to them in favour of the Africans. But first, said the (Indian) politicians, they must be elected to the Legislative Council' (Jagan, 1963:43). Candidates from the League of Coloured Peoples made similar communal appeals.

In light of the 1947 election experience, the task of the PAC was to forge a multi-ethnic image by recruiting an African leader who had the same magnetic appeal among Africans that Cheddi Jagan had among Indians. The search ended with the selection of Forbes Burnham, who was an outstanding London-educated Guyanese lawyer and orator. With Jagan and Burnham, a 'dual charisma' was installed within the leadership of the PPP. Indians and Africans, who together constituted over 80 per cent of the population, could now be theoretically mobilised to provide the PPP with multi-racial support and victory at all foreseeable general elections.

The final lesson that the PAC learned from the 1947 elections was that its political reform programme would fail if its contemplated political party was organised haphazardly and staffed by persons whose sole interest in the party was to capture political office. The Labour Party set up for that election quickly disintegrated, substantially because of its loose selection of candidates and weak leadership. The PAC's organisational strategy was to recruit for its top echelon leadership persons who were solidly committed to socialist ideals and who were willing to work at the grass roots level with the people. The PAC's aim was to have an agitational party which would work with the people at all times, regardless of whether elections were imminent or not.

When in January, 1950, the PAC finally launched its own party – the People's Progressive Party – its organisational, 'infiltration', and leadership strategies derived from its participation in the 1947 elections had already been worked out and implemented. The *PAC Bulletin* was renamed *Thunder*, which became the official organ of the Party. The central ideological aim of the PPP was similar to that of the PAC, although it was stated with greater cogency and clarity. Said the PPP:

> ... the final abolition of exploitation and oppression will be achieved only by the Socialist reorganisation of society. (The PPP) pledges to build a just socialist society, in which the industries of the country shall be socially and democratically owned and managed for the common good (Thunder, 1950:6-7).

41

The unity of the various ethnic sectors, or at least the unity of Indians and Africans, was essential to the Party's success as a means of preventing voters from casting their ballots for uni-ethnic parties, which were expected to mushroom at any forthcoming elections. The Party's programme declared:

> The PPP will strive for unity of workers, farmers, co-operatives, friendly societies, progressive businessmen, professional civil servants, and co-operation of all racial groups (Ibid.).

The organisation of the PPP was highly centralised, with the Secretary-General (Janet Jagan) co-ordinating the various party groups which were formed among Indians and Africans in the urban and rural areas. Two auxiliary arms of the party, the Women's Political and Economic Organisation and the Progressive Youth Movement, were set up to mobilise the women and youth in the population to join or identify with the PPP. The Party had a central office in Georgetown which, although staffed mainly by part-time volunteer workers, was in continual operation.

More by deliberation than by accident, the formation date of the PPP coincided with the anticipated appointment of a new constitutional commission which was scheduled to visit Guyana. On December 16, 1948, in his address to the Legislative Council, the Governor of Guyana promised that a constitutional commission would visit the country 'shortly', to look into the possibility of granting greater participation to the Guyanese in governing the country (Report, 1950). The Franchise Commission of 1941 had come close to granting universal adult suffrage; it had received several petitions demanding the removal of all property, income, and literacy qualifications for the franchise. The PPP anticipated, therefore, that a new constitutional commission would most probably grant this request at last.

Agitational activities by the PAC, particularly the Enmore incident, hastened the tardy implementation of the promise to send a new constitutional commission to Guyana. On October 8, 1950, the Waddington Commission was appointed to 'review the franchise, the composition of the Legislature and of the Executive Council ... and to make recommendations' (Ibid., p.iv). The representatives of the PPP, L.F.S. Burnham and Cheddi Jagan, appeared before the Commission and lodged a strong petition for universal adult suffrage and self-government.

The report of the Waddington Constitutional Commission, which was appointed during the government of Britain's Labour Party, resulted in the granting to Guyana of the most liberal constitutional arrangement given to any British territory in the Caribbean. Two crucial aspects of the new constitution were:

(1) introduction of universal adult suffrage; and (2) a limited cabinet ministerial system intended to concede the right to govern most of the internal affairs of the colony to an elected majority. New general elections were set for April 27, 1953, and the PPP, more than any other group, was prepared for the contest. In spite of its organisational preparedness, however, the leaders of the PPP did not anticipate victory. The Party had expected to win only enough seats to constitute a respectable opposition. From the Legislature, the PPP had planned to continue its 'politics of protest', as Janet Jagan, the General Secretary, described the orientation of the party during its first few years of existence (Jagan, 1963:11).

The 1953 elections produced a large array of independent candidates and political parties, essentially similar to the participants in the 1947 elections. The main difference was the emergence of the PPP, a political party with a strong organisational apparatus, guiding ideology, and grass roots support. Thus, the first mass party appeared in Guyana. For all practical purposes, the PPP had been in existence since its embryonic nucleus was launched in 1946, and by 1953 it was ready to dislodge the older style political movements which appeared and disappeared equally quickly before and after each election.

The overwhelming victor in the election was the PPP, which won eighteen of the twenty-four seats in the Legislature. The most significant fact of the result of the 1953 elections showed that in several constituencies where PPP candidates obtained victories, the only explanation for these outcomes was strong Indian-African inter-ethnic co-operative voting behaviour. The most dramatic example of this Indian-African intersectional voting behaviour occurred in the Indian dominated Demerara/Essequibo constituency, where the PPP experimentally placed an African candidate, Fred Bowman, to face Dr. J.B. Singh, an Indian, who was endorsed by the EIA. Mr. Bowman won.

In the wake of the PPP victory, three years before the 1953 elections and more than a year after, unprecedented co-operation and mutual support between the African and Indian sectors, prevailed. As a part of this study, interviews were carried out among Africans and Indians who were adults in 1953. Almost invariably, these Guyanese say they believe that a 'Golden Age of Racial Harmony' in Guyana existed during the time that Burnham and Jagan were allies (Skinner, 1960).

The PPP savoured their victory and had held office for approximately six months when British warships with heavily armed troops supervised the eviction of the party from power. Arrests, prison terms, detentions and house confinements of PPP leaders quickly followed. Physically separated from each other in this grave crisis – Dr. Jagan was in jail and Mr. Burnham was under house arrest – the PPP leaders soon started to openly express their differences regarding the tactics and strategy of the independence movement generally, and, in particular, the manner in which certain PPP functionaries conducted themselves in office. Eventually, these differences widened to fateful schismatic factional infighting for the PPP leadership. Dr. Jagan and Mr. Burnham parted company, formed their own parties, and Guyana was launched into decades of bitter and at times bloody inter-communal strife.

It is not difficult to unravel the combination of factors which were necessary for the party to unite the two major ethnic parts in the Guyanese population, mobilising them for national development unhindered by intersectional strife. It is very clear that the victory of the PPP was due mainly to the inter-communal charismatic leadership of Burnham and Jagan. Even before the PPP was launched, the PAC had such characteristics as a strong organisation and a revolutionary ideology, appropriate for colonial Guyana. Yet, this was not enough to unite the two major parts of the Guyanese population. With the change of the leadership of the PAC group, however, the fortune of its successor, the PPP, improved dramatically. Both Jagan and Burnham were dynamic sectional leaders whose private political futures would have suffered immeasurably had they contended the elections as individual candidates. The social structure, with its inherent communal predilections, would inevitably have given only sectional support to each leader. However, the unity of the two leaders overcame the strong communal voting pattern embodied in the social structure and consequently resulted in inter-ethnic political co-operation among Africans and Indians.

III   The Fateful Fall into the Spiral of Ethnic Politics: The Role of Party Organisation

The moment of opportunity to build a new basis for inter-group relations and a new society was lost forever it seemed, when the two sectional leaders parted company, formed their own parties and pursued their own ambitions for personal acclaim and power. The moment of reconciliation is a rare event in a multi-ethnic state suffused with all sorts of underlying predispositions for ethnically-inspired divisive behaviour. What makes the loss of that opportune moment even more unbearable is the following sequence of events in which the old divisions embedded in the social structure were exploited and exacerbated by a new form of mass politics. A new type of party emerged, constructed on the discrete ethnic fragments into which the old unified party had been broken. Mass politics invite rival mass organisations to capitalise on ethnic loyalties for votes. The new system of politics is adopted from a model of political competition derived from European contexts marked by unity and consensus.

Many colonies with fragmented ethnic sections were bequeathed political institutions designed around adversarial zero-sum politics. The new parties in Guyana were encouraged to design vote-getting campaign strategies aimed at capturing a government and vanquishing an opponent as in a war of all against all. To win is to conquer; to lose is to die. Ethnic conflicts that are organised and acted out in an arena of partisan competition bound by zero-sum rules of rivalry tend to exacerbate the underlying deep divisions of the society. Party organisation and electoral competition together consign an ethnically multi-layered polity to a route destined to self-destruction. It seems that once the moment of reconciliation is lost, the ethnic monster is let loose in the theatre of mass politics and manages to negate all efforts at development. In this chapter, we will look at the role of party organisation in contributing to Guyana's gallop into intensified ethnic conflict.

45

In Guyana, like other Third World multi-ethnic states, competitive parties formed around a nucleus of members from one or another sub-system, do not serve to unify the society, nor do they establish legitimate authority. In societies which are relatively well integrated and already bound by a widely shared body of basic values, political parties serve as effective linkages between the identity of citizens and the policies of decision-makers at all levels of government. In such states, 'national integration (is) reasonably resolved some time before political parties (make) their appearance' (La Palombara and Weiner, 1969:28). Hence, when groups of individuals begin to work together to capture power in elections, the resulting parties act within the boundaries of an established political and social consensus rather than expending energy in trying to impose one and, in the process, polarising each grouping around the cultural, social and economic interests it represents. What is equally significant is that in such countries, by the time mass politics have emerged as a fact of political life, the legitimacy of political authority has already been accepted.

The party system which evolved in Guyana embraced these norms of the political culture. Legitimacy did not – and can not – reside in a regime controlled by one portion of the citizenry to the exclusion of another or of all the others, especially where the excluded groups constitute separate sub-societies. Competitive parties that are formed from exclusive ethnic blocs in internally fragmented states such as Guyana do not serve as agents of national integration, and do not mobilise energies and scarce resources for national development. Instead, they exacerbate the underlying cleavages and sectionalism. The way they organise their lives and those of their constituents in a competitive arena of zero-sum stakes results in the destruction of all efforts aimed at developmental amelioration. The new competitive parties in Guyana illustrate this well.

Following the historic split of the national independence party, the PPP, two new factional parties emerged around the leadership of Dr. Jagan and Mr. Burnham. Each claimed the mantle of the old, popular and victorious PPP so that at least temporarily there was a Burnhamite and a Jaganite PPP. Later, the Burnhamite faction would alter its name to the People's National Congress (PNC hereafter), while the Jaganite faction retained the PPP label (PPP for Jagan's faction hereafter). After the 1955 split, a general scramble commenced between the Jaganite and Burnhamite factions to ensure that Indians and Africans respectively stayed with their ethnic leaders. This occurred at the same time that each partisan grouping proclaimed its adherence to socialist ideals and programmes. The new party formations that were erected were then invested with socialist aims. But it was clear that this meant different things for each leader. Mr. Burnham, the PNC leader, conceived of 'socialism' in less of a doctrinaire Marxist sense than did Dr. Jagan. Mr. Burnham believed, like

46

Dr. Jagan, in the general improvement of economic and living conditions for the Guyanese, but he subscribed to a 'mixed' economic system to achieve this goal (PNC, 1964). He argued for a government that 'will own and run outright those industries which the circumstances and facts suggest', as well as a sector constituted of 'enterprises in which the Government will share as partners with private investors and entrepreneurs, and yet others which will be run entirely by private enterprises' (Burnham, 1968:18)). He contended that 'in the mixed economy, no rigid ideological dogma binds the state to nationalise or not to nationalise, to initiate and develop or not to initiate and develop, industries' (Ibid.). He felt that the mixed economic approach 'is flexible, in that it allows for various combinations of state and private initiatives in fulfilling the objectives of high economic productivity and a rising standard of living' (Ibid.).

For Dr. Jagan, on the other hand, the socialist model in the Soviet bloc provided the best guideline for developing Guyana's private capital investments, particularly foreign investments; he advocated a centrally planned economy that would operate with more regard for human welfare than for profits (Jagan, 1970).

Importantly, however, the PPP leader did not preclude the participation of domestic capital enterprises in the productive process in the short-run. As set forth in a famous 1956 Congress speech, 'the socialist economy on the model of the USSR. is a long-term objective' (*Chronicle*, 1956:1). Presumably in time, private capital would be abolished regardless of whether it was owned by domestic or foreign investors.

The two principal objectives of the PPP and PNC – capturing the governmental decision-making body, and implementing a 'socialist' society – governed the behaviour of the two parties' organisations in relation to the population. Both parties unequivocally rejected overt appeals to racism to achieve either or both of their key objectives. The parties committed themselves formally and publicly to the view that racism could not be tolerated in Guyana. Nearly every speech and major party document produced by the parties denounced racism vehemently. Outwardly at least, ethnic unity was crucial to the two parties for the political and economic development of Guyana. In practice, the situation was rather different.

Both the PPP and PNC provided for open membership to their organisations. In their efforts to increase the number of persons who were members of and/or identifiers with their party, the PNC and PPP made formal appeals to various classes and sections of the population. For instance, although the PPP proclaimed itself as a working class organisation, it defined itself formally as 'a broad allegiance of democratic sections – working class, peasantry, middle-class, native businessmen, and capitalists – opposed to imperialism. As such, communists, social democrats, native capitalists, civil servants and professional men could play their part in and belong to such a party' (Ibid.). The appeal of the Marxist PPP to inherently diverse ideological groups – capitalists and working – class individuals for instance – did not mean that the party had surrendered its formal socialist goals. Non-working class elements were encouraged to join or identify with the party only because this improved the chances of the party to ultimately realise its socialist goals in the long run. Dr. Jagan indicated clearly, however, that the orientation of the PPP would continue to be in the direction of catering to working class interests (Ibid.). Dr. Jagan displayed open contempt for the middle-class elements to which his party appealed saying:

> One of the main characteristics of the middle-class is its opportunisms, its tack-and-turn, its vacillations to put itself always in the best position in order to get the greatest possible gains (Ibid.).

Clearly then, the leader of the PPP viewed the coalition of diverse supporters of his party as a temporary arrangement until the party was in a position to implement its working-class society.

Formally, membership and identifier prescriptions for the PNC were as free from sectional appeals as those of the PPP. The PNC membership and identifier formula did, however, differ from the PPP's in one important respect, with regard to the middle-class. Mr. Burnham had set forth his party's attitude to the role and importance of the middle-class, pointing out that workers 'are not the only inhabitants of British Guyana. There are the peasants, the civil servants and the white collar workers and local businessmen. Some of these may be lumped into what is described as the middle class here' (Burnham, 1955:4). But he qualified his position on the middle class saying that it 'has usually shown a distrust of and contempt for the workers and their aspirations' (Ibid.). He then proceeded to underscore the importance of this stratum of the electorate to the future fortunes of the PNC, insisting that '(It) has its part and an important one to play' (Ibid.).

For Mr. Burnham, the middle-class was not seen as a menace to the PNC's ultimate goals. Indeed, if it could be won over, the middle-class would be integrated as an important part of the PNC's strategy to acquire power. Clearly, Mr. Burnham's party was committed formally to an alliance between workers and middle class individuals in a co-operative effort to realise the goals of the party. Thus, like the PPP, the PNC did not formally and overtly appeal or cater to ethnic supporters. Theoretically, both parties were built upon neutral, non-ethnic bases and aspired to implement social systems free from ethnic and sectoral cleavages. On the surface, the organisational activities of the two parties were geared to realising the economic and political goals of the party without eliciting or tolerating ethnic differences and sentiments.

On paper, the most powerful and important unit in the hierarchy of each party was its Congress. The members who attended the all-important annual party Congress were drawn from the basic organisational unity of the party – the Group. At the grassroots level, the members of the parties were organised into small subdivisions called groups. A certain number of members (about 12) constituted the minimum required to form such a party group. Each party had a network of party groups that provided the information and personnel necessary to carry out grassroots party activities. The PNC and PPP attached immense importance to the role of groups in the operation of the party organisation.

Each party had its auxiliaries or specialised sections – its youth groups and women's groups. The youth groups of the PPP and PNC were the Progressive Youth Organisation (PYO) and Young Socialist Movement (YSM), respectively. The women's auxiliaries were the Women's Progressive Organisation (PPP) and the Women's Auxiliary (PNC). These organisations were not autonomous, but acted as specialised bodies, recognising the existence of particular categories of members in the parties' organisations. Both the PNC and PPP had two other activities which were of considerable importance to the operation of the parties. These were the party newspapers and the *ad hoc* committees. Each party had its own newspaper; the PPP published *The Mirror* daily, and the PNC produced *The New Nation* weekly. These organs were distributed not only through regular newspaper stands, but also by the party groups.

Notwithstanding the appeals of the PPP and PNC for supporters in all classes and from all communities, the reality was that each party attracted virtually only Indians or only Africans. With the historic split in 1955, the coalition of African and Indian votes that supported the old PPP was destroyed. Progressively from 1955 to the present, Africans and Indians not only consolidated and completed their move to the Burnham and Jagan parties respectively, but also, and most importantly, ethnic declarations for these leaders and their charismatically-led parties by the Indian and African communities became overt and vociferous.

Sectional identification with the two major parties became a fundamental fact of contemporary Guyanese politics. Paradoxically, in a political field of self-declared socialist parties, class criteria as a determinant of party identification was practically negligible or absent. *Apanjaat*, the local colloquial term for 'vote for your own kind,' was the dominant factor which governed the political choices of nearly all Guyanese. Everyone expected an Indian to support and vote for the PPP and an African for the PNC.

However, not every African had become a member of the PNC, nor every Indian a member of the PPP. Both parties had a very small handful of the 'other side's' natural supporters in its fold. Usually these persons held high official positions in the 'other' party, and were exposed constantly to the public as evidence of the 'multi-racial' following of the party in question. For example, in the PPP, an African had traditionally held the position of party chairman since 1957, and, in general, Africans who supported the PPP found it easy to hold jobs in the highly visible central headquarters of Freedom House (the name of the PPP's headquarters). In the PNC camp, similar practices generally prevailed. For example, at 'Congress Place' (the PNC headquarters) Indians were found visibly in office jobs; in fact, for a number of years, an Indian held the very important job of manager of Congress Place.

The practice of publicising Indians in the PNC and Africans in the PPP was extended beyond providing visible office jobs for these persons at the respective party headquarters. In the Executive Committee and General Council of the PPP and PNC, a multi-racial image was also projected. Both parties could boast to the public that their top echelon official posts were filled by an ethnically mixed staff. The party organs *The Mirror* and *The New Nation*, did not fail to convey this picture in each of their publications.

Significantly, the two parties' efforts in projecting multi-racial images had practically no impact on voter identification. Election results (to be discussed in detail later in this chapter) clearly indicated that in the case of the PPP and PNC, cross-communal voting was virtually absent. At public meetings, group meetings, and party conventions, the paucity of cross-sectional attendance was obvious. Informal interviews and discussions carried out among a broad class and cultural range of Guyanese as part of this research project, attest to the fixed attachment of Indians to the PPP and Africans to the PNC. Rarely would a respondent to a question on party identification declare his or her support for his/her sectional party on ethnic lines, however. Typically, an Indian or African pointed to the economic program of the party of his choice (which was almost invariably the party that was associated with his ethnic group) as the basis for his party support or identification. In fact, because of the differing urban or rural interests of the two parties' distinct clienteles, their programs might well have reflected the real requirements of their members.

The official multi-ethnic image of the PNC and PPP, coupled with the insistence of the Africans and Indians that support for these parties was based on economic considerations, was contradicted by (a) the almost total association of Indians with the PPP and Africans with the PNC, and (b) the close resemblance of the PNC and PPP programs. Indians and Africans did not belong to separate monolithic economic groups. Each sector was differentiated internally into various economic classes. From an economic standpoint, big Indian landowners, rice millers, and businessmen, as well as Indian professional men should identify with the PNC. Similarly, African sugar workers should identify with the PPP, whose economic program and political pressures had dramatically improved the well-being of all sugar workers. But

50

when tested for their relevance to political affiliation, these economic and class criteria consistently provided negative correlations. The economic variable simply did not explain party identification. Instead, ethnic identity was the most consistent factor that was associated with voting behaviour. The facts above showed that, in Guyana, the party claims to a multi-racial following were simply not true.

More than any other structure, the party group reinforced sectoral identification with the parties. Where it was active, the party group linked the party with the population, but many groups were not as active on a regular basis as the parties claimed. The group and its officials were the major links between the party and the people. Where the group did not exist, village or community leaders served as the main link between the party and the people. What went on in the group – the appeals, the propaganda, education – directly and indirectly determined to a substantial extent whether the party intensified sectional sentiments and ultimately destroyed or built the basis for developing consensual political beliefs among all Guyanese. The leadership of the PNC and PPP groups almost invariably was African and Indian, respectively. Group leaders tended to be outstanding community leaders, so that generally they commanded great respect among their ethnic communities. The PNC tended to recruit school headmasters, middle to high echelon civil servants, and trade union officials for group leadership; the PPP recruited pundits, trade union officials, school teachers, and some middle-class landowners.

To a substantial extent, the uni-ethnic composition of group leadership and group participation was traceable to the sectoral divisions in the social system. Conceivably, this position could exonerate the parties from any responsibility in determining the ethnic composition and leadership of their groups. The facts indicated otherwise, however, for in recruiting members for their groups both the PNC and PPP had the same general principle: 'Organise our own people first, then try to persuade others to join us after.' (*Apanjaat*). In other words, to ensure that they could at all times command the allegiance of at least a major segment of the voting population, the parties deliberately (but unofficially) pursued a policy of fostering sectional party identification. This *Apanjaat* policy was initiated after the party split between Burnham and Jagan.

Following the 1955 PPP split, , most Indians and Africans followed their respective communal leaders without much persuasion. Significantly, however, some voters initially adopted a less emotional view. On the basis of the 1957 general election results, the evidence suggested that a sizeable segment (about 25 per cent) of all Indians and Africans were either undecided or unconcerned as to party preference. But this group was not allowed to remain uncommitted. This non-committed and/or lethargic group together constituted together an important part of the electorate, which if activated to Guyanese politics non-sectionally, could have decided whether or not the

51

country's party programs would have taken an ethnic bias. By virtue of the increasing intensity of organised communal politics between the PPP and PNC from 1955-1961, members of this group were forced to relinquish their non-commitment and unconcern and seek shelter under the party of their ethnic identity. Neither the PNC nor the PPP operated on the principle that an African could be for the PPP and an Indian for the PNC. Rather, they plunged head on into organising the electorate, seeking followers according to ethnic identity and paying little immediate attention to ideology or class in their recruitment fervour. As a result, the non-committed/lethargic elements were left without an organisation to articulate and represent their views.

Acting through their leaders and volunteer activists, both parties' groups were able to single out for 'special treatment' those persons in villages and towns who failed to follow the ethnic line. The group activists applied various forms of pressure, including open attacks on the persons or homes of the uncommitted, as a means of persuading them to behave according to the tenets of *Apanjaat*. The election results from 1957 to 1964 clearly showed clearly a tightening pattern of ethnic voting behaviour. Voting turn-out rose from 57 per cent in 1957 to 97 per cent in 1964, with the PPP and PNC receiving respectively approximately as many votes as there were adult voting-age Indians and Africans in the population.

A network of party groups had successfully organised themselves into tight ethnic patterns of political allegiance. Although generally attended by only a small number of persons of any village or town, group meetings constituted the centre from which party messages emanated. Notwithstanding the PPP and PNC claims to socialist labels, on the group level where the parties' grassroots activities were carried on, the evidence showed beyond a doubt that the parties were more communalist than socialist.

To be sure, both parties distributed race-free ideological material imported from abroad to their grassroots group-members, who in turn distributed it to others in the villages and towns. This is particularly true of the PPP which, like the PNC, pointed to its distributed ideological literature as adequate evidence of its non-ethnic character. In spite of the massive number of ideological pamphlets and books distributed, the fact was that party activists peddled communalist attitudes first and ideology second. The socialist message in the literature was subordinated to the ethnic identity of the media (the activists) through which it was distributed.

The organisation of the population into a network of sectional groups, and the consistent surreptitious propaganda peddled by group activists, literally exposed Indians and Africans to only a single set of political views and attitudes after 1955. The resultant hardening of communal attitudes, exacerbated by the activists of the party groups, frustrated the efforts of the PPP and PNC to induce members of the other side to join with their parties.

Having accomplished Phase I (ethnic consolidation) by which they had successfully corralled Indians to the PPP and Africans to the PNC, phase II (conversion) became an impossible task.

Periodically, a conversion was made in a village or town. Typically, a rare African worker decided to join the PPP, or a middle-class Indian civil servant entered the PNC, or more likely, the United Front (UF). The parties had ways of learning about such conversions and, in most cases, prevented them from becoming permanent. Generally, some form of victimisation or violence was applied to recapture the deviant. If the PPP or the PNC was in power, and the convert in any way depended upon the government for his livelihood, he was put under governmental pressure. If the party could not reach the defector through the government, community pressure was applied. This could take the form of ostracism, or verbal or physical attack on the convert and his/her family. Wherever possible, both government and community pressures were applied simultaneously.

The intermediate echelons in the parties' decision-making hierarchies generally had little direct contact with the broad base of the population. In particular, activities of the regional committees, general councils, and executive councils had little direct influence on the voting behaviour of the ordinary Guyanese. They were internal party decision-making structures, dominated by the all-pervasive personal will of the party leader. These intermediate echelons, particularly the Executive and General Councils, were staffed with a multi-ethnic membership, so they served as fronts to uphold the parties' claims to a multi-communal following.

The impact of the parties' several inter-ethnic fronts on structuring voter preferences along non-ethnic lines was cancelled out by the grassroots racist activities of the groups. Overtly, both Dr. Jagan and Mr. Burnham discouraged the use of race as the basis of voter identification with any party. But, given the highly personalist control each charismatic leader had over his party, including over the manner in which the party groups operated, room existed to question the sincerity of this formal discouragement. Significantly, neither Dr. Jagan nor Mr. Burnham had taken any steps to dissuade the groups from peddling an ethnic line or even from using coercive means in enforcing each party's *de facto Apanjaat* policies.

One other intermediate decision-making structure – the party sections – was of some importance with regard to voter identification. The PPP sections (PYO, WPO) and the PNC sections (YSM and WA) had grassroots organisations which paralleled the parties' network of groups. Among the party sections, the youth auxiliaries of the PNC and PPP (the YSM and PYO, respectively) were of the greatest importance with regard to the persisting sectional voter behaviour in Guyana. These youth sections were the 'organised violence' arms of the parties. They were militant, rash and quick to enforce the overall party lines at the local level, wherever it was violated. For this reason, neither the YSM under the PPP regime, nor later the PYO under the PNC regime, was numerically strong or operated openly. In order to carry out unpunished some of the grassroots hatchet work of the party with the violent militancy the political culture seemed to call for, the youth auxiliaries received protection from the government. Consequently, the PYO and YSM were strong during the regime of their own parties, but not at other times. The PYO flourished and grew very powerful during the PPP regime, just as the YSM flourished and grew under the PNC-UF regime that began in 1965. Like their parent parties, the PYO and YSM also sought to present a dual image to the public. They attempted to staff their headquarters leadership with persons from other ethnic groups but, at the grassroots level, maintained a uni-ethnic staff and an almost completely uni-ethnic membership.

Finally, let us look at the women's sections, the WPO (of the PPP) and the WA (of the PNC), for their impact on ethnic voting behaviour. The women's auxiliaries were not as militant or active as the youth sections. The WPO, in particular, was very unstable and sporadic in its attempts to serve the political needs of women. The WPO operated in a cultural context that not only bound the Indian woman to implicitly and *in toto* accept the political views of the husband, but also literally barred the woman from participating in men's activities, that is, politics. For this reason the WPO was a relatively weak organisation that made little difference in the political preferences among Indian women.

The Women's Auxiliary (WA) of the PNC, on the other hand, was an ultra-militant organisation whose activities closely rivalled those of the YSM and PYO. Operating in a cultural context that accorded the African woman the dominant role in the family, the Women's Auxiliary operated without inhibition as to which sex should monopolise politics. The WA was very strong; its important role in the PNC was attested to by the nomination of its members as legislative candidates and their appointment to head ministries, to ambassadorial positions, and to high positions in the PNC's officialdom. In all its activities, the Women's Auxiliary acted in communalist ways similar to that of the PYO and YSM, through a network of local organisations, particularly in Georgetown.

The Party Congress did not add to ethnic division in Guyana in any significant way. It was held annually and attended by members of the press and by special international guests. Both the PNC and PPP took special measures to prevent any overt display of the parties' *de facto* sectional policies or free expression of communalist sentiments by members attending the Congress. Elections for the highest party positions held at the Congress were virtually pre-arranged. Interviews conducted among delegates to the parties' Congress confirmed that the party leaders made their preferences known before the

54

election of party officials occurred. Defiance of the leaders' preferences was rare.

The activities of the Congress resulted in the election of a multi-ethnic body of officers to staff the intermediate echelons of the party organisation. The press reported the events, which the parties hoped would indicate how inter-communal in composition and anti-racial in program the parties were. Because of this, the annual party Congress could easily be deemed the greatest farce that the parties mounted annually, in particular for the benefit of international reporters. The ideological programs and speeches so well prepared and oratorically articulated at the Congress were definitely not meant for the guidance of the grassroots groups of the parties.

The party newspapers played a subtle and indirect role in hardening the differences between the Indian and African sections in Guyana after 1955. *The Mirror* and *The New Nation*, the PPP and PNC's newspapers respectively, were almost exclusively purchased by and distributed to Indians and Africans. This had become an established fact of Guyanese political life; neither the PNC nor the PPP attempted to distribute the bulk of its newspapers through regular news stands, but instead, both relied on direct sales to party activists. For example, in the African and Indian villages where part of this research was conducted, copies of *The Mirror* and *The New Nation* could be obtained only by contacting the chief party activists in these areas. In Georgetown, news stands that sold non-ethnic all-Guyanese newspapers (for example, the *Daily Graphic*) distributed *The Mirror* and *The New Nation* only to a limited extent. As in the rural areas, party activists supplied the bulk of these party newspapers to party supporters and identifiers.

The distribution of party newspapers to predominantly one section did not, in itself, add to the growing ethnic bifurcation in Guyana after 1955. It was the content of the party organs which mainly determined whether their influence on political opinions among Indians and Africans was decisive in developing sectional attitudes. An analysis of the *New Nation* and the *Mirror* after 1955 revealed two crucial patterns of political editorialising which upheld the view that the party newspapers added deliberately to ethnic divisions among Indians and Africans. The first pattern referred to the continual charge by *The Mirror* and *The New Nation* that the PNC and PPP, respectively, were communalist organisations. In nearly every issue that it printed, each of these party organs hammered relentlessly on the biased ethnic outlook of the other party. The same issue that condemned the other party, carefully mentioned the new decorative Africans in the PPP or Indians in the PNC to prove to readers that its party was multi-ethnic.

The second pattern of political editorialising provided additional convincing evidence of the communalist role of *The Mirror* and *The New Nation*. With very few exceptions, when the PPP was in power, every action by the government was given a sectional interpretation by the PNC's *New Nation*. Programs by the PPP government to improve the living conditions of African urban dwellers (e.g. the building of low cost housing) were given little or no credit by the *New Nation*. The PPP government was accused of being a 'Rice Government' or a 'Coolie Government', even when its actions resulted in undeniable gains to Africans. The PNC could simply not afford to lose its 'natural' supporters because of the economic or social benefits that the Jagan government offered Africans. The *New Nation's* interpretations of the government's actions were quite clearly intended to keep Africans in the PNC.

In subsequent years after the eviction of the PPP from power, with the PNC as the major partner in the PNC-UF coalition government (1964-1968), the *Mirror* assumed the communalist role that the *New Nation* had played when the PPP was in power. Similarly, since the advent of the exclusive PNC government after the December 15, 1968 general elections, the PPP's *Mirror* pounded incessantly on the theme that the Burnham government was a 'Blackman or Racist Government'. Regardless of how salutary its effects for the interests of Indians, no program advanced by the PNC regime was given a fair analysis in the *Mirror*, based on economic or social consequences. Ethnic affiliation was the medium of analysis. The same motive – to keep Africans with the PNC and Indians with the PPP – operated in the editorial lines of *The Mirror* and *The New Nation*.

In summary, with the division of the old PPP, the two leaders, Dr. Jagan and Mr. Burnham, organised their own parties which competed for votes among the population. The need for each party to survive and maintain a strong measure of assured electoral strength necessitated their appealing to sectional sentiments as a basis of popular party identification. Through the party apparatus, particularly the party group, the auxiliary sections and the party newspapers, ethnic sentiments were evoked, nurtured, and manipulated for party ends. The parties utilised informal methods both when they were in and out of the government to control and compel Indians and Africans to vote for the party of their community.

As a consequence of party organisational behaviour at the grassroots level, political choices were restricted for citizens and, more importantly, inter-communal fears and distrust were cultivated. The basis of Indian-African co-operation and community action was therefore sabotaged, and the chances of national consensus-building virtually eliminated. In the end, when one party obtained control of the government, its regime enjoyed virtual non-recognition from the defeated sector in the elections. In these circumstances, problems of political legitimacy arose, and government programmes were continuously in danger of sabotage from the 'out' section.

IV The Fateful Fall into the Spiral of Ethnic Politics: The Role of Elections and Political Campaigns

In Guyana, the new ethnically-based competitive parties formed by Jagan and Burnham in the quest of electoral votes deepened the divisions in the social system. Election periods were particular moments when the greatest harm was done. After 1955, election campaigns would contribute significantly to the spiral of tightening ethnic politics. Each new election campaign drove one more nail into the coffin of inter-ethnic unity. The following discussion describes the activities of the two major parties in Guyana during a typical election campaign. It seeks to demonstrate how and why party competition during the electoral contest accentuates inter-sectional suspicion and hostility, weakening the integrity, legitimacy and stability of the political system. But first, it will be useful to briefly review the theoretical claims and limitations of competitive parties in ethnically fragmented states.

In most democratic, integrated political systems characterised by a sharing of fundamental social values among the population, elections serve a salutary purpose. They not only reaffirm the commitment and involvement of the citizen to the prevailing political system by the ritual act of voting participation, but simultaneously legitimise the means and processes by which political values are authoritatively allocated (Milnor, 1969).

Elections and voting 'draw attention to common social ties and to the importance and apparent rationality of accepting the public policies that are adopted' (Adelman, 1964:3). Because of the body of shared values that underlies a relatively integrated political system, competition among parties tends to be limited as regards issues, so the electoral contest tends to be relatively low-keyed in intensity. The losers in the party competition at elections do not seek to sabotage the government, but 'when the campaign is

57

over ... the intensity of emotion on the part of the losers tends to evaporate and they salve their wounds with various psychologically soothing devices. The losers find that they didn't care so much, or see aspects of the situation they did not see before' (Lane, 1965:165). Results of party competition are accepted without the loss of face partly because of the pluralistic social infra-structure in most integrated polities. Voter preference are not rigidly determined by a single and compelling particularistic value such as ethnic affiliation, but are the function of multiple group interests and identification. The inherent institutional pluralism of integrated political systems results not only in citizen membership and identification with several diverse organisations and interests but, most importantly, dictates that political parties seriously interested in governing the state be broadly-based in their appeal (Lipset, 1960). In these circumstances, parties tend to campaign for votes on issues that do not advocate a radical restructuring of the social and political order. Nor do they threaten the survival and social and economic well-being of the losers. Consequently, the major parties tend to be relatively similar and the stakes involved in the competitive struggle are not high. In other words, each of the major parties is essentially acceptable to most citizens.

In an integrated political system, therefore, competing parties serve several constructive functions simultaneously. Legitimate decision-makers are elected; a sense of citizen participation is imparted; the citizen re-affirms his/her commitment to the political system; and the ultimate stability of the political system is assured. These roles of parties and elections are, however, limited only to certain types of societies which are integrated. It suggests that competitive parties and periodic elections are not always useful to certain polities. Indeed, the above introductory discussion was careful to delineate these conditions under which competitive parties and periodic elections can be of value to a specific type of social and political system. As a corollary, the commentary raises implicit questions about the limitations of competitive parties and elections in promoting political integration and stability in states that are not (a) socially pluralistic, and (b) bound by a body of shared beliefs and values. La Palombara and Weiner raised this question when they noted that:

> where the central values concerning the political process are not adequately shared, we often find unstable political systems in which the continuation of competitive parties is somewhat problematical (La Palombara and Weiner, 1969:28).

More particularly, in terms of the present study, the hypothesis is advance that in a cleavage-ridden state such as Guyana, political parties engaging in competitive elections tend to accentuate ethnic differences. In Guyana, the country's political parties do not operate in an integrated political system with a pluralistic social infrastructure, and do not possess a racially over-lapping membership. In Guyanese elections the political campaign for votes after the 1955 split in the independence movement was bitterly fought, and its outcome was not accepted as the legitimate decision of all the people. Party competition evokes the most hostile inter-community sentiments during elections. Campaign tactics are inordinately disruptive and covertly appeal to ethnic instincts.

In countries with unintegrated political systems, class, regional, ethnic, or religious predispositions which have been stimulated during heated political campaigns are not readily suppressed or forgotten. In Guyana, as for other similar Third World countries, each succeeding election campaign raises the level of inter-group distrust and fear to a new high point until, after several elections, inter-community differences become so intolerable that continued mutual coexistence among the sub-groups in the society is close to impossible. Figure 4.1 illustrates the point graphically.

Figure 4.1: **Levels of Ethnic Tension Generated by Three Successive Election Campaigns**

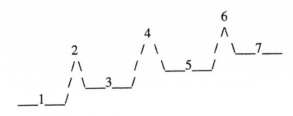

---------------- Level of Tolerance

1: Pre-election level of inter-community tension
2: Unprecedented level of tension created by election campaign.
3: New level of inter-community tension created in the wake of last election campaign.
4: Unprecedented level of tension created by new election campaign.
5: New level on inter-community tension.
6: Unprecedented level of tension created by new election campaign.
7: Intolerable new level of inter community tension.

For Guyana, 2, 4, and 6 would represent the elections of 1957, 1961, and 1964. Number 7 represents the general intolerable situation that was transformed into civil war. Since 1964, a crisis situation has existed, requiring an unprecedented number of police and army regulars to prevent the disparate sections in the population from resorting to full physical confrontation.

This chapter is divided into two parts. The first part provides a statistical description of voting participation. Specifically, the variable ethnic identity is correlated to voter preferences, to show the increasing intensity of sectional voting patterns, particularly since the dissolution of the old PPP in 1955. The second provides a detailed analysis of campaign tactics, to show how they deepen ethnic cleavages between Indians and Africans in Guyana. One additional development needs to be mentioned before we commence. In 1960, a new party called the United Force was formed. It was constituted mainly around the interests of Europeans, Amerindians, Portuguese, and light-skinned mixed race persons. It was an unabashedly *laissez-faire* capitalist party and therefore attracted a number of well-off Indians and Africans to its fold. But in essence, it was an 'ethnic' party and its presence attested to the further fragmentation of the social system.

A.   Statistical Analysis of Ethnic Voting Patterns

Following the PPP split in February 1955, the Jaganite and Burnhamite factions scrambled for supporters, mainly in the Indian and African communities respectively. The Jaganite PPP and the Burnhamite PPP had become *de facto* ethnic parties; those voters who had been attracted to the older, more inclusive version of the PPP in the 1953 general elections, chiefly because of the party's ideological programme, were left without any meaningful partisan choice in the 1957 elections. Most of these persons stayed home on election day, which resulted in the lowest voting participation in Guyanese history from the time that universal adult suffrage was introduced in 1953 to the 1964 general elections.

For the 1957 general elections, the country was divided into 14 constituencies. The results are presented on Tables 4.1 and 4.2. In this interpretation, the 55.8 per cent turnout of electors essentially represented votes cast for ethnically-oriented parties. The parties which contested these elections, the Jaganite PPP (Indians), the Burnhamite PPP (African), the National Labour Front (Indian middle-class), and the United Democratic Party (African Middle-class) all pitched their appeal in ethnic terms. The two PPPs did this covertly, but the practice became so widespread that the ethnic appeals of these parties soon became an open secret. The National Labour Front, an offspring of the middle-class East Indian Association, and the United Democratic Party, a product of the middle-class League of Coloured People, did not provide an acceptable non-ethnic alternative programme to the two PPPs for those voters who sought ideologically or non-racially oriented parties. In other words, voting choice was between ethnically-based parties in the 1957 general elections, and the two major parties of this type were led by Jagan and Burnham.

Table 4.1:   Voting Turnout

Electoral District	Number of Electors	Ballots Cast	%
1. Eastern Berbice	31,794	18,877	59.4
2. New Amsterdam	5,879	3,192	52.8
3. Berbice River	5,429	3,015	55.5
4. Western Berbice	8,324	6,041	72.6
5. Eastern Demarara	18,295	11,151	60.95
6. Central Demarara	25,137	14,427	57.4
7. Georgetown North	10,444	5,960	50.5
8. Georgetown Central	12,473	6,800	54.6
9. Georgetown South	24,244	12,299	50.7
10. Demarara River	26,972	12,461	46.2
11. Demarara/Essequibo	15,182	9,041	59.55
12. Essequibo River	13,649	7,026	51.5
13. Western Essequibo	11,215	6,799	60.6
14. North Western	3,481	1,619	46.5
District Total (Average)	212,518	118,708	55.8

Source: *Report on the General Elections of 1957*, Government Printery, Georgetown, 1958, Appendix II, Table I.

Table 4.2:   Parties and Results

Party	Number of Candidates	Ballots	%	Seats Won
1. PPP (Jaganite)	13	55,552	47.50	9
2. PPP (Burnhamite)	13	29,802	25.48	3
3. National Labour Front	14	13,465	11.51	1
4. United Democratic Party	8	9,564	8.18	1
5. Guiana National Party	1	199	0.17	0

Source: *Report on the General Elections of 1957*, Government Printery, Georgetown, 1958, Appendix II, Table II.

Many voters responded to their limited range of choice in the 1957 elections by staying home. To be sure, other reasons might have contributed to the low voting turnout. After the suspension of the constitution in 1953, British troops paraded the coastal plains frequently and after their departure, a larger than usual security presence was installed, a factor that may have deterred voters from going to the polls in 1957. Another reason advanced was that voters were so confused by the presence of the two PPPs in the 1957 elections that many preferred not to vote at all.

- In order to account for the low voting turn-out in the 1957 general elections, reasons other than the security factor or the presence of the two confusing PPPs must be found. The thesis advanced here is that the low voting participation can be traced to the limited range of political choices offered to the Guyanese voting public. This reasoning is based primarily on information gathered through direct interviewing conducted from 1967-1968.

In the five villages studied (two predominantly African, two predominantly Indian, and one mixed) both persons who voted in 1957 and individuals who were eligible to vote but did not cast their ballots were interviewed. Both voters and non-voters expressed sentiments deploring the in-fighting between Dr. Jagan and Mr. Burnham for the PPP's leadership. Nearly all voiced the hope that the two leaders would get together again. Most African and Indian voters had decided to support Burnham and Jagan respectively. For their part, the non-voters were emphatic in stating that in 1957, they had been psychologically unable to bring themselves to vote for either Dr. Jagan and Mr. Burnham, since this would necessarily entail disrupting the relatively peaceful inter-ethnic harmony that existed between African and Indian communities at that time.

This point cannot be over stressed. Put differently, the resulting movement of comprehensive ethnic politics went through a stage of ambivalence before sectional voting patterns became consolidated in the next election campaign. Not only 1957 non-voters, but voters as well, stressed that, at the time of the election, they had feared that the inter-communal *modus vivendi* that had existed between Africans and Indians was threatened by the racial nature of the choice presented by the two PPPs. For this reason, a significant minority of both Africans and Indians simply decided to stay home rather than vote for ethnically oriented parties.

The second set of data shows that by 1961, the non-voters of the 1957 elections had been eliminated by the intensification of *Apanjaat* politics. The PPP and PNC (The Burnhamite PPP altered its name to PNC in 1958) continued and completed their efforts to organise nearly the entire Guyanese electorate into ethnic political blocs. Each party wanted to ensure that all members identified with it ethnically would, in fact, vote for it. Neither the PPP nor the PNC expected that this would result in the formation of inflexible ethnic voting blocs. Rather, they counted on persuading persons not identified with them ethnically to join them, but only after each had corralled their respective ethnic sections behind them. In the four years after 1957, then, the reluctant non-voter of that year's election practically disappeared. Because of the growing pervasiveness of *Apanjaat* politics, he/she was forced to seek personal and family security by conforming to the predominant political norms of his/her ethnic sector. As pointed out in Chapter 3, local party organisation, mainly at the group level, isolated non-conformists for special persuasion. By 1961, the process of total ethnic commitment of Indians and Africans to the PPP and the PNC respectively was almost complete. We shall utilise results of the 1961 elections to demonstrate this.

In the 1961 general elections, the colony of British Guyana was divided into 35 constituencies. The candidate who received the highest number of votes among the contenders won a constituency, regardless of whether this number was a majority or plurality. Considering the new kinds of party allegiance, this 'first-past-the-post' system meant that a party could predict the outcome of an election by ascertaining the ethnic distribution in any constituency. Both the PPP and PNC possessed this information.

The election law required each candidate who contested a constituency to make an initial deposit (in 1961, $240 British West Indies currency) and, win or lose, to obtain a certain minimum percentage of the votes cast in order to have his/her deposit returned. By using its constituency ethnic distribution data, a party could decide whether or not running a candidate in a particular constituency was a practical investment. This the PPP did; it placed candidates in only 29 of the 35 constituencies. On the other hand, in order to avoid charges of racism, the PNC competed in all thirty-five constituencies. In 1960, the United Force, the new party constituted mainly of Europeans, Portuguese, Amerindians, many lightly pigmented mixed race persons, as well as a small number of well-off Indians and Africans, entered the 1961 elections and competed in 34 of the 35 constituencies.

For statistical analytical purposes, the main consequence of selective constituency competition was the great difficulty this posed for comparing electoral gains of the parties against the percentage distribution of Indians and Africans in the population as a whole. Since the PPP competed in only 29 constituencies, the overall number of votes amassed by that party could not be used to represent the total it might have received by competing in all thirty-five constituencies. On the other hand, because the PNC competed in all thirty-five constituencies, the conclusion that the total votes cast for that party represented approximately the size of its ethnic voting bloc seemed justified.

The results are shown in Table 4.3.

Table 4.3: **Votes Received by the Two Major Parties in the 1961 Elections**

Party	Number of Candidates	Ballots	%
PPP	29	93,085	42.6
PNC	35	89,501	41.0

Source: *Report on the General Elections of Members of the Legislative Assembly, 1961*, Government Printery, Georgetown, 1962:7-12.

These figures clearly did not reflect the Indian-African communal distribution which, according to the 1960 census was as follows: (Table 4.4).

Table 4.4: **Indians, Africans and Mixed as a Percentage of the Total Population**

Ethnicity	Percentage of Population (1960)
Indian	47.79
Negro	32.83
Mixed	11.99

Source: *1960 Census*, Vol. 2, Table 5, Government Printery, Georgetown, 1961.

The 'Mixed' category is included because at least half of this group tended to identify with the PNC. In 1961, with ethnic feelings rising high, ambivalence regarding sectional identity was not the safest personal policy for 'Mixed' individuals to follow, except for those who obviously could claim affinity to the Portuguese or European group by virtue of very light skin texture. Hence, in electoral terms the African voting segment was at least:

32.83 per cent + 1/2 (11.99 per cent) = 38.72 per cent (approximately 39 per cent)

Conceivably, the 2 per cent differential between the votes obtained by the PNC (41 per cent) and the electoral strength of the African sector (39 per cent) could be accounted for by one or both of two reasons: (a) the percentage of the 'mixed' who voted for the PNC was higher than 50 per cent; (b) African voting turnout was higher than Indian voting turnout. In any event, a comparison between the population of the African section and the votes gained by the PNC in 1961 showed a very close correlation.

In the 1964 elections, when both the PPP and PNC competed in all 35 electoral districts and ethnic animosities had reached their highest peak in Guyanese history, the results more faithfully displayed a very close correlation between the size of the ethnic sector and partisan voting patterns. The 1964 results are presented on Table 4.5:

Table 4.5: **Votes Received by the Two Major Parties in the 1964 Elections**

Party	Percentage of Ballots Obtained
People's Progressive Party	45.84
People's National Congress	40.52

Source: J.E. Greene, *Race versus Politics in Guyana*, University of the West Indies, Jamaica, 1974:26.

Voting turn-out was a phenomenal 96.98 per cent, despite the fact that voting was not compulsory. Comparing these results with the census data in Guyana revealed the very close correlation between ethnic identity and voting preference. The 45.84 per cent performance of the PPP, instead of the 47 per cent which was estimated as the size of the Indian population in 1964, was accounted for mainly by the fact that nearly half of the Indian population was below 21 during the 1960s. The 40.52 per cent of the PNC came closer than the 1961 figure in reflecting the size on the African voting bloc.

The above aggregate data comparisons showed the affinity between ethnic identity and party. By themselves, these figures were not necessarily conclusive proof of ethnic voting preferences in elections, though they were very suggestive of sectional voting patterns in Guyana. In order to provide additional data that incontrovertibly establishes the extremely close correlation between ethnic identity and voting choice, an analysis of the 1961 results for a select number of African, Indian and mixed Indian-African villages will be provided.

The 1961 data is used because the official electoral records provide a poll by poll breakdown of the election returns. This is the only election since universal adult suffrage was introduced in 1953 for which this kind of information was available, including the 1968 contest. In 1961, the 35 constituencies were divided into sub-divisions called polling divisions. Altogether, 688 polling divisions were created in the country, with rural and urban polling divisions covering about 400 and 600 electors, respectively.

Because a polling division in the rural areas tended to cover one or two entire villages, and villages tended to be either predominantly Indian or African, by comparing polling results with the ethnic composition of specific villages, a researcher could discover whether or not voting preferences reflected ethnic identity. Only a small number of polling divisions (and their corresponding village or villages) were selected for analysis. Included are (1) a predominantly African village; (2) two predominantly Indian villages; and (3) two more-or-less equally mixed (Indian-African) villages.

Table 4.6:   Type I - Predominantly African Polling Divisions and Villages

Case I

1. Electoral District No. 2:	Polling Division No. 2
2. Place of Polling Division:	Church of Scotland School, Kildonan
3. Candidates:	Cheddi Jagan (PPP)
	W. D. Mendonca (PNC)
	Muldeo (UF)
4. Race/Name Distribution* :	127 Indians
	280 Africans
	5-8 Others
5. Official Results:	123 votes - PPP
	262 votes - PNC
	7 votes - UF
6. BC/LT$^+$:	393/416
7. Non-Voters:	23

* Ethnicity/Name distribution refers to the estimated number of Indians to Africans in a polling division as derived by examining name types (Christian names, Indian names) as registered in the official lists.
$^+$ BC/LT refers to Ballots cast out of List Total of eligible voters

Source: Table constructed by the author from the *Report on the General Elections of Members of the Legislative Assembly, 1961*, Government Printery, Georgetown, 1962:7-12.

To discover how many Africans and Indians resided in a village or set of villages covered by a polling division, official Electors' Lists containing the names of voters were procured. By counting the number of Christian and Indian names in a polling division, a relatively accurate distribution of African and Indians in a polling division could be obtained. One of the uncontroversial aspects of the Guyanese political culture is the fact that Africans who reside in villages tend to carry 'English' or 'Christian' names, while Indians have Hindu or Muslim names. Because Englishmen and Europeans do not live in the villages studied here, the English names found in Electors' Lists obviously belonged to Africans. To ensure that the correlations and conclusions drawn from the results of the polling divisions analysed here were valid, this researcher visited and lived for varying periods in the villages covered by the polling divisions. This was done in order to confirm that the ethnic distribution deduced from the Electors' Lists was correct, and to interview party activists about voting patterns in the villages. The villages studied are presented in 'cases' and 'types' in Tables 4.6, 4.7 and 4.8. Type I, Case I, is the predominantly African Village; Type II, Cases II and III are the predominantly Indian Villages; and Type III, Cases IV and V are the mixed African-Indian villages. The data found in lines 4 and 5 in each case are crucial in this analysis.

Table 4.7:   **Type II – Mixed Indian/African Polling Divisions and Villages (Two Cases)**

Case II

1. Electoral District No. 2:   Polling Division No. 2
2. Place of Polling Division: Village Office, Limliar
3. Candidates: Cheddi Jagan (PPP)
                                     W. D. Mendonca (PNC)
                                     Muldeo (UF)
4. Race/Name Distribution: 120 Indians
                                     180-185 Africans
5. Official Results: 121 votes - PPP
                                     159 votes - PNC
                                     8 votes - UF
6. BC/LT :   288/305
7. Non-Voters: 17

Source: Table constructed by the author as in Table 4.6.

67

Case III

1. Electoral District No. 2:   Polling Division No. 10
2. Place of Polling Division: Union Lodge, No. 53
3. Candidates: Cheddi Jagan (PPP)
                                 W. D. Mendonca (PNC)
                                 Muldeo (UF)
4. Race/Name Distribution: 249 Indians
                                 209 Africans
5. Official Results: 234 votes - PPP
                                 186 votes - PNC
                                 13 votes - UF
6. BC/LT: 434/458
7. Non-Voters: 24

Source: Table constructed by the author as in Table 4.6.

Table 4.8:   Type I - Predominantly Indian Polling Divisions and Villages (Two Cases)

Case IV

1. Electoral District No. 2:   Polling Division No. 8
2. Place of Polling Division: Canadian Mission School, Villages Nos. 47-48
3. Candidates: Cheddi Jagan (PPP)
                                 W. D. Mendonca (PNC)
                                 Muldeo (UF)
4. Race/Name Distribution: 501-503 Indians
                                 4 Africans
5. Official Results: 438 votes - PPP
                                 4 votes - PNC
                                 49 votes - UF
6. BC/LT: 492/507
7. Non-Voters: 15

Source: Table constructed by the author as in Table 4.6.

Case V

1.	Electoral District No. 2:	Polling Division No. 3
2.	Place of Polling Division:	Health Centre, Bush Lot
3.	Candidates:	Cheddi Jagan (PPP)
		W. D. Mendonca (PNC)
		Muldeo (UF)
4.	Race/Name Distribution:	479 Indians
		5 Africans
5.	Official Results:	459 votes - PPP
		5 votes - PNC
		6 votes - UF
6.	BC/LT:	472/484
7.	Non-Voters:	12

Source: Table constructed by the author as in Table 4.6.

The above cases do not constitute the total number of cases studied by this researcher, but only a few of those which were selected from a larger number and presented here because they are relatively representative of the three village types. In cases I, IV, and V, representing voting patterns in African and Indian villages, Items 4 and 5 illustrate that neither party received votes in excess of the number of Indians or Africans in the village. In fact, the same pattern holds true for all five cases presented. Even more importantly, for Cases I, IV, and V, as for the other cases, the correlation between the official results and race/name distribution was very close. Because this pattern repeated itself as it did, for nearly all the polling divisions in the country where race/name analysis is feasible and justified, the close correlation can not be easily dismissed. Indeed, for Cases I, IV, and V, as for other representative cases presented here, Items 4 and 5 of the tables were convincing evidence for the proposition that the *Apanjaat* politic had become universal in Guyana by 1961.

In Cases II and III, representing the mixed Indian-African villages, ethnic voting patterns as shown by lines 4 and 5 were maintained, notwithstanding African-Indian daily interactions. In these mixed villages, nearly everyone interviewed during 1968 as part of this research project glorified 'the happy, good old days' when the PPP and PNC leaders worked together on the old, pre-1955 PPP. Despite this nostalgia, the African and Indian communities had moved apart since the inception of *Apanjaat* politics as practised by the two contemporary parties. Indeed, during the four-month GAWU strike in 1964, ethnic violence was so widespread that most mixed communities became uni-ethnic when houses owned by Indians were moved from African areas, and

African-owned houses were moved from Indian areas. In a number of cases, insecure Indians and Africans would simply exchange houses to move into a predominantly Indian or African part of the village. In 1961, as shown in Cases II and III, political opinion in mixed villages was already polarised; the 1964 strike speedily aroused intersectional animosities because the foundations for this sort of conflict were laid as far back as 1961. The 25-30 per cent non-racial, non-voting group found in nearly every village at the time of the 1957 election had been eliminated. No buffer of electoral inter-ethnic reasonableness remained by 1961.

The fourth and final set of data compares the electoral results of 1961 with those of 1964 to show the persistence of the solidified ethnic voting patterns established since 1961. This is done is by placing side by side the percentage of votes received by the parties in each constituency in 1961 and 1964, as shown in Table 4.9.

Table 4.9: **Constituency Comparisons of Votes Obtained by the Major Parties in the 1961 and 1964 Elections**

Constituency	PPP		PNC		UF	
	1961	1964	1961	1964	1961	1964
1. Corentyne River	79.0	76.68	13.5	13.72	7.5	6.82
2. Corentyne East	73.6	77.54	23.0	18.61	3.4	1.74
3. Corentyne Central	82.6	82.74	23.0	18.61	3.4	1.74
4. Corentyne West	78.0	78.17	19.3	17.79	2.7	2.5
5. Berbice East	75.7	74.78	20.4	19.17	3.9	3.49
6. New Amsterdam*	--	19.70	63.5	62.83	36.5	15.99
7. Berbice River	38.3	36.93	46.7	45.29	15.0	16.22
8. Berbice West	70.2	72.91	24.0	22.33	5.8	2.98
9. Abary	35.2	36.36	59.1	57.06	5.7	5.79
10. Mahaicony	58.5	60.45	32.0	31.59	9.5	6.99
11. Mahaica	51.1	50.03	41.9	43.04	7.0	6.03
12. Demerara Coast East	61.0	61.14	39.0	35.43	--	2.96
13. Demerara Coast Central	50.6	51.59	43.6	43.56	5.8	3.72
14. Demerara Coast West	62.6	65.39	28.47	28.3	9.0	5.69
15. Kitty	31.1	34.69	51.1	50.11	7.8	14.45
16. Campbellville	26.4	27.86	53.8	55.52	19.8	16.0

Continued/...

17. Georgetown North*	--	15.79	49.8	52.41	50.2	30.7
18. Georgetown Central*	--	15.77	45.2	48.02	54.8	35.22
19. Werk-en-Rust*	--	12.31	65.9	66.04	34.1	21.11
20. Georgetown South	24.9	25.77	52.9	56.07	22.2	17.29
21. La Penitence-Lodge	18.9	18.5	68.5	71.67	12.6	9.17
22. Ruimveldt*	--	23.44	72.4	69.52	7.6	6.5
23. Huston	50.1	48.32	44.0	45.9	5.9	4.95
24. Lower Demerara River	55.0	59.11	33.0	31.29	12.0	8.81
25. Upper Demerara ++ River	12.3	1.18	76.5	87.35	11.2	11.15
26. Canals Polder	59.7	59.86	37.0	35.83	3.3	3.23
27. Vreed-en-Hoop	62.0	63.46	29.5	27.33	8.5	7.26
28. Leonora	64.6	61.46	31.7	34.17	3.7	3.01
29. Boerasirie	70.3	72.75	25.6	21.5	4.1	3.2
30. Essequibo Is.	68.9	70.70	19.7	118.9	11.4	6.85
31. Suddie	63.1	62.64	30.3	28.95	6.6	6.5
32. Pomeroon	42.7	41.57	34.5	34.91	22.8	22.84
33. North-West	61.6	63.59	30.9	25.33	7.5	9.14
34. Mazaruni-Potaro	11.0	8.81	63.9	60.46	25.1	29.58
35. Rupununi	--	2.18	28.3	18.96	71.7	77.96

* Indicates constituencies in which the PPP did not compete in 1961. In these constituencies comparisons between the percentage of votes the PPP received in 1964 and would have received in 1961 cannot be made. As pointed out earlier, for financial reasons, the PPP did not place candidates to compete in a number of constituencies in 1961. However, in 1964 the PPP competed in every constituency because a system of proportional representation under which the seats in the legislature were to be allocated was introduced. Under the 1964 proportional representation system the votes cast in all constituencies were added together and then divided into equal parts - 53 being the number of seats in the 1964 legislature.

++ The PNC increase here is caused by the emigration of nearly all Indians out of the predominantly African Upper Demerara Constituency after riots in which several Indians were killed.

Source: Table constructed by the author.

As can be observed, in nearly every constituency where PPP and PNC figures are provided for 1961 and 1964, the percentage of votes cast for these parties remained remarkably similar. On the other hand, the UF lost votes in nearly every constituency. This occurred because ethnic animosities had reached such heights by 1964 that nearly all Africans and Indians who supported the UF in 1961 (mainly upper class or upper middle class types) were forced to revert to the party of their ethnic community to ensure their own physical safety.

In the 1964 elections, voting turn-out was again very high, totalling 96.98 per cent. This figure even more than the 1961 vote of 89.4 per cent indicates the intensity of interest in the outcome of the 1964 campaign. Unlike 1961, when the election was relatively peaceful, during 1964 violence was common and inter-ethnic hostilities reached their highest peak in Guyanese history. *Apanjaat* politics, which had dominated the 1961 elections, continued to do so in 1964 and even seemed to have increased in intensity, as witnessed by the reduction of the UF's voting percentage (12.41 per cent in 1964 as compared with 16.4 per cent in 1961). Generally, as shown by the constituency comparisons above, the 1961 results had not significantly altered 1964; ethnically-based electoral behaviour continued without change from 1961 to 1964.

B. Political Campaigns and Ethnic Allegiance

Let us now describe and analyse a typical election campaign to show how ethnic differences and sectional consciousness between Indians and Africans were evoked by the parties between 1955 and thereafter. As pointed out at the beginning of the chapter, sectional hostilities provoked during the six-month period immediately preceding each election were not forgotten after the attitudes engendered carried over, leaving a significantly higher level of communal antagonism between the Indian and African sections in inter-election periods. Over a period of three elections, the consciousness of Africans and Indians had become so saturated with mutual hate that my interviews showed that inter-sectional violence became common and talk of partition became current.

In Guyana, the intensification of racial animosities was substantially traceable to political campaigns waged by the parties during election years. From 1957 to 1968, three general elections were held; each election drew more voters than the previous one (55.8 per cent in 1957; 89.4 per cent in 1961; and 96.9 per cent in 1964). We shall not concern ourselves with elections after 1968 since all of these were conducted fraudulently. The increase in voting participation after 1957 attested not so much to growing political sophistication of the Guyanese electorate as to the intensity and pervasiveness of inter-ethnic hostilities and, concomitantly, to the grave importance Indians and Africans attached to electoral outcomes.

Political campaigns primarily between the two major competing parties (the PPP and PNC) evoked acute consciousness of the ethnic cleavages in Guyanese society. To assure its continued existence, each party wanted a sizeable segment of votes in the electorate at a minimum. Ideally, each party wanted a majority, in order to win control over the government. In the Guyanese context, the two objectives were inconsistent, considering the 1964 population distribution, which gave neither Indians nor Africans an electoral majority at the polls. Indeed, as pointed out earlier, the two objectives were inconsistent, given the manner in which the two parties vied for votes. Each party first sought to organise under its own umbrella the ethnic community identified with it, and then proceeded to attempt cross-sectional conversions. This resulted in a stalemate, with each ethnic group standing as a cohesive voting bloc behind its respective party. To understand why this occurred, the manner in which a typical campaign was conducted must be understood.

Dualism pervades Guyanese politics. Just as each party tried to camouflage its uni-ethnic predominance by displaying African and Indian personnel in its offices, during elections each party projected a public image of waging a clean, issue-oriented campaign but underneath, conducted a sordid appeal to sectional sentiments. In fact, each party allocated most of its grassroots campaign resources to soliciting votes. The two faces of each campaign were accompanied by two campaign strategies. The campaign organisation of both the PPP and PNC approximated the Figure 4.2.

Figure 4.2:   Campaign Organisational Chart of the PPP and PNC

OVERALL CAMPAIGN CO-ORDINATOR
('Advised' by Party Leader and assisted by a staff)
|
REGIONAL CO-ORDINATORS
|
SUB-REGION (A set of villages) ACTIVIST OR 'PRECINCT' CAPTAIN RESPONSIBLE TO REGIONAL CO-ORDINATOR
|
LOCAL AUXILIARIES MOBILISED TO ASSIST IN CAMPAIGN
(Pundits, school-teachers, civil servants, YSM, PYO, women's section groups)

The public aspect of each campaign was directed mainly by the party's overall campaign co-ordinator. The clean campaign typically (a) utilised the best party speakers at public meetings, (b) defined its appeals in terms of well-reasoned arguments over various issues, (c) reported party speeches at length in the party news organ, and (d) vehemently denounced racism. The party distributed thousands of pamphlets elucidating its positions, bought advertising space in newspapers, and used the free radio time allocated to it by the Government to disseminate its views. All these activities pointed to the clean face of a Guyanese political campaign.

If Guyanese national elections were contested solely by the application of the clean campaign tactics, the probability that ethnic identity would be the determining basis of party preference would be very small. Not that sectionalism would not be a main variable accounting for party preference in such a circumstance, but that the incentives for doing so would be limited and minimised. Unfortunately, in Guyana, political campaigns were not conducted on a clean level only. In fact, the clean campaign methods were relatively unimportant in the overall repertoire of activities carried out by the PNC and PPP to win votes. In Guyana, the major parties depended on a different set of tactics to mobilise support for themselves. While the clean campaign strategy was directed and executed solely by the overall campaign co-ordinator's staff, the 'informal' campaign was left to the regional managers, assisted by grassroots party activists and volunteer personnel, including teachers and civil servants. Planning and tactics of political campaigns at the grassroots involved the participation of the regional campaign managers, who were paid party activists normally assigned to the region permanently; these were assisted by representatives of the auxiliaries and the youth sections of the parties, and other influential persons such as local teachers or civil servants who normally were not affiliated openly with a party during off-election years. A region covered as many as fifty to sixty villages and small towns; the regional manager functioned to direct and co-ordinate the activities of the party campaign in a specific region. Each of the regularly paid party activists was subordinate to the regional manager; as such he was given responsibility over a number of villages and towns contiguous to each other in a particular region. The activities of the volunteer party workers in villages and towns – the group leaders, teachers, civil servants, etc., were in turn supervised by the paid party activist.

One of the consequences of the regional campaign strategy was the intense political pressure upon most parts of the Guyanese electorate by the parties during the political campaigns. From 1957 to 1963, the intense campaign coverage of the electorate was concentrated mainly in certain constituencies; from 1964 to the present all areas in Guyana were subjected equally to intense racial political campaigning tactics and methods. This shift in tactics occurred because of the change in 1964 from the 'first-past-the-post' system to proportional representation. Under the 'first-past-the-post' method used from 1953 to 1961, a party could decide not to contest a constituency because the ethnic distribution of the population in the constituency did not indicate an outcome favourable to it. Consequently, most of the competitive party battles were concentrated in constituencies with large numbers of Indians and Africans. However, under the 'proportional representation system', introduced in 1964, the entire country became a single constituency, so every vote became important to the party, regardless of where it was located. In the 1964 elections, therefore, intense grassroots campaign strategy was extended to the entire country by all parties. While the electoral evidence showed no significant change in voting patterns between 1961 and 1964, ethnic feelings were extended over a greater area of the coast. To be sure, by 1961 ethnic voting preferences had solidified, but proportional representation intensified campaigning by exposing the entire electorate equally to intense *Apanjaat* politics. With nearly all of the small Guyanese population concentrated in villages and towns on the coast, and with roads providing easy access to any coastal area, the grassroots campaign strategy of the parties was carried out easily and thoroughly, literally leaving no area unmapped or untended.

The appeals employed by grassroots party workers were of two varieties. The first variety involved invoking old negative stereotyped views held by Indians and Africans, to reinforce community solidarity of a particular sector. The second variety concerned making economic promises which said that if the party should win, the resources of the government would be channelled for the improvement of the African or Indian section. Let us briefly recapitulate these appeals, for they offer important insights into the actual workings of ethnic politics.

Over the years of their common existence in Guyana, Indians and Africans developed certain stereotype views of each other. Typically, an Indian conceived of an African as (1) physically strong and powerful. (Most Indians are relatively small in stature as compared with most Africans.) While this appeared to be a positive stereotype with regard to the African's physical endowment, most Indians viewed the physical power of the African as a threat to their security. (2) The Indian saw the African as economically undisciplined. Indians viewed the high consumptive habits of the African as irresponsible behaviour. Instead of saving some of the high earnings which came from good civil service and teaching jobs, as well as from cane-cutting on the sugar estates, the African as seen by the Indian, spent all his/her money on liquor, dances, and good clothes. For the Indian, the 'economic extravagance' of the African accounted for the many shabby houses in which Africans lived, and the paucity of the African business enterprises. In holding this economic stereotype of the Africans, Indians obviously failed to consider the numerous cases which attested to the economically conservative behaviour of many Africans. For Indians, the 'economic irresponsibility' stereotype was not peculiar to a segment of the African population but was true of all Africans generally. (3) Indians viewed Africans as culturally inferior. Most Indians regarded the wholesale adoption of 'British' ways by Africans as a mark of the African's inferiority. Although in some ways just as bastardised as Africans by British norms, Indians considered the African inferior, seemingly for not

75

retaining any cultural traits of his/her African heritage. (Some cultural traits which were retained were either not recognised by Indians, or were condemned as 'juju' culture.)

On the other hand, Africans typically conceived of Indians as (1) physically weak and inferior. Widespread African disrespect of Indians substantially stemmed from the rather frail physical features of the Indian. Indians were 'dhall and rice coolies', a slur phrase which pointed to the dietary habits of Indians who habitually ate split peas, rice, vegetables and fish, and less pork and beef. (Most Hindu Indians do not consume beef, and similarly, Muslim Indians do not consume pork). (2) The African considered the Indian economically miserly. Africans viewed the Indian as a miserly person who would sacrifice his/her dietary well-being and clothing adornment for saving a few cents from every pay package. While this appeared as a positive stereotype, most Africans viewed this (exaggerated) behaviour trait as a threat in the long run to the superior status of the African in the colonial social hierarchy which had accorded the lowest rung to the Indians. (3) The African held the Indian as culturally inferior. Most Africans prided themselves on having acquired the English Language and English norms (which in colonial British Guyana were the criteria for status and jobs), and regarded the 'retarded' acquisition of English ways by Indians as a mark of the Indian's inferiority. Hence, Indians were frequently called derogatory 'coolie babu', and Indian ways 'coolie culture'.

These stereotypes were rarely expressed openly by Indians to Africans or vice-versa, but party activists exploited them for political ends. On the part of the PPP activists, Indians were told that the PNC government run by 'Africans' would transfer their sectional stereotyped traits to the government. That is, the PNC government would (a) be economically irresponsible and extravagant, spending public tax money for dances and other such activities; (b) favour persons who were Christians and had adopted British values in the allocation of government jobs and privileges; and (c) allow Africans to intimidate Indians and threaten their property. On the part of the PNC activists, Africans were told that a PPP government would (a) recognise Indian values and consequently eliminate the old English criteria for government jobs, allowing Indians to take over the civil service and teaching professions; (b) enable Indians to use their savings to buy land and property at low prices, resulting in the economic pre-eminence of Indians in Guyana; and (c) allow Indians to become the most dominant ethnic group in Guyana notwithstanding the obvious physical weakness of Indians in general.

In the clean campaign, both the PPP and PNC displayed concern for the economic welfare of all citizens, regardless of ethnic affiliation. However, at the grassroots, these cross-sectoral appeals were forgotten. Indians were told flatly by PPP activists that, should the PPP win, the government would be 'ah'we government' (our government). Indians were promised more land, high prices for the rice they produced, and more government jobs. On the other hand, Africans were told just as brazenly that a PNC government would concentrate on urban needs such as housing and would expand the government to provide more jobs for Africans. Above all, an African government would keep the Indians 'in their place' referring to the fear of Indian domination.

The appeals of the parties at the grassroots level were conveyed through small, semi-private meetings and by door-to-door canvassing. Small meetings were held in back or front yards in an area where, tacitly, only individuals of one ethnic group could attend. At the small meetings, issues were hardly discussed; instead, the stereotypes were invoked to secure votes.

Door-to-door canvassing was carried out not only to make appeals for votes, but also to inquire into (a) party preference, and (b) difficulties a family might have in getting to the polls on time. A canvasser typically entered a house where he or she generally urged that 'ah'we people must stay together or else the (coolies) or (black people) go tek (take) over.' The entire stereotyped syndrome was gradually expressed to remind the voter to vote for his/her own kind (Apanjaat).

Overall, the appeals of the two parties tended to emphasise and exploit the sectional differences between Africans and Indians. A campaign waged intensely along these lines at the grassroots level for six months before elections, and for three consecutive elections over a decade, inevitably deepened the differences between Africans and Indians. The parties succeeded in assuring themselves of a minimum number of votes by invoking the differences between Africans and Indians. In the end, this resulted in the expression of unprecedented, intense inter-communal hostilities and violence. Most importantly, each party discovered, to its 'amazement', that once in power, its grassroots appeals succeeded in intensifying sectional divisions in the polity, rendering effective and legitimate government literally impossible without the use of force.

Probably more than any single party activity, the 'informal' political campaign evoked the historical and social differences between Africans and Indians and provoked intense and even violent pitches. As demonstrated by the statistical evidence on voter preference, these social differences were reflected politically in the development of rigid ethnic voting patterns from 1957 to 1968. In a competitive game, the 'vote-getting motive' of the PPP and PNC compelled these parties to utilise unclean campaign methods to obtain a minimum of votes. Consequently, after the elections were over, the few inter-sectional community norms and understandings that might have existed between Africans and Indians before each election period were put to a severe test and not restored to the *status quo ante*. After several elections, nearly all inter-sectional norms were destroyed for all practical purposes. More than ever before, the ethnic division in Guyana was unmediated by any reliable cushion of understanding to keep Africans and Indians from violent warfare. The integrity and stability of the state was severely impaired severely by party competition for votes.

V   The Fateful Fall into the Spiral of Ethnic Politics: The Role of Voluntary Associations and Pressure Groups

The fateful fall into the spiral of intensifying ethnic politics was also facilitated by the role of voluntary associations after the 1955 leadership split of the independence movement. Thereafter, the relationship between political parties and voluntary associations accentuated the continued ethnic bifurcation in the Guyanese cultural system. All major economic and cultural intermediate associations became affiliated directly or indirectly with one or another of the political parties in Guyana. The rigidity of this close affiliation was underlined by the consistent similarity of policy positions on issues of public concern between particular parties and specific interest groups.

Much of the political science and sociology literature on voluntary associations and pressure groups has underlined the utility of interest groups in integrating the state and promoting democratic practices. In an integrated society, the pluralistic social structure allows the multiplicity of voluntary associations formed around overlapping and interlocking memberships to serve as a cushion of moderation by which citizens relate to each other. Voluntary associations do not make total and exclusive demands on the loyalty of its members, who in turn belong to many intermediate groups. In ethnically fragmented societies, these associations tend, however, to be exclusive.

In Guyana, the network of voluntary intermediate associations caters primarily to members of one of the ethnic sections. To a substantial extent this is inevitable since historically, each section gravitated to and developed around a particular occupation. Forming as they generally do around clusters of similar interests, voluntary organizations could not help but be uni-sectional in membership. In Guyana, the major intermediate associations are therefore preponderantly uni-sectoral in membership (Truman, 1967). The large economic organizations such as trade unions and the more important cultural groups such as religious associations are identified today by the public as belonging to the 'blackman,' the 'Coolie,' or the 'Potagee.'

Voluntary associations are formed to promote the interests of their members. Consequently, one expects that these groups would fight to maintain at least a considerable amount of autonomy so as to improve their bargaining position and influence with political parties and the government. The bargaining strength of interest groups is related to the extent to which they are able to commit or withdraw their support to any party, or other institution with which they negotiate for policy favours. In Guyana, voluntary associations lack the independence of action essential for effective leverage with regard to influencing the policy positions taken by political parties. The associations are captive to the parties; they dare not defy the parties with which they are identified.

Mainly because of the dependency relationship of voluntary organisations with political parties, divisions in the Guyanese social and political system are enhanced and perpetuated. If the voluntary associations were free agents capable of bargaining firmly with either party for policy favours, particular uni-sectional organisations might affiliate with parties on a non-ethnic basis. All the parties – the PPP, PNC and UF – have at one time or the other offered programmes which, on the face, were very attractive to interest groups not ethnically associated with them. Indeed, each party tried to outdo the others in providing incentives to win support from voluntary organisations with which they were not linked ethnically. Even when the offers made by one party significantly exceeded those made by the party identified with a particular interest association, the association usually did not alter its informal affiliation to its own ethnic party. The reason lies in the political realities of the environment.

The close relationship between parties and particular intermediate associations reflected not only their interlocking ethnic membership but, most importantly, was guaranteed by certain means which the parties utilised to ensure their stranglehold over the will of the associations. Two factors coerced voluntary associations into permanent affiliation with the parties. First, the parties co-opted important members of the associations into their leadership structure. This was done by giving the presidents or secretary-generals of the important interest groups party seats in the national legislature and/or by granting them important status positions in the party's organisational hierarchy. Second, the parties infiltrated the associations so their agents could participate in determining the officers of the organisation. This simplified the final co-optation process by rendering the elected officers of an association indebted to the party for their positions. Simultaneously, this ensured that the policy positions of the association were in alignment with, or at least did not conflict with the policies of the party.

From 1955 onwards, the period that coincides with the Jagan-Burnham split, the parties succeeded in capturing all the major voluntary organisations in Guyana. This chapter describes the most critical associations in Guyana during the decade after the leadership split, and aims to show how the parties succeeded in capturing or co-opting them. The broader objective of the chapter is to demonstrate that, after the 1955 split, certain institutions and practices threw the parties into what appeared to be an irreversible spiral of ever increasing ethnic conflict. To the role of party organisation and election campaigns is added the part played the uni-sectional voluntary associations. The relationship between the parties and the interest groups structured the political differences between Indians and Africans, reinforcing bifurcation in the Guyanese polity. In effect, at a very critical period when new political structures were being formed, certain voluntary associations and pressure groups, had they acted independently free from ethnic influence, could conceivably have moderated the headlong plunge of the society into irreversible forms of ethnic political choices.

A.   Voluntary Associations and Ethnic Memberships

In the first chapter, we attempted to show that, as the immigrants took roots in Guyana, they gradually developed voluntary associations to serve their specific interests. Before 1910, very few voluntary associations existed; the freed slaves and indentured immigrants stabilised themselves around specific occupations and lived in particular and exclusive geographical areas. By 1920, Indians, African, Chinese, and Portuguese – the main labouring groups imported into Guyana – had defined their occupational interests and started to build community organisations to institutionalise their separate ways of living. Cultural organisations such as the League of Coloured People, the East Indian Association, the Chinese Association, and the Portuguese Club sprung up to cater to the religious and cultural interests of the several ethnic groups.

The Great Depression of the 1930s produced an unprecedented number of labour unions. Most of these disappeared as quickly as they had appeared, but particularly after World War II, during the full scale drive for independence of the colonies, new voluntary associations of all sorts developed rapidly in Guyana. The Depression greatly emphasised the economic precariousness of Guyanese dependence upon the world market for survival and, consequently, underlined the need of labourers to organise to protect their economic interests. Similarly, the end of World War II drew attention to the political and cultural dependence of Guyana upon Great Britain and thereby stimulated the growth of political and cultural associations to assert the political and cultural identity of the Guyanese people. The Political Affairs Committee (PAC) was the classic example of a political and cultural association which was formed after World War II in order to agitate for national independence.

Unfortunately, but almost inevitably, the formation of voluntary associations followed ethnic lines in Guyana. The two major ethnic groups, Indians and Africans, had become not only predominantly rural and urban dwellers respectively but, simultaneously, had become identified with specific occupations, because the economic interests of Africans and Indians had been separated by the historical patterns pointed out earlier. Since voluntary organisations tend to form around clusters of similar interests, the intermediate associations unavoidably became uni-sectoral in composition. Practically, all the major intermediate organisations reflected the historical development of separate economic and cultural interests among Africans, Indians, Portuguese and Chinese. In the next part, we describe the strategic importance of nine associations in the Guyanese polity and point to the nature of each group's party connection. The broader aim is to show in some detail how parties co-opted and captured intermediate associations and rendered them subservient to party goals and interests in Guyana. In the end, ethnic loyalties were more comprehensively and securely linked to the sectional parties in a deeply divided state.

Strategic Voluntary Associations and their Party Affiliations

In the formative decade after the 1955 leadership split, about nine voluntary associations could be classified as extremely important to the PPP and the PNC, which sought to win their support. These were: (1) The Civil Service Association; (2) The Federated Unions of Government Employees; (3) The Trades Union Council; (4) The Guyana Mine Workers' Union; (5) The Guyana Agricultural Workers Union; (6) The Rice Producers' Association; (7) The African Society for Cultural Relations with Independent African; (8) The Maha Sabha; and (9) the Anjuman.

Both the PPP and PNC attempted to capture these nine associations. About a decade after 1955, the PNC was safely in control of five, while the remaining four were similarly controlled by the PPP.

i) The Civil Service Association (CSA)
The CSA was a trade union which represented the interests of senior civil servants whose positions were listed under the rubric 'Personal Emoluments' in the Annual Estimates of Guyana. Membership in the CSA was voluntary, although a nominal fee was required to become a formal member of the organisation. Most of the members of the CSA were Africans; many senior Indian civil servants who were eligible to join the organisation tended not to do so because the CSA was generally viewed as African-run and dominated.

Because of the senior positions of the CSA members, nearly all of them held important and responsible supervisory and executive posts in the governmental bureaucracy. Consequently, the CSA was potentially capable of immobilising a regime if it chose to do so via a prolonged strike, such as the ones called against the Jagan Government in 1962 and 1963. The leadership of the CSA maintained a close but informal political relationship with the PNC. This was facilitated mainly by the interlocking ethnic identity of CSA leaders and Mr. Burnham's party. The PNC ensured that the CSA was kept under its control by intervening indirectly in the internal elections of the senior civil servant organisation. This was not necessarily done by endorsing candidates for the CSA's governing council, but by blacklisting or expressing disapproval of certain individuals in the organisation. Particularly since 1962, when the CSA for the first time demonstrated its capacity to immobilise a government, the PNC ceased to take the CSA election of officers for the organisation for granted.

The close political relationship of the CSA to the PNC was demonstrated by the strikes called by the CSA against the PPP government in 1962 and 1963. Determined to embarrass the PPP regime as incompetent and unsuited to lead Guyana into independence, the PNC utilised the PPP's 1962 annual budget (known as the Kaldor Budget) as the occasion for calling the CSA out on strike (Report, 1962b). The Jagan government was paralysed and rescued from political disaster only by the intervention of British troops which were summoned to restore order (Ibid.). Similarly, in 1963 the CSA was called out on strike to protest the PPP's attempt to pass a Labour Relations Bill that would have tried to solve jurisdictional disputes among unions by submitting each union's claim to represent workers to a popular industry-wide ballot (Chase, 1964). A similar measure introduced in 1953 by the old PPP had been supported by Mr. Burnham, but ten years later the PNC leader opposed it. The CSA's strike in 1963 again immobilised the PPP government and required the intervention of British troops to maintain basic law and order. The strategic position of the CSA, coupled with its close informal association with the PNC, made it impossible for any government to rule Guyana without the consent to the PNC. Far from acting as professional and politically neutral bureaucrats who recognised an obligation of loyalty to the government in power, the CSA became highly politicised and almost subservient to the policy of the PNC (Ibid., pp.193-197).

ii) The Federated Unions of Government Employees (FUGE)
While the CSA represents the interests of upper echelon senior civil servants, the FUGE catered to the welfare of lower-echelon and lower-paid civil servants. Together, the CSA and the FUGE covered virtually all civil servants in Guyana. The FUGE however, was not a single, unitary union. It was a

federation of specialised trade unions which covered various aspects of the government bureaucracy. The specialised unions affiliated with the FUGE were:

1) the Post Office Workers' Union;
2) the Medical Employees' Union;
3) the Transport Workers' Union;
4) the Public Works, Pure Water Supply, and Sea Defence Workers' Union;
5) the Government Employees' Union; and
6) the Airways Corporation Employees' Union.

These separate unions federated because they felt that as individual units each was relatively weak in negotiating with the government in any dispute.

Like the CSA, the FUGE was predominantly (85 per cent) African in membership (Ibid.). Hence, the overlap of attitudes, if not of immediate working conditions interests, between members and supporters of the PNC and the FUGE was overwhelming. If the CSA was strategically placed in the operative machinery of the government bureaucracy, the FUGE was no less significant to the continuity of smooth and uninterrupted government operations. The FUGE members' political actions complemented the activities of CSA members. Neither could operate without the other; they were mutually interdependent. A strike called by FUGE could be just as crippling to the governmental bureaucracy as a strike by the CSA.

The FUGE was more overtly oriented to and controlled by the PNC than was the CSA. The General-Secretary of the FUGE was an ex-General Secretary of the PNC, while the General Secretary of one of the FUGE's affiliates, the Transport Workers' Union, was a PNC parliamentarian who served in 1969 as the PNC cabinet minister responsible for Labour and Social Security. In 1968, the General Secretary of FUGE, Mr. Andrew Jackson, was a member of a a sub-committee that drew up a statement issued by the Trades Union Council (the federation of most trade unions in Guyana) officially endorsing the PNC in national elections which were held in December 1968. Apart from the interlocking leadership between the PNC and FUGE, this researcher observed that several officers of the FUGE affiliated unions served as precinct activists for the PNC.

Mr. Burnham's party generally did not interfere, at least overtly, in the elections of the FUGE's leadership hierarchy. Important leaders of the FUGE's affiliates were simply co-opted by the PNC into the party's leadership hierarchy, or served in Parliament on behalf of the PNC. The FUGE participated in the 1962 and 1963 strikes against the PPP government in the same way the CSA did on those occasions (Report, 1962b; Chase, 1964).

iii) The Trade Union Council (TUC)

The TUC was the largest federation of unions in Guyana. As of 1966, 24 unions were affiliated with the TUC out of a total of 59 registered unions then in existence (NW, 1966b). The General Secretary of the TUC estimated the membership of the organisation at 50,000, although the sum of the membership figures given by the individual unions affiliated to the TUC fell considerably short of this total (Ibid.). Even if the real membership figure of the TUC were half as much as the sum given by the TUC's General Secretary, the union would still be the largest organisation of labourers in Guyana.

On paper, the largest union affiliated with the TUC was the MPCA, the company union which had been recognised as the official bargaining agent of sugar workers. The Guyana Agricultural Workers' Union (GAWU), which enjoyed *de facto* popular support among sugar workers, was not a member of the TUC. Apart from the MPCA, nearly all the other unions associated with the TUC were African dominated. Since the MPCA did not have the confidence of the Indian sugar workers who it supposedly represented, for all practical purposes the TUC was lopsidedly African in real membership. The general leadership structure of the TUC was dominated by Africans; the President and General Secretary of the TUC were both Africans.

The TUC was not a politically neutral organisation. Noted one observer:

> . . . the concept of the separation of unions from political parties has been corroded in the last few years by the inter-related roles of the TUC, the UF and the PNC in the campaign against the PPP government. This has created a situation in which the TUC leadership has become a kind of salient partner in the (PNC/UF) coalition government (Graphic, 1968:8).

In 1968 the TUC took an unprecedented action when it published as widely circulated document endorsing the PNC as the best party in the 1968 elections (Chase, 1964; TUC, 1964; UFP, 1964). Even earlier, in 1962 and 1963, in support of the PNC and UF efforts to bring down the PPP government, the TUC had called a general strike which brought the PPP government to a standstill. The Unions which were formed to represent the employees of the government (the CSA and the FUGE) were affiliated with the TUC.

iv) The Mine Workers Union (MWU)
The MWU represented bauxite workers who were employed by two foreign companies, the Demerara Bauxite Co. (a subsidiary of the Aluminium Company of Canada) and Reynolds Metals Co. (U.S.). The bauxite industry was the largest producer of foreign exchange in Guyana (over G$77 million in 1966, over one-third of all foreign exchange earned that year (GIS, 1966). Because of this fact, strikes called by the MWU could create serious revenue problems for any government in power.

The bauxite companies were located in two settlements which were almost exclusively populated by Africans. Consequently, the MWU was almost completely African in membership. The connection between the MWU and the PNC was not only established by the interlocking ethnic membership of the two groups, but by the fact that the President of MWU was also president of the Trades Union Council. Apart from this, many members of the MWU leadership hierarchy were also open PNC activists. In 1963, the MWU participated in the general strike against the PPP government, although no legitimate interests of the MWU had been affected by PPP governmental policies. A year later, in the 1964 general elections, the bauxite settlements voted overwhelmingly (98 per cent) for the PNC.

v) African Society for Cultural Relations with Independent Africa (ASCRIA)
ASCRIA was the major African cultural organisation in Guyana. Early in the 20th century, a middle-class African organisation, the League of Coloured Peoples (LCP) served as the most important cultural group for persons of African descent. During the 1950's the LCP fell into disrepute among lower-income Africans because in 1957 it supported the National Democratic Party, which opposed Mr. Burnham's PPP faction in the same way it had opposed the old pre-1955 PPP, which was co-led by Mr. Burnham and Dr. Jagan.

ASCRIA was formed as the substitute for the moribund LCP. Unlike the LCP, ASCRIA based its strength primarily on lower-income African support. Also unlike the LCP, ASCRIA did not scorn its ethnic African connection with Africa, and in fact rejected European values. ASCRIA was militantly proud of its African heritage and set out to recapture and implement among Africans in Guyana, the cultural practices found in contemporary Africa. Hence, ASCRIA promoted a programme to urge Africans to drop their Christian names and assume African ones, and convened classes to teach Africans Swahili. In this way, ASCRIA had hoped to make Africans proud of their 'Africanness' and regain something of their original cultural identity.

ASCRIA was an enormously popular African organisation in Guyana (ASCRIA, 1968). At no time in its history did the LCP attain such high regard among Africans as ASCRIA did. Headed by Eusi Kwayana (formerly Sidney King), who was militantly anti-Jagan, ASCRIA took a vehement stand against the PPP, which it deemed as a racist party. Eusi Kwayana held several important posts in the PNC government. Mr. Burnham appointed Kwayana as head of the Government Marketing Corporation, and also as the chairman of the Security and Migration sub-committee of the Interior Corporation.

ASCRIA had other connections with the PNC. In an interview with the Secretary-General of the Young Socialist Movement (YSM), the youth auxiliary of the PNC, this researcher learned that over one-third of YSM's members belonged to ASCRIA. At least one PNC parliamentarian, Mr. L.

John, was an overt and active member of ASCRIA. In the 1968 elections, ASCRIA openly endorsed and campaigned for the PNC.

Most Indians in Guyana were very afraid of ASCRIA, which was viewed as 'the vanguard of African racism.' Because of this, the PNC overtly sought to disassociate itself with the activities of ASCRIA, saying that unlike ASCRIA, it believed, not in building a separate identity for Africans, but a common identity for all Guyanese. Nevertheless, the popularity of ASCRIA forced the PNC to Co-opt its leader and several of its members into the PNC government.

vi) Guyana Agricultural Workers Union (GAWU)

Formed in 1946 as the Guyana Industrial Workers Union, GAWU was the *de facto* representative of the interests of the sugar workers. It sought to replace the MPCA, several of whose officers were found to be on the payroll of the Sugar Producers Association, the employers' organisation with which the MPCA was supposed to negotiate to protect and improve sugar workers' interests. The formation of GAWU triggered one of the bitterest and most prolonged jurisdictional disputes in Guyanese labour history. Indeed, efforts of the PPP government, first in 1953 and later in 1963, to pass a Labour Relations Bill which would have resolved the jurisdictional dispute by submitting both unions (the MPC and GAWU) to a rank-and-file vote among sugar workers, precipitated the suspension of the Guyanese constitution by Britain in 1953 and eleven years later produced a four-month strike which brought unprecedented inter-ethnic rioting to Guyana in 1964.

GAWU was unrecognised by the Sugar Producers Association as the Union officially entitled to represent the sugar workers. This was the case even though, since its inception in 1946, GAWU had consistently demonstrated that it had the loyalty of nearly all sugar plantation labourers. GAWU could call a strike and workers would respond unquestioningly. Similarly, GAWU could call off a strike and expect immediate compliance. In contrast, the MPCA had absolutely no control over the actions of most sugar workers.

Because sugar production was the most important economic activity in Guyana, employing more workers than any other single industry, any union that enjoyed the overwhelming confidence of sugar workers must be regarded as politically potent. As evidence of the powerful position of sugar workers, whenever an industry-wide strike occurred, practically all other economic activities came to a standstill in Guyana, apart from bauxite production. As far back as 1945 Cheddi Jagan, recognising the strategic position of sugar workers in the economy, sought an official position in the MPCA. That is, before the formation of the Guyana Industrial Workers' Union, GAWU's predecessor. Dr. Jagan held the position of Treasurer of the MPCA from 1945-46 during which time he disapproved of the friendly relations between MPCA officials and the Sugar Producers' Association. When the Guyana Industrial Workers' union

(GIWU) was formed to replace the MPCA in 1946, Dr. Jagan was one of the co-founders. Ever since its formation, GIWU, and its successor, GAWU, had maintained an intimate relationship with various Indian-oriented political groups, the Political Affairs Committee (1946-1950) and the PPP. When the PPP divided into factional parties in 1955, the GIWU, being predominantly Indian, supported the Jaganite PPP.

In the 1960s, the PPP maintained control over the GIWU which was renamed GAWU. Throughout the 1960s, the Secretary-General of GAWU was a PPP parliamentarian and a member of the PPP's official leadership hierarchy, holding a position in the party's General Council. Dr. Jagan was the honorary President of GAWU, while two of GAWU's most popular leaders were PPP parliamentarians. Moreover, several field secretaries of GAWU appeared on the PPP list of candidates who competed in the 1968 general elections.

The evidence that the GAWU was controlled by the PPP was overwhelming. Secretary-Generals and popular officials in the GAWU had always found it easy to obtain high positions in the PPP leadership hierarchy, and to secure good jobs in the government when the PPP was in power. In a sense, this relationship between the PPP and GAWU was unavoidable, not only because of the inter-locking ethnic identity between GAWU members and PPP members and supporters, but also because the cornerstone of the PPP's historic strength was laid when Cheddi Jagan began his agitation by championing the cause of sugar workers.

vii) The Rice Producers' Association (RPA)
Formed by statute in 1948, the RPA was commissioned by the government to protect and promote the interests of rice farmers, as well as with educating farmers about new techniques, seed varieties, and other aspects of rice husbandry. As an 'official' agency, over half of the RPA's operating costs were paid by the government. All these points clearly showed that the RPA was neither 'voluntary' nor 'independent'. The operations of the RPA suggested, however, that it was in fact a 'voluntary' organisation. First, the organisation was not controlled by the government beyond the broad stipulation of its main functions. Second, a sizeable part of the RPA's budget came from members of the association, for all members were assessed an annual fee. Third, rice farmers were not required to be members of the association.

Other factors pointed to the quasi-voluntary nature of the RPA. As originally conceived, the RPA was supposed to be a politically neutral organisation. From 1948 to 1964, the RPA did not operate under any party government apart from the PPP regime (1953, and from 1957-1963). During the latter PPP regime (1957-1963), the RPA became involved in politics rapidly favouring Dr. Jagan's party. Mr. Burnham's PNC could not prevent the PPP government from continuing its financial support of the RPA during the

PPP regime. With the inauguration of the PNC-UF coalition in 1964 and the PNC government in 1968 however, the RPA gradually, but steadily, lost its government support. In 1968, all government financial support was terminated and the peasant rice farmers' association became totally dependent on its members for its operational expenses. The RPA continued to exist as it did before, but thereafter it was a completely self-supporting organisation. The RPA was the only peasant rice farmer association in Guyana after World War II. It had over 15,000 dues- paying members in a rice farming population that included 45,000 rice growing families (RPA, 1968). Since there was no other rival rice farming organisation, the RPA monopolised the representation of rice farmers' interests vis-à-vis the government, which purchased all rice produced for sale in Guyana.

Formally, the RPA was constituted quite democratically. Its members elected the officers of the organisation, as well as field representatives, who were full-time paid RPA personnel posted in various parts of the country to advise and aid farmers with their farming problems. Less formally, we shall see that the PPP exercised a degree of influence over RPA officials. The field representatives were the link between the RPA's leadership hierarchy and the rice farmers. The RPA produced a monthly journal, the *Rice Review*, which was distributed to its members by the field representatives.

Like the GAWU, which enjoyed immense popularity among sugar workers, the RPA was well-known and highly regarded by most rice farmers. As for the GAWU, this placed the RPA in a strategic position to influence the behaviour of rice farmers. Recognising this fact, the PPP at an early date sought to capture the RPA and make it its own. The first step in this direction was taken in 1957, when Dr. Jagan utilised his general popularity among Indians to become the RPA's president. Since 1957, the PPP had maintained consistent control over the RPA although Dr. Jagan relinquished the Presidency of the RPA in 1961.

Apart from Dr. Jagan's Presidency of the organisation from 1957 to 1961 and the interlocking ethnic similarity of the PPP supporters and RPA members, several political connections had linked the RPA to the PPP since 1957. The most important link was the Rice Committee within the PPP organisation (*Sunday Argosy and Evening Post*, 1963). Apart from the general concern of this committee with the overall welfare of the rice industry, field interviews suggested that the Rice Committee screened and approved all officers and field representatives who were elected to the RPA. Other kinds of political connections existed between the PPP and RPA. For example, the President of the RPA in 1969 was a PPP parliamentarian, while the General Secretary was a member of the Board of Directors of the PPP's huge import-export firm, GIMPEX. Moreover, examination of the *Rice Review* for the last decade showed that the rice policies propounded by the RPA and PPP had been identical on every point. Further, since 1964 when the PPP lost control over the government, the *Rice Review's* editorials policy had indiscriminately attacked all the PNC's rice policies. Perhaps the latter fact accounted for the RPA losing its subsidy from the PNC government.

viii) *The Guyana Sanatan Dharma Maha Sabha*
The Maha Sabha was the most important cultural and religious organisation for Hindus in Guyana. Although its headquarters were located in Georgetown, a predominantly African city, the Maha Sabha had regional branches located in various parts of rural Guyana (Maha Sabha, n.d.). The formal membership of the Hindu association was small, as compared to the large numbers of Hindus who participated in activities sponsored by the organisation. The basic unit of the Maha Sabha was the 'temple organisation'. The Maha Sabha aspired to build in every Hindu village a temple around which its members could gather to teach and carry out basic Hindu practices. Nearly every Indian in Guyana was within easy access of a temple organisation. The fact that the Maha Sabha could rely on local Hindus to provide funds and voluntary labour to build temples helped explain its broadly-based and country-wide strength.

The activities of the Maha Sabha were both religious and cultural in nature. Apart from building temples and disseminating religious knowledge to Hindus, the Maha Sabha announced the dates and declared the importance of Hindu religious holidays; it also organised social community groups to celebrate Hindu festivals. Since the formation of ASCRIA, the African cultural association, the Maha Sabha particularly intensified its organisational efforts at Hinduisation in Guyana.

Educational activities became a major preoccupation of the Maha Sabha. For example, in Georgetown the Sabha ran a large high school and awarded scholarships to Hindus from all over the country for study there. In various other areas, the Sabha set up elementary schools which provided basic education in English, accompanied by a heavy dose of Hindu cultural teachings. Several educational committees were established throughout the country to co-ordinate and organise the educational programme of the Sabha. Finally, the Sabha arranged for missionaries and Hindu celebrities from India to come to Guyana for brief periods of time.

The strength of the Maha Sabha reflected not only its popularity among Hindus, but also the fact that over 85 per cent of all Indians in Guyana were Hindus or were identified as such. Given the ethnic basis of voting preferences in the Guyanese political system, nearly all Maha Sabha members were obviously supporters of the PPP as well. The connection between the PPP and Maha Sabha was more explicit than this coincidence of ethnic similarity between Maha Sabha members and Dr. Jagan's party, however, because of overlapping leadership. The Sabha's President was a lawyer who regularly pleaded for PPP members who were in trouble with the law. In 1969, when the PPP challenged the validity of the December 1968 general elections in court, he acted as the PPP's chief counsel. Further, he was the PPP's nominee on the Public Service Commission. Finally, the Secretary-General of the Maha Sabha was a PPP parliamentarian.

Other political connections linked the Maha Sabha to the PPP. My field observations showed that pundits from the Maha Sabhas' temple organisations were open activists in PPP election campaigns. Similarly, examination of numerous issues of the Maha Sabha's weekly newspaper, the *Amar Jhoti*, demonstrated that the political positions taken by the PPP were repeated in the Sabha's news organ. All these points clearly indicate the informal political support that the Maha Sabha gave the PPP.

ix) *The Anjuman-E-Islam*
The Anjuman was the most important cultural and religious organisation among Muslims in Guyana. Because of the small size of the Muslim population in Guyana (about 15 per cent of all Indians are Muslims), the Anjuman did not have as large and comprehensive a network of local sub-units as the Maha Sabha had for Hindus. Nevertheless, the Anjuman was popular among Muslims and engaged in promoting cultural and religious activities similar to the Maha Sabha. For example, the Anjuman attempted to organise the building of mosques in villages where Muslims were in substantial numbers, as well as to offer evening classes on Muslim religion and culture. Moreover, the Anjuman brought missionaries from Pakistan to Guyana to aid the Muslim community in maintaining their religious connections with Islam. In Guyana Muslims shared a basic and common 'Indian' cultural identity with Hindus. Because of this fact, most Muslims were supporters of the PPP. On the other hand, the PPP in its political thinking, did not take the Muslim community for granted. Several Muslim names always appeared on the PPP's list of candidates at general elections, and several PPP paid group activists and parliamentarians were Muslims. The main symbolic connection between the Anjuman and the PPP was the co-optation of the President of the Anjuman to serve as a PPP parliamentarian.

Apart from these nine bodies, the economic associations of the Portuguese and the Europeans were employers' associations which served as countervailing forces to the labour unions of African and Indian labourers. The Sugar Producers Association was the organisation that represented sugar estate managers and producers; by virtue of the strategic significance of sugar to the economy, the Sugar Producers Association was a very significant pressure group in Guyana.

The Chamber of Commerce consisted of large industrial manufacturers, dealers, wholesalers, and retailers. This group was dominated by the

Portuguese businessmen. The Consultative Association of Guyanese Industry was the political arm of the Chamber of Commerce. Instead of the latter body pressuring for both political and economic advantages, it divided its functions artificially, restricting the parent body, the Chamber, to economic affairs, and delegating political and labour disputes to its unofficial subsidiary, the Consultative Association of Guyanese Industry.

Traditionally, Portuguese and European cultural interests had been served by the Catholic and Episcopal Churches. Until 1953, these churches were given special representation in the colonial legislature. Although 'serving' primarily Africans and Indians, the Catholic and Episcopal Churches had Portuguese and European leaders whose political views and orientations were generally at variance with those of their congregation.

B.   Parties, Voluntary Associations, and Bifurcation

The foregoing discussion illustrates that the voluntary associations, formed around the most important activities in which Indians and Africans were engaged for a livelihood and for cultural attachment, were closely linked to Guyana's political parties. Indians were predominantly rice farmers and sugar workers; their voluntary associations, the RPA and GAWU, were intimately connected with the PPP. Similarly, Africans were predominantly civil servants and industrial workers; their associations, the CSA, FUGE, MWU, TWG, etc. were very closely linked to the PNC. The leaders of the Indian cultural associations, the Maha Sabha and the Anjuman, were PPP parliamentarians. In almost similar fashion, the leader of the African cultural group, ASCRIA, was co-opted into service at a high level in the PNC government, as Director of the Government Marketing Division and President of the Security and Migration sub-committee in the Interior Corporation.

Undeniably, the basis for the close relationship between the parties and the voluntary associations was their interlocking ethnic membership. The parties did not create the ethnic voluntary organisations, but the relationship between the parties and interest associations strengthened and structured the bifurcation between the Indian and African political and social subsystems in Guyana. Both major parties contributed to the split through the implementation of two interconnected, unofficial policies. First, their overall goal of seeking control over at least one section of the Guyanese population for electoral ends caused these parties to pursue a deliberate policy of aligning and capturing the interest associations ethnically identified with them. The second policy was concerned with the manner in which the first policy was implemented. By intervening indirectly in the elections of the voluntary associations and/or co-opting their key leaders, the parties exerted dominant influence over the associations.

The interlocking personnel and policy links between the major intermediate groups and the parties hardened over the years and became institutionalised over a decade of this sort of relationship. All through the 1960's, particularly during the 1962 Kaldor budget crisis and the bloody 1963 and 1964 labour disputes that intensified inter-communal conflict, the parties maintained very close relations with the major associations. By prescription and precedent then, all the major voluntary organisations solidified their close relationship with the PPP and PNC. In Guyana therefore, these associations were perceived by the population as belonging either to the 'Blackman party' or the 'Coolieman party.'

With regard to the problem of the deepening communal division, two major consequences followed from the close affinity between parties and associations. First, the voluntary associations became very politicised. In a sense, this was unavoidable because of the intensity and pervasiveness of political feelings in Guyana, and because of the interlocking ethnic membership affiliation between the associations and the parties. But politicisation was exacerbated by the co-opting of the association leaders into the parties and/or by the interference of the parties in the electoral procedures of the associations. The parties carried their struggle for electoral survival to the associations, whose support they needed.

The second major consequence of the close relationship between parties and associations related to the bargaining position of the voluntary organisations vis-à-vis the parties. Since none of the major voluntary associations had ever threatened nor, much less, tried to align themselves with a party not ethnically identified with their membership over the ten or fifteen years of their existence, it would appear that a high degree of permanence had developed in the relationship between the parties and the associations. The close alignment of the voluntary associations with the parties strengthened the cohesion within the Indian and African communities in Guyana. In turn, this strengthening of internal sectoral cohesion had set the two major ethnic communities even further apart because of their mutual hostility to each other. Inter-ethnic voluntary organisations were conspicuously few in Guyana. An Indian or African had to join an Indian or African intermediate organisation to protect his /her economic or cultural interests.

By capturing the major voluntary associations, the parties rendered them subservient to party goals and interests. The existence of a stratum of independent intermediate associations could force parties to abandon their informal racial policies. Independent associations could commit or change their support for a party to best suit their economic or cultural interests. When the voluntary associations became captive to the parties, however, then a main source of political restraint was eliminated and parties pursued extreme unmoderated policies. Because the parties had succeeded in capturing all the major intermediate groups in Guyana, they could pursue unrestrained their *Apanjaat* policies, which separated the Indian ethnic section from the African. The captive relationship between the groups and parties allowed the latter to use the former to execute *Apanjaat* party policies, which further deepened the divisions in Guyana.

VI Ethnic Conflict Explodes into Civil War

The spiral of intensifying ethnic conflict, slowly but inexorably exacerbated by the way the political parties organised the lives of their constituents, the manner in which election campaigns were waged, and the method by which voluntary associations were enlisted in the struggle for communal ascendancy, led almost inevitably to cataclysmic inter-ethnic confrontation and civil war. Between 1961 and 1965, the screws of communal conflict were slowly tightened so that few persons could escape being co-opted participants in a system of mutual communal hate. Inter-ethnic relations, especially between Africans and Indians, were increasingly marked by covert contempt and deceptive distrust. The elements of an impending explosion were registered first in the fear of ethnic domination of Indians by Africans and of Africans by Indians. A new drama was unfolding in which the main motif was a struggle for ethnic ascendancy compounded by a politically instigated terror of internal communal colonisation. While inter-ethnic interaction was still carried on in the familiar routine of daily life, the same persons in the privacy of their homes and communities enacted a script of racist and communal antipathy, drawing perilously closer to open conflagration with each passing day. In public, the political drums continued surreptitiously to beat on the theme of ethnic claims and exclusivity; in public interaction each side had contrived a set of secret intra-communal symbols, idioms and nuanced expressions to silently communicate group solidarity erected on an understanding of collective contempt for the other side. Dual roles and schizophrenic personalities dwelt simultaneously in an ethnically split society. Forced to live together by the designs of a colonial conqueror, the sectional elements possessed no experience for inter-communal accommodation. Introduced mass politics were betrayed by sectional leaders jockeying for power. A moment of opportunity for reconciliation and reconstruction was squandered and the innocence of legitimate inter-ethnic suspicion was nurtured into a monster obsessed with the fear of communal dominance. One cleavage after another which separated the ethnic segments – race, traditional values, religion, residence and occupation – was reinforced by a mode of modern mass ethno-nationalist politics that drove the society to the brink of self-destruction.

After the 1961 elections, in the aftermath of an intensively organised, ethnicised election campaign, and with the promise of independence soon thereafter, the victory by Cheddi Jagan's Indian-based PPP posed a fundamental threat to the survival of Africans, Mixed Races, Europeans, Amerindians, Chinese and Portuguese. The system of electoral politics enabled the victor in a zero-sum game of competition to assume complete control of the resources of the government. The chance – even a slim one – that this power could be perversely applied to systematically and permanently exclude political and communal opponents was all that was necessary to mobilise massive and crippling opposition to any ethnically-based government. In the multi-layered communal order established by the colonial power, an inter-dependent economy of specialised parts, each part dominated by one ethnic group, was institutionalised. No ethnic group could live without the other. Fear of ethnic domination was also a critical feature in the politics of independence after the accession of Jagan to power in 1961. That the British promised independence to the victor of the 1961 elections brought with it a more magnified fear that the party in power would be able to re-define the rules of the game permanently without colonial external intervention. Independence evoked visions of ethnic discrimination, repression and servitude in the functional equivalence of a new kind of internal colonialism.

The impending ethnic catastrophe in Guyana following the 1961 elections was compounded by a second factor, apart from the inter-communal conflict and the attendant fear of ethnic domination. Ideology assumed a salient role, for Dr. Jagan's PPP unabashedly espoused a Moscow-oriented socialist policy for the transformation of colonial Guyana. More specifically, Guyana, under the avowed Marxist-Leninist Cheddi Jagan, sought a radical new direction at the inopportune time when Cuba under Castro had become an acutely uncomfortable thorn in the side of the United States. After the Bay of Pigs fiasco, President Kennedy had firmly decided that there would not be another Cuba in the Western Hemisphere. Defiantly, Dr. Jagan declared unreserved support for Fidel Castro, calling him the greatest liberator of the twentieth century. Guyana was still a colony at the time. Hence, the PPP government posed a triple threat to various opponents, both internal and external. First, the Burnham-led PNC, representing mainly the African section, saw Jagan's PPP as a communal threat to the possibility of permanent ethnic domination. Second, the *laissez-faire* capitalist-oriented United Force (headed by Portuguese businessman Peter D'Aguiar), representing for the most part the well-off, non-African, non-Indian sections of the Guyana population, feared the PPP because of the communist threat to private property. Third, the Kennedy regime feared the PPP because of its threat to the geo-political security interests of the U.S. in the Western Hemisphere in the context of Cold War politics. In this chapter, we shall describe and analyse how the external ideological interests of the United States were manipulated so as to exploit the ethnic and ideological divisions in Guyana, in order to remove the PPP from power. In particular, we shall describe how the underlying ethnic malaise was manipulated so that inter-communal civil war would ensue, allowing one ethnically-based party to dislodge another, while simultaneously solving the problem of a communist menace in Guyana for the United States. The following discussion focuses on three major, violent crises that occurred during the Jagan administration of 1961-1964.

Three Crises

a) The 1962 Crisis

In March, 1960, the main political leaders in Guyana convened in London to discuss with the British Colonial Office 'what measures of constitutional advance should take place in British Guyana' (Report, 1960:3). One must recall that the 1953 Constitution, which had been suspended, was the most advanced constitution granted to Guyana by Britain up to 1960. Since its suspension, a new constitution, elaborated in 1957 and known as the Renison Constitution after the name of the British governor of British Guyana, Sir Patrick Renison, had been in effect. Under it, new national elections took place. The Renison Constitution was, in essence, similar to the constitution granted in 1928. It severely restricted the responsibilities of elected representatives of the people. While the 1953 constitution had granted internal self-government, the new constitution did not do so. In this respect, the Renison Constitution of 1957 represented a definite constitutional setback in Guyana's efforts to win independence.

After three years of working with the 1957 constitution, at the insistence of both Dr. Jagan and Mr. Burnham, Britain was persuaded that Guyana was ready for a new advance in constitutional self-government. Hence the 1960 Constitutional Conference was called to work out not only the immediate changes of government that should occur, but also to set some tentative timetable for Guyana's eventual independence. At the end of the 1960 Constitutional Conference, two major gains were conceded by the British Colonial Office. First, after new elections scheduled for 1961, a new constitution granting complete internal self-government to Guyana would be implemented. The 1961 Constitution was more advanced than that of 1953,

97

since the former granted control over all aspects of Guyanese political affairs except defence to the party that won. Second, for the first time Britain formally conceded that 'Her Majesty's Government accepts the principle of independence for British Guyana' (Ibid.:6). In pursuance of the second objective, the Colonial Office specifically said that the subject of the independence date would be set 'at any time not earlier than two years after the first General Election held under the new constitution or upon it being decided that the West Indies Federation should attain independence' (Ibid.).

For all practical purposes, the party which would win the August 21, 1961 elections would lead Guyana into independence. All the parties anticipated this and stated the point repeatedly and clearly in their election campaigns of 1961. Confident of victory, the PNC not only anticipated that Mr. Burnham would govern, but also went so far as to suggest a specific date when Britain would grant Guyana full independence under the victorious PNC government (Report, 1962c). Mr. Burnham's party based its electoral predictions mainly on the assumption that the United Force would win no seats in the 1961, elections and that several marginal constituencies with close African-Indian rations would vote for the PNC. The outcome of the elections disappointed the PNC immensely. The UF not only captured four seats in the 35 seat legislature, but played an important role in deciding four out of five of the marginal seats in the PPP's favour. The outcome of the elections gave the PPP 20 seats, the PNC 11 seats, and the UF four seats. The PNC had anticipated winning not only the four seats taken by the UF, but also swinging at least three additional seats in the marginal African-Indian constituencies to give it a majority of 18 seats (Bradley, 1961). When all the votes were tallied, the PPP obtained 42.5 per cent of the popular vote, the PNC 40 per cent and the UF 17 per cent.

Prior to the 1961 elections, both the PNC, the PPP and even the UF had predicted victory for themselves. During their campaigns, while the outcome of the elections was still to be decided, the parties did not indicate what they would do if they did not win. After the elections were over however, all the fears of the defeated parties were openly vented and the fundamental fissures which underlaid the sectionally-ridden Guyana social system were resurrected. The UF, in particular, became hysterical. This party which, it will be recalled, represented the economically well-to-do groups in Guyana, including Europeans, Portuguese, as well as many upper and upper-middle-class Indians and Africans, saw a bleak future for itself under a PPP government. During the 1961 elections the UF made Communism a major issue (Ibid.:12-17).

The UF brought literally tons of anti-Communist literature into the campaign, and also obtained the direct and open help of the Christian Anti-Communalist Crusade Movement based in the U. S., as well as that of the Catholic and Anglican Churches in Guyana (Ibid.). In the light of Castro's recent success in Cuba, the UF painted a picture of 'atheistic Communism' in

Guyana under Jagan, who had openly expressed unreserved admiration for the government of the Cuban Premier. For the UF then, the PPP government was an ominous threat to the security of its supporters and to private enterprise. The PNC did not react as hysterically to the PPP victory as the UF, particularly since the UF had labelled both the PPP and PNC as Communist parties (Ibid.:13-14). But the PNC was deeply worried. During the 1957-1961 PPP regime, Mr. Burnham's party had protested vigorously against the 'agricultural bent' of the PPP's development plan, charging the PPP with running a 'Coolie Government' or 'Rice Government' (Ibid.:14-16). Now that the PPP was in power again, and this time with independence probably imminent, the PNC saw its prospects of ever governing Guyana diminishing rapidly – unless something was done.

With an intense interest in keeping the PPP out of power permanently, the UF, in particular, awaited an occasion to bring the Jagan Government down. One way to do this would be to create enough disturbances in Guyana to prove that the PPP could not govern the country, and that an independent Guyana under Jagan would be highly unstable. If this could be done, Britain might be persuaded to postpone independence for Guyana indefinitely. The occasion for the UF to initiate its disruptive tactics was presented when the PPP announced its annual budget for the fiscal year 1961-1962. This budget was known as the Kaldor Budget, after its formulator, the distinguished Cambridge economist, Nicholas Kaldor, whose services were acquired by the Jagan Government through the United Nations. It attempted to raise funds for economic development, mainly through tapping domestic sources of capital. Specifically, the budget attempted (a) to close tax loopholes which had traditionally have been exploited by businessmen; (b) to establish exchange controls in order to prevent massive outflows of capital; and (c) to impose a compulsory five per cent savings on all incomes which were above $100 (British West Indies currency) per month (Report, 1962b). These savings were to be invested in Government bonds which would be redeemable in seven years at three-and-a-quarter per cent interest. No taxes were to be levied on the interest obtained for these savings (Ibid).

The Kaldor Budget was praised editorially by the *New York Times* and the *London Times* as a commendable effort at self-help by an emerging country to fund its own developmental programme. Professor Newman, who conducted a systematic inquiry into the Kaldor budget described the reaction of the UF and its news organ, *The Chronicle*, as 'hysterical' concluding that 'there was no basis for the storm of virulent criticism which the United Force let loose on the budget' (Newman, 1964:93). Newman quoted directly from the editorial of *The Chronicle* to demonstrate that the source of the UF's criticisms were its ideological differences with the PPP:

'A vindictive and malicious spirit . . . prowls though the Budget . . . . The Budget's tax reform proposals are merely the transcription of doctrinaire Marxism into the fiscal policy of this poor country', said the *Sunday Chronicle's* editorial of 4 February (Ibid.).

Newman went on to impeach the motive for political implicit in the drive to destabilise the Jagan government:

In the next ten days, the criticism mounted to increasingly hysterical levels, and it became clear that the UF was seizing the opportunity that the Budget had presented to force the PPP government from power by the wave of 'popular' anger over the new taxes (Ibid.).

Newman proceeded to implicate the actions of the PNC which was initially reluctant to join the UF's attack on the Budget:

The PNC ... eventually joined in ... probably because it too saw a chance to topple the Government; the leaders Burnham and D'Aguiar were photographed ostentatiously shaking hands with each other, after jointly leading an illegal procession around the Government buildings (Ibid).

The African-dominated civil service associations, the CSA, the FUGE and other unions federated with the TUC, called a strike, and joined the PNC and the UF in demonstrating and protesting against the Jagan regime. The disturbances culminated in widespread violence and arson in Georgetown on February 16, 1962. When local police were unable to restrain protesters, British troops were called in to maintain basic law and order. When 'Black Friday' came to an end, the toll read as follows: five men killed, eighty injured, and over $11.5 million dollars (British West Indies currency) worth of property destroyed in the business centre of Georgetown. For a small country, this was a significant loss. More importantly, the biggest damage was done to the PPP regime, which was unable to maintain elementary order in Georgetown with its own domestic resources. The PPP charged that the only reason it had summoned the support of the British authorities whom it habitually attacked was because the African-dominated police force had failed to suppress the riots for political reasons.

Following 'Black Friday', several events occurred that partially fulfilled the aims of the UF and PNC during the February riots. These events, together with the aims of the several factions, are discussed in the *Report of the Inquiry Commission* cited below. First, a Constitutional Conference which was scheduled for May, 1962, to discuss and fix the date of Guyana's independence was postponed until October, 1962. The reason for the postponement given by the Colonial Office was that a Commonwealth Commission of Inquiry was to be sent to Guyana to investigate the February riots. This Commission, composed of three persons – one from Ghana, one from India, and one from Britain – had to submit its report before a conference on the independence of Guyana was rescheduled. The second aim that the riots fulfilled for the PNC and the UF was to open the new Constitutional Conference to discussion, not only of the date of Guyana's independence, but also of matters regarding Guyana's future stability, given the leadership of the PPP in the government.

The Commonwealth Commission of Inquiry conducted extensive hearings in Guyana; it submitted its report in October, 1962. The basic findings of the Commission underscored the ulterior political motives of the UF's and PNC's reaction to the Kaldor Budget. On Mr. Burnham's participation in the riots, the Commission commented:

> The real motive behind Mr. Burnham's assault was a desire to assert himself in public life and establish a more important and more rewarding position for himself by bringing about Dr. Jagan's downfall (Report, 1962b:19).

On Mr. D'Aguiar's role, the Commission said:

> The view taken by Mr. D'Aguiar was that it was not enough to make any modifications in the budget, and the only course open to the Premier was to resign. He intended to use every means to bring down the government (Ibid.:27-28).

Finally, commenting on the role of the unions in striking against the Government, the Commission observed that:

> despite the loud protestations of the trade union leaders to the contrary, political affinities and aspirations played a large part in shaping their policy and formulating their programme of offering resistance to the budget and making a determined effort to change the government in office (Ibid.:64).

The Commission's report submitted and published, the postponed Constitutional Conference was finally held on October 23, 1962. At the conference, the position taken by Dr. Jagan was stated as follows:

> I submit, Sir, that the struggle for power between the various political factions at home should not properly form part of the deliberations of

this conference. Rather, my Government conceives this to be a domestic matter to be hammered out at home (Ibid.:7).

For Dr. Jagan, the primary business of the conference was to set an independence date and to agree on a constitution for Guyana. The PPP leader argued that by virtue of winning the 1961 elections his party was entitled to lead the country into independence, since during the 1961 electoral campaign, 'the opposition parties in appealing to the electorate made it clear that whichever party won the elections would be leading the country to independence' (Ibid.).

Mr. Burnham and Mr. D'Aguiar disagreed with this. Mr. D'Aguiar contended further that:

No single party won an overall majority ... and therefore it is a matter of principle for us that a minority party should not have the right to change a constitution vitally without getting a further mandate from the people. Our basic stand is the demand for new elections before there is a new constitution (Ibid.:14).

Not only were new elections demanded by the two opposition leaders but, equally important, they insisted that the elections be held under a new voting system. They supported proportional representation instead of the first-past-the-post procedure which had given the PPP a majority of seats in the 1957 and 1961, elections despite not polling a majority of votes cast. One must recall that in 1957, the PPP obtained nine out of the fourteen seats in the legislature although it received only 47 per cent of the popular vote, and in the 1961 elections the party won 20 out of 35 seats even though it obtained only 42.6 per cent of the votes. Mr. Burnham stated his position for the introduction of proportional representation:

For us, proportional representation is a means of ensuring co-operation. It is our conviction... that a multiplicity of parties is an expression of existing fissiparous tendencies in a given community, and proportional representation merely gives further expression to certain of these fissiparous tendencies (Ibid.:12).

In response to the demands of the opposition parties' request for proportional representation, the PPP not only pointed out that no colony to which the British had granted independence had ever been put under this electoral system, but offered a counter-demand as well. Dr. Jagan suggested that under a new constitution, the suffrage should be extended to persons eighteen years old. The aim of the counter-demand was to neutralise the effects of proportional representation, should it be granted, by allowing Indian youths, who greatly outnumbered African and Portuguese youths, to vote in all foreseeable elections. For example, one of the reasons why the PPP did not receive over 50 per cent of the votes in the 1964 elections, although Indians made up a little more than half the Guyanese population, was because over half of the Indian community was under 21 years old.

The upshot of the diverse demands offered at the London Conference was a stalemate. No agreement could be reached unanimously (the Colonial Office insisted on unanimity to validate final decisions reached at the Conference). The Colonial Secretary, Mr. Duncan Sandys, dismissed the conference as deadlocked, with no decision made on : (a) future elections; (b) independence date; (c) proportional representation; and (d) voting age.

b) The 1963 Crisis: The Eighty-Day Strike

The decisions of the 1962 London Conference were still to be announced. While the PNC and the UF had succeeded in postponing the date of independence for Guyana, they had not yet fully accomplished their goal of denying the PPP control over the government. The fear that the Jagan government might lead Guyana into independence, and conceivably remain in power for many years, was not abated after the London Conference. In fact, although the opposition parties were still uncertain about the possible outcome of any future conferences, they suspected that the Colonial Office had become receptive to their arguments against the Jagan regime, especially after the riots of February, 1962.

One of the most crucial lessons that the PNC and the UF learned from the riots of Black Friday was the vulnerability of the PPP government, because of its location in Georgetown, the capital city. Overwhelmingly, the PPP supporters were Indians who resided in rural areas, while PNC and UF supporters were urban residents and non-Indians who lived mainly in Georgetown. Further, by striking in February, 1962, the CSA and the FUGE, the predominantly African civil service associations, demonstrated to the PNC the crippling effects on a government when civil servants cease to work. Together, these two factors – the location of the Government in Georgetown where the PNC and UF supporters predominate, and the strategic position of the CSA and the FUGE vis-à-vis the continued operations of the Government – provided the opposition parties with potentially debilitating artillery against any government that the UF, and particularly the PNC opposed. These basic facts of political power emerged even more clearly in the 1963 strike.

The return of Guyana's political leaders to Georgetown after the London Conference was followed by a very brief period of relative peace. Within four months the peace was broken and a new strike called against the PPP government. This time, ethnic animosities, particularly between Indians and Africans, soared to unprecedented heights. For all practical purposes, over a period of 80 days, basic law and order broke down in Guyana and civil war was in progress. Ethnic fears were harnessed to tangible political objectives. The struggle was over control of the government. The political parties directed this struggle, throwing the entire society into crisis.

The 80-day strike stemmed from the introduction during March, 1963, of a Labour Relations Bill into the legislature by the PPP. This piece of legislation was similar in nearly every respect to the Labour Relations Bill proposed by the old PPP in 1953. At that time, Mr. Burnham and Dr. Jagan were co-leaders of the PPP, and Mr. Burnham was one of the chief party spokesmen on behalf of the Labour Relations Bill. The Bill attempted to resolve jurisdictional disputes between unions by submitting the claims of contending labour organisations to an industry-wide poll which would decide which group would represent the workers. As in 1953, one of the key political objectives of the Labour Relations Bill of 1963 was to replace the company union, the MPCA, with the GAWU, which not only was popular among sugar workers, but was controlled by the PPP.

The PPP's reason for introducing the Labour Relations Bill was expressed by Dr. Jagan as follows:

The intention of the Party to introduce this type of labour legislation had been embodied in its manifestos in 1953, 1957, and again in 1961. It can therefore be said that the PPP government had a mandate to enact a Labour Relations Bill by virtue of three successive general elections which the party had won (Jagan, 1966:271).

In 1953, the TUC did not object to the Bill, but in 1963, when this union was under virtual control of the opposition parties and when Mr. Burnham and Mr. D'Aguiar expressed opposition to the Bill, the TUC came out against the Labour Relations proposal. The TUC's main objections against the Bill were (1) that it placed too much power in the hands of the Minister of Labour, who had the prerogative of initiating inter-union polls to decide which union should represent workers in jurisdictional disputes, and (2) that there had been a lack of consultation between the government and the TUC on the Bill (Chase, 1964; C. Jagan, 1966; TUC, 1964). It was clear that strong ulterior political motives underlaid the PNC and UF opposition to the Labour Relations Bill. Mr. Burnham confirmed this point of view himself, when he said that the Labour Relations Act was not the *causa belli*, but the *casus belli*, not the cause of, but the occasion to form the strike (Chase, 1964).

As in the February riots of 1962, the PNC and UF were not so much interested in the particular issue that triggered off the 1963 strike, as in disrupting and possibly overthrowing the PPP government. As in 1962, the 1963 incident was aimed at demonstrating the inability of the Jagan regime to govern Guyana, and to postpone independence, change the electoral system, call new elections, and ultimately remove the PPP government from power. In sum, the PNC and UF's distrust of a PPP regime in an independent Guyana precipitated violence and sabotage against the Jagan government.

In the 1963 crisis, the forces that were arraigned against the PPP regime were formidable. First, the TUC called a general strike in which the CSA, FUGE, BGTA and MPCA participated. Because it was a company union, the MPCA failed to mobilise the sugar workers, who were preponderantly Indians, to join the strike against the Indian-based PPP government. In the case of the CSA and FUGE, African civil servants went on strike but most Indian civil servants did not. Further, the Teachers' Association (the BGTA), which was called out against the PPP government, failed to mobilise the strikers since over one-third of the members were Indian school teachers. These points vividly attest to the underlying ethnic structures that fuelled the fires of the 1963 strike.

The second force that opposed the PPP regime came from external sources which would reveal the destabilising role of the United States and the internationalisation of the conflict. This assumed the form of the ICFTU, ORIT, and AIFLD. The ICFTU, ORIT, and AIFLD were a series of interconnected international trade unions which had official links with the TUC in Guyana. The International Confederation of Free Trade Unions (ICFTU) was formed in 1949 as a break-away splinter union from the World Federation of Trade Unions (WFTU). The ICFTU was constituted as a separate trade union movement after the WFTU was divided into Communist and non-communist blocs over guerrilla insurgency operations in Malaysia. The ICFTU had since been recognised as the Free World counterpart of the WFTU, the so-called Communist international trades' union movement. The American Federation of Labour (AFL) in the United States was one of the largest affiliates of the ICFTU. The Guyana Trades Union Council was an affiliate of the ICFTU. The Inter-American Regional Organisation of Workers (ORIT) was a regional branch of the ICFTU associated with trade union movements in the Caribbean. The Guyana TUC was affiliated with ORIT. Finally, the American Institute of Free Labour Development (AIFLD) was formed in 1962 to aid Latin American and Caribbean unions in their 'development.' On the surface, this union was subsidised by labour and business in the United States (Lens, 1965; Sheehan, 1967; Pearson, 1964; Chase, 1964).

The Guyana TUC was an affiliate of the International Confederations of Free Trade Unions (ICFTU) which sympathised with the strike by organising a general blockade of air and sea traffic to Guyana. Ships carrying food to

Guyana from Caribbean ports ceased coming to Guyana, as did all the airlines, which the ICFTU threatened with boycotts if they did not co-operate (Chase, 1964). Food became scarce in Georgetown, and in the absence of oil, vehicular traffic virtually came to a standstill throughout Guyana. Furthermore, without oil several governmental operations were in danger of breakdown. During the strike, the AIFLD supplied money and food to the strikers, which aided in prolonging the strike (Ibid.).

Under these circumstances, the Jagan regime solicited the help of the Cuban and Soviet Governments. A Cuban vessel with oil arrived to break the blockade and later a Soviet vessel with wheat followed. These two events created rumours of a Communist take-over, triggering full-scale ethnic violence in Guyana. In Georgetown, Indians were beaten and killed, while in rural areas Africans were subjected to similar treatment. Shootings and bombings became commonplace. Civil war had commenced.

The third force that opposed the PPP government was the Georgetown Chamber of Commerce (GCC), the sugar companies, and the bauxite companies. All three of these groups closed their stores and manufacturing operations during the strike. In the case of the GCC and the sugar companies, when workers refused to strike the companies simply closed operations. Both of these groups, which represented the traditional status quo interests in Guyana, were motivated more by fear of the 'Communist' PPP than by anything inherent in the Labour Relations Bill.

Finally, the police force, overwhelmingly staffed by Africans, again refused to enforce the law impartially. Janet Jagan, who was then Minister of Home Affairs and therefore in charge of internal security, resigned during the 1963 crisis, charging that the police refused to co-operate with her. At several critical points in the early period of the strike, pleas by the PPP government for British troops were turned down. Those pleas became especially desperate after the entire Indian community in Wismar-Mackenzie, a bauxite town with a predominance of Africans, was uprooted, some were massacred, and the remainder were brutally forced to leave. This particular incident is remembered by Indians in Guyana even today. When Indians are queried about future African-Indian co-operation, they are invariably reminded of Wismar-Mackenzie, which has become a symbol of inter-ethnic animosity. Africans also point to specific events which carry similar symbolic connection.

The strike came to an end on July 7, eighty days after it started. The British TUC was called in and successfully mediated the dispute. The Labour Relations Bill, which had triggered off the strike, was lapsed in Parliament on June 18, when the Premier prorogued the legislature after a parliamentary dispute. The continuation of the strike until July 7, nearly three weeks after the Labour Relations Bill was thrown out, was another indication of the political nature of the strike.

The 1964 colony-wide civil strife brought Mr. Duncan Sandys, the British Colonial Secretary, to Guyana. Mr. Sandys came to inspect the situation in the British colony and confer with political leaders. From his visit, Mr. Sandys was persuaded to hold in the fall of 1963 another independence conference. The Guyanese leaders, Dr. Jagan, Mr. Burnham and Mr. D'Aguiar, attended the conference, which was held in October, 1963, and repeated the arguments made at the 1962 conference. This time however, the PNC and the UF based their demands for proportional representation and new elections before an independence date was set on the incidents of 1963, which shook the Jagan Government. Now, no one could ignore their arguments.

As in 1962, the conference was deadlocked and about to be dismissed again. On this occasion, however, the Colonial Office persuaded the three leaders to sign a document that would entitle the British Government to arbitrate the issues which arose at the conference. All three leaders attached their signatures to the document, which stipulated that whatever decision the Colonial Office made was binding on all parties. When the Colonial Office announced its decision, all the demands of Mr. Burnham and Mr. D'Aguiar were conceded, and none of Dr. Jagan's requests were granted. The British Government stipulated that (a) new elections were to be held, (b) a new conference subsequent to the elections would be convened to decide on the independence date, (c) proportional representation was granted, and (d) the voting age remained at 21. The decision infuriated the PPP, which charged the Colonial Office with a breach of faith. The decision of the Colonial Office set the stage for the 1964 crisis, of which neither the PNC nor the UF, but instead the PPP were the main instigators. In the meanwhile, ample evidence was assembled by the *New York Times* and the *Washington Post* to show that the strikes in Guyana against the PPP were sponsored by the CIA (Sheehan, 1967; Pearson, 1964). Furthermore, strong evidence existed to point to the role of the U. S. in influencing Britain not to concede to any of the demands of the PPP at the London Conference. One notable piece of evidence came from A. Schlesinger's memoirs on his days as Special Advisor to the Kennedy administration. Schlesinger said to Kennedy that 'an independent Guyana under Burnham would cause us many fewer problems than an independent Guyana under Jagan' (Schlesinger, 1965:779). He then argued for a change:

And the way was open to bring it about because Jagan's parliamentary strength was larger than his popular strength. He had won 57 per cent of the seats on the basis of 42.7 per cent of the vote. An obvious solution was to establish a system of Proportional Representation (Ibid.).

In October 1963, the British government introduced proportional representation into Guyana and, as Schlesinger reported, with that act 'British Guyana seemed to have passed out of the Communist orbit' (Ibid.).

c) The Crisis of 1964: The GAWU-Inspired Strike

The Sandys' decision, which was announced in late November, 1963, favoured the PNC and UF parties and consequently sparked immediate verbal denunciations of the British Government by the PPP. However, this was only the initial response by the Jagan regime, which decided to wait until the Christmas holidays were over before embarking on a course of practical action to agitate against Sandys' one-sided concessions to the opposition parties. The PPP recognised, in the same way that the PNC and UF had during the 1962 and the 1963 crises, that a PNC/UF government was essentially unacceptable to it. To the PPP, a PNC/UF coalition symbolised a return to the political and economic status quo that existed before 1950; equally as important, such a regime represented the institution of practices which would be detrimental to the economic interests of the Indian community. In late January, 1964, the PPP launched what Dr. Jagan called 'a hurricane of protest' in order 'to afford our supporters the opportunity to demonstrate their confidence in the leaders of the party in the face of the British Government's betrayal at the London Conference' (Jagan, 1966:350).

When the marchers, who were nearly all Indians, finally arrived in Georgetown, Dr. Jagan addressed the group, clearly stating the intention of the demonstration:

> I am not going to promise you that the fight will be easy. Our masters will fight back ruthlessly. If, however, you are prepared to fight, if you are prepared to struggle, if you are prepared to die, know that I am with you 100 per cent (Ibid.:351).

The effectiveness of the march was buttressed by the renewal of the call by the PPP-controlled GAWU for recognition by the Sugar Producers Association (SPA). At Plantation Leonora, strike action against the sugar industry was initiated on February 11, 1964, and formally became industry-wide on March 4. Under the direction of the GAWU and PPP activists, workers demanded that the company union, the MPCA, be replaced by the GAWU and the weekly union dues, which were automatically withdrawn from the more than 20,000 sugar workers' pay packets and given to the MPCA, be handed over to the GAWU. The SPA did not accede to the GAWU's demands which, in any event, were made at this particular time in order to call an industry-wide strike in support of the political grievances of the PPP against the British government. The PPP sought to create widespread disruption in the colony to dissuade Britain from implementing the Sandy's decision. Civil strife would therefore continue.

The strikes on the sugar estates did not come to an end until July 25, 1964. During the four-month period such widespread ethnic violence again occurred in civil war proportions. On this occasion, however, with the possible exception of the 80-day crisis in 1963, all preceding crises looked relatively insignificant by comparison. One journalist on the spot reported that:

> The newspapers throughout 1964 hardly have a day without some incident. Frequently for three or four days running the stories of violence are so ghastly that they took precedence over everything else (Simms, 1966:175).

Another observer reported the events for a part of the strike period during June and July 1964 as follows:

> 48 persons were killed in the worst disturbances yet witnessed in Guyana. The disturbances were racial and political. Bombings, shootings, and savage assaults were the order of the day. Arson was rampant. Physical partition in certain areas came into being with the rapidity of lightning (Chase, 1964:305).

When the strikes came to an end, no one was sure of the extent of the physical damage that the inter-communal civil strife had left in its devastating wake. Estimates of total deaths range from 150 to 200, injuries from 900 to 2,000, homes destroyed from 1,400 to 2,000, displaced persons from 10,000 to 20,000, and physical property damage from G$5 million to G$20 million (Glasgow, 1970; C. Jagan 1966; UFP, 1964). More important than physical damage however, was the complete political and social division that resulted between Indians and Africans. For all practical purposes, the state was completely bifurcated and demands for partition became commonplace. During the strike period, several important political events occurred. First, by May 23, at about mid-point during the strike period, conditions had deteriorated so badly that a State of Emergency was declared, British troops were made available to cope with the situation, and internal security of the colony was placed completely in the hands of the British governor, Richard Luyt. As long as the strike continued, however, the new security measures were unsuccessful in stopping the ongoing inter-ethnic warfare. Second, in June, 1964, over 30 persons were detained by the police; all but two were PPP members. Among those arrested were PPP parliamentarians, PPP Cabinet members, and the PPP Deputy-Premier.

Finally, through Orders-in-Council, Britain announced the date of new elections for December, 1964. Although on a much decreased level, inter-racial violence continued until the elections were over in December 1964, even though the strike had ended on July 24, 1964. After that, peace returned to the Guyana coastland, but more than ever before, the colony was divided into distinct political and communal groups. The results of the elections gave the PPP 45.8 per cent of all votes cast, the PNC 40.5 per cent, and the UF 12.4 per cent. When these votes were proportionately allocated (under the new 1964 Constitution arrangement) among the 55 seats in the legislature, the PPP obtained 24 seats, the PNC 22, and the UF 7. The PNC and UF joined forces to form the coalition government that ran Guyana from 1964 to 1968.

While the December 1964 elections were being conducted, Guyana continued to be under a State of Emergency, which had been declared by the Governor in May, 1964. This state continued until December 31, 1966, during which time several PPP activists remained in detention without trial at the Mazaruni Prison in Essequibo. During this period Guyana was granted its independence on May 26, 1966 – that is, while the State of Emergency still existed in the country. Because a State of Emergency continued to exist after the elections, tight security precautions across the country, bolstered by the availability of British troops to suppress internal disruptions, prevented the PPP from mounting another set of disruptive strikes and demonstrations against the new Coalition Government formed by Mr. Burnham and Mr. D'Aguiar. However, the PPP did withhold its support of the new government by several symbolic acts which potentially held negative consequences for the future stability of Guyana. First, immediately after the 1964 elections, PPP supporters held several peaceful demonstrations across the country, chanting 'We were cheated, not defeated.' Second, when the new legislature was convened early in 1965, the PPP boycotted the assembly by refusing to take the seats they had won during the last elections. Third, when the Colonial Office called a new Constitutional Conference to discuss Guyana's independence, the PPP boycotted the conference. The Colonial Secretary made a personal appeal to Dr. Jagan to attend the conference (Report, 1965b), but because the PPP leader felt that the British Government had delivered a biased decision against him in 1963, when proportional representation had been introduced in Guyana, and since no prospect of reversing this decision was foreseeable at any future conferences, Dr. Jagan felt he had reasonable justification for not co-operating with the British authorities any more (NW, 1965a). Finally, when independence was granted on May 26, 1966, PPP supporters, who constituted over half of the Guyanese population, refused to partake in the celebrations. Many PPP activists and supporters had taken the open stand, 'No independence under Burnham,' prior to the independence conference (NW, 1965a:1 and 1965c:4-6). Evidently, the Indian community was very despondent because their own leader, Dr. Jagan, was not the Prime Minister when Guyana obtained independence.

The actions taken by the PPP following the 1964 elections clearly indicated that Dr. Jagan would not co-operate with the PNC-UF regime in governing Guyana. Indeed, the non-co-operative attitude of the PPP underlined the attitude of unacceptability and non-legitimacy of the PNC-UF government of over half of the Guyanese population. This was hardly surprising, for the parties had organised the Guyanese population along tight ethnic lines for over a decade before independence (1955-1956), so that no government was likely to be accepted by the Indian and African community together.

Many actions taken by the PNC-UF coalition during their post-independence regime were initiated mainly to consolidate their fragile position or to appease their supporters. Such acts did nothing to assuage the fears of the Indian community. First, several additional PPP activists were arrested by the coalition government and placed in confinement at the Mazaruni Prison. Second, the rice industry, controlled mainly by small Indian peasant farmers, came under attack by the PNC-UF coalition. Subsidies on petroleum and other rice-related concessions and loans which had been granted by the PPP government were withdrawn by the PNC-UF coalition. The Rice Marketing Board, the governing board that has exclusive authority to buy and sell rice in Guyana, was re-organised to eliminate PPP control over it, and placed in turn under the control of PNC activists (NW, 1965b). Even more importantly, the Cuban market for rice, which yielded a high price to the rice-farmers for their product, was eliminated by the coalition government (NW, 1966a). These actions taken by the PNC-UF regime were aimed partly at destroying an important base of PPP financial and popular support, but were ostensibly implemented in order to put the rice industry on a sound financial footing by making it independent of government subsidies (Reid, 1968; RPA, 1968).

While certain actions could be explained by the coalition government, the termination of trade with Cuba was an act which they were unable to explain. Overall, the economic features of the post-Jagan regime figured into the ideological aspects of the political crisis in Guyana. What was more significant was the drastic deepening of the ethnic cleavages as a consequence of the inter-communal violence and civil war. This fact would remain a permanent symbolic feature in any future attempt to reconcile the two major ethnic communities

VII Ethnic Domination, Rigged Elections and Communal Repression

The fear of ethnic domination was, in part, responsible for the breakdown of law and order which led to civil war in Guyana. Almost universally, the multi-ethnic states of the Third World are confronted with the problem of establishing a legitimate government. Without an underlying cushion of consensual values, it would appear that a system of domination by one communal group or the other is inevitable. This view had become part of the orthodox doctrine propounded by plural society analysts. In Guyana, ethnic domination was first practised by the European section. The successor PPP government of Cheddi Jagan (1957-1964) allegedly possessed the fundamental features of an ethnically-oriented regime despite its socialist claims. Following Jagan's eviction from office, the Burnham-led coalition government would soon thereafter also assume the form of an ethnically directed dictatorship. Throughout the years of Burnham's rule, the cornerstone of regime survival was erected upon the reliance on communal support. To the plural society theorists, this was inevitable; it fitted in nicely with their plural society paradigm. However, as true believers they had failed to explore the alternative of a broadly-based co-operative arrangement to secure a legitimate government. It will be useful to look quickly at the arguments of the plural society analysts before we proceed to describe how Burnham established a very sophisticated form of control by which to govern.

A.   The Domination Model

The theoretical literature on communal politics in the Third World is replete with formulations on how to solve the problem of maintaining order. Maintaining order and stability are universally perceived as the primary problems in unintegrated deeply divided societies. From the time of Furnivall, who first enunciated 'the plural society model', the answer was deemed to reside in a system of domination (Furnivall, 1948; Furnivall, 1939; Rabushka and Shepsle, 1972). In its early formulations, the plural society was considered to be structurally characterised by the presence of 'distinct racial sections with an elaborate western superstructure over native life' (Ibid.). Without such a superstructure, the society 'must collapse and the whole system crumble into dust' (Ibid.). In effect, societal integration in the colonised plural society was maintained according to this view, because of the political and economic domination of the coloniser. Furnivall's 'domination model' was justified and legitimated on the proposition that the ethnic sections constituted 'a medley, for they mix but do not combine' (Ibid.) and that this segmented condition required an 'umpire' to maintain elementary order. Nothing was said about alternatives to colonial European minority domination or about the policies of divide and rule practised to justify continued colonial domination. To be sure, Furnivall anticipated that turmoil would eventuate in a post-independence context unless the society was able to 'organise a common social will' (Ibid.). What is important to us, however, are the overall conditions which made 'domination' and 'control' by a minority feasible in the plural society. A fuller development of Furnivall's domination model pointed to the existence of a number of factors which facilitated control. First, cultural pluralism did not, by itself, inevitably lead to a demand for supervision or control by a third mediating party (Lijphart, 1977). The fact must be emphatically registered that the 'third party' – the coloniser – had a vested interest in promoting its 'mediation' role. This, in turn, underscored colonial policy that aroused and agitated communal groups to be conscious of their identity and interests. It was the coloniser who instigated self-conscious segmentation. This, in laying out the prerequisites for domination by a third party or mediator, it is important to identify the policy of divide and rule as a *sine qua non* in the total scheme of colonial domination. Simply put, domination was facilitated by the coloniser exploiting the divisions in the society. Second, domination and control became easy because of the dependence of the dominated group on the coloniser for its economic existence. The colonial economy became export-oriented built around one or a few crops which were marketed at cheap prices to metropolitan centres. The re-design of most colonial economies from a subsistence structure to one that was monetarised, specialised and highly dependent on external markets placed the levers of control in the hands of the coloniser. Not only was the economic structure rendered dependent, but so were political and to a lesser extent, social organisations linked to the new colonial state for favours. In time, the values of the coloniser became pre-eminent in allocating resources and these too assisted in rendering domination easier. Finally, the colonial state was centralised and backed up by a powerful arsenal of coercive means to execute the will and policies of the coloniser.

Together then, colonial domination was made possible not just by the fact that a plural society existed, but especially by the practise of divide and rule, coupled with economic dependence of the colonised and the use of superior force by the coloniser. We shall argue later in the text that the persistence of these features – a dependent economy, centralisation, and a monopoly of coercive force – in the post-independence period would also facilitate the emergence of a repressive regime. In effect, the nature of control in the pre-independence colonial system bore an essential structural continuity with that of the repressive post-colonial state. They both sought stability by exploiting the communal structure, but found this easy or tempting to do because of structural features which were bequeathed by the colonial state.

Furnivall was followed by a wide variety of theorists who, in addressing the issue of stability in communally-bound states, posited different domination and control models. M. G. Smith spoke of the need for some sort of 'central regulative organisation' which would differentially incorporate the structures of pluralism to maintain order (M.G. Smith, 1965:32-33). Smith, closely following in the footsteps of his intellectual mentor, Furnivall, developed this idea of ethnic domination. Said Smith:

> Given the fundamental differences of belief, value, and organisation that connote pluralism, the monopoly of power by one cultural section is the essential pre-condition for the maintenance of the total society in its current form (Ibid.).

Furnivall and Smith were not the only scholars to have fallen into the trap of confusing description with prescription. It is fallacious to argue that because multi-ethnic societies tend to throw up ethnically repressive regimes, that that is the way these societies should be governed. Leo Kuper pointed to a system of domination which strengthened and exploited the diversity among the subordinate communal groups while promoting 'intercalary structures' to mediate and control group contact (Lustick, 1979:330). Work by Van den Berghe described stable governance in plural societies as 'pluralistic despotism' (South Africa's version as 'Herrenvolk democracy') marked by political subjection, coercion and economic interdependence (Ibid.). Herbert Adams describes his control model as 'pragmatic race oligarchy' under which communal domination is thorough-going and constantly modernised to extend its rule (Ibid.). Milton Esman's 'institutionalised dominance' stresses monopoly of privilege by the dominant group while the dominated groups are isolated and kept under close political control (Ibid.). Finally, Rabushka and Shepsle, in designating their type as 'dominant majority configuration', emphasised the role of the majority communal group using violence, rigged elections and repression as the mode of rule (Ibid.). In all of these models, the common features are the acceptance of some sort of communal domination as almost inevitable in multi-ethnic states. These authors differ mainly in the form they believe domination will take and the instruments that will be utilised for effective control.

B. Prelude to Full-Scale Ethnic Domination: The PNC-UF Coalition

After the historic 1964 elections which witnessed the defeat of Jagan's PPP, the new coalition of Forbes Burnham and Peter D'Aguiar acceded to power. No attempt was made by the two largest sectional parties, the PPP and the PNC, to forge a grand coalition in a new government of national unity. Neither Burnham nor Jagan would serve in a subordinate role to each other even though a grand coalition needs not involve a hierarchy of leaders. The trajectory of events after the 1955 leadership split clearly indicated that Jagan and Burnham held irreconcilable personal and programmatic differences. The upshot was a re-affirmation of the plural society expectation, if not prescription, of a system of government based on ethnic domination. It would not be until the middle 1970s that the two leaders would be forced by circumstances to come close to reconciliation. In the meanwhile, however, Burnham would proceed to erect, slowly initially, a thoroughgoing system of ethnic control in Guyana. We will examine how this was done.

In December 1966, the State of Emergency declared by the Governor in May, 1964 was lifted, but only after a National Security Act was passed on December 11, 1966, granting the government the powers to arrest and detain anyone suspected of engaging in subversive activities. The PPP protested against the National Security Act, which could be applied arbitrarily and when applied involved the suspension of *habeas corpus* rights of the individuals arrested. The PNC and UF supporters did not see anything wrong with the National Security Act since they felt that 'the Bill will and can only be used against "opponents"' (NW, 1966c:5).

Because a State of Emergency continued to exist after the elections, tight security precautions across the country, bolstered by the availability of British troops to suppress internal disruptions, prevented the PPP from mounting another set of disruptive strikes and demonstrations against the new Coalition Government formed by Mr. Burnham and Mr. D'Aguiar. But the PPP did withhold its support of the new government by several symbolic acts which held potentially negative consequences for the future development and stability of Guyana, by threatening the legitimacy of the regime.

Regardless of how beneficial certain actions by the PNC-UF regime might be, the PPP attacked government policy decisions as anti-Indian in the same way that the PNC had attacked the PPP policies when Mr. Burnham's party was in the opposition. The PPP could not afford to lose its 'natural' supporters because of the policies by the PNC-UF that were beneficial to Indians.

Two policy actions taken by the PNC-UF coalition did not fail to intensify the apprehension of Indians in Guyana. First, the Commission appointed by the International Commission of Jurists (ICJ) to look into the question of 'racial balance' in Guyana's public service departments recommended that the African dominated Police Force and Guyana Defense Force be balanced by the rapid recruitment of Indians to these agencies of the government. This recommendation was not implemented, leaving the coercive arm of the government virtually under the PNC control. Second, the issue of federation, which could have involved the massive movement of African West Indians to Guyana to offset the Indian majority, was resuscitated under the PNC-UF regime, particularly after the exclusive PNC regime was inaugurated following the controversial elections of 1968. Under the PPP regime, the federation issue had been avoided in so far as it involved the movement of people among the units which were to be integrated. The Jagan government had as much political interest in keeping Guyana out of a West Indians Federation as the Burnham government had in joining a West Indian federation (NW, 1968). Since the UF's position as a partner in the government would be jeopardised by the massive infusion of Africans into Guyana under any federal or immigration arrangement, during the PNC-UF regime, the UF opposed immigration. However, when the exclusive PNC government took office in December, 1968, indications became clear that the entry of Africans into Guyana either under a simple immigration policy or under a federal arrangement would be forthcoming (*The Graphic*, 1969; *Sunday Mirror*, 1969).

Field research in Guyana during the 1967-1969 period underscored the widespread non-acceptance of the PNC regime by the Indian community. Without exception, every Indian interviewed said that (a) the Burnham government was anti-Indian and pro-African exclusively, and (b) that they favoured a physical and political partition of Guyana dividing the country into two separate and sovereign entities. On the part of the PNC government, Mr. Burnham made several calls for national unity. This pattern was very similar to that established by the Jagan regime which attempted to woo Africans into joining the PPP and/or supporting the PPP government. As under the Jagan regime, many efforts were being made by the PNC to win Indians to the government. But the PNC regime was no more successful than the PPP government in broadening its base of popular support.

When the Burnham-D'Aguiar coalition acceded to power, it inherited a country that was in considerable economic and political disarray, much of which had been caused by their own efforts to destabilise the Jagan government. Among the first political acts of the new regime was the repression of the PPP organisation. When Guyana obtained independence in

116

1966, the State of Emergency declared earlier was still in effect, and numerous PPP activists were confined to jails without trial. In a few years, the vibrant PPP grassroots organisation was reduced to a shambles through systematic jailing, harassment, and economic victimisation. Externally, the country charted a strong pro-Western position, severing all relations with Cuba and following the voting pattern of the United States with regard to the seating of the People's Republic of China in the United Nations.

In the field of economic development, Guyana adopted a strategy of 'industrialisation by invitation.' Essentially, this economic strategy aimed at attracting foreign investment by providing incentives in the form of tax holidays and duty-free concessions to foreign businesses. The government's major preoccupation was the development of an infrastructure of roads, electricity, ports, education and other basic services. The fact that Peter D'Aguiar controlled the finance ministry underscored the strong private enterprise bias of the country's chosen path to economic salvation. Burnham summed up his regime's position as follows: 'Regardless of ideology, whether it be the USSR, UK, USA or elsewhere, maximum productivity is accepted as the national objective' (Burnham, 1968:18).

By 1968, private investment had reached over G$62 million annually, of which G $32.4 million was from foreign sources. While complaints were loud and frequent from the PPP, the coalition partners boasted of unprecedented prosperity in Guyana. Communal peace was restored, the PPP was practically silenced, and a pro-Western economic and foreign policy was solidly launched.

Burnham's relationship with D'Aguiar however, was an uncomfortable one. Burnham was embarrassed by the fact that D'Aguiar symbolised the remnants of Guyana's colonial plantocracy, which derived privileges partly from a colour-class stratification system. To compound the discomfort from his association with D'Aguiar, the PPP never permitted Burnham to forget that, in terms of the Prime Minister's earlier professed ideology, the United Force was anathema and the enemy. Burnham was, however, temporarily willing to pay the price in reputation in return for the consolidation of his power. Reflecting on the problems at a later time, Burnham commented:

From 1964 to 1968, our participation in government, with the millstone of the United Force around our necks, was very much a question of survival... in harness with another political party whose philosophical and social objectives were not really coincident with our own (Burnham, 1970:153).

Sociologist Percy Hintzen put the matter more bluntly, describing D'Aguiar's party as 'privileged groups...aligned to foreign business interests...favoured in a colour-class system...[and] inclined to oppose any attempt at restructuring the colonial political economy' (Hintzen, 1976:12-13). Because the PNC needed D'Aguiar's support to remain in power, 'the coalition was an effective monitor and control over PNC policy' (Ibid.). According to this view, the coalition resulted in the restriction of the PNC's 'more socialist policies' and 'limited the extent (Burnham) could favour his black supporters through biased legislation and patronage' (Ibid.).

Disenchantment between the UF and PNC grew to intense proportions the longer the coalition lasted. The UF charged that the PNC was heavily pro-African and biased therefore, not only against Indians but against UF supporters as well (*The Sun*, 1968a:1; *The Sun*, 1968b:7). The meaning of this separation of the UF from the PNC was clear. Now not only Indians, who made up over 50 per cent of the population, were against the PNC but also UF supporters, who were about 10 per cent of the population. With over 60 per cent of the population against it, the PNC regime was in greater danger of political disruption than ever before. Elections were scheduled again for mid-1968 and the PPP, although substantially weakened, berated the PNC association for allowing 'a splinter group' to run the government. About six months before the elections, party crossings in Parliament, giving the PNC a majority, allowed the party to evict the UF from the coalition government. With D'Aguiar out, the PNC for the first time gained sole control over the government.

The PNC reconstituted the Electoral Commission, staffing it with its own sympathisers and changing the procedures of administering the elections (*Sunday Times,* 1968). In the 1968 elections, in what would be incontrovertibly established as rigged elections, involving tens of thousands of fictitious votes, an astounded UF and PPP witnessed a PNC 'victory' at the polls. We refer to the 1968 elections as 'a seizure of power.' The electoral fraud was committed under the tight supervision of a politicised, communally-lopsided police and military force. The central election office in Georgetown was barricaded like an impregnable fortress with high security fences, barbed wire, flood lights, and armed guards protecting its activities under utmost secrecy. The 'overseas vote' was a new creation literally extending the domestic electorate to England and the U.S. It was wholly administered by the PNC politically-appointed ambassadors to the U.K. and U.S.A. It supplemented padded domestic voter lists. The PNC won nearly all the overseas votes and in a number of local constituencies, it alone won more ballots than eligible votes on the roll. Both the PPP and the United Force were shocked by the results, but they could do nothing against a government that now controlled both 'the ballots and bullets.' Hence, after the 1968 elections, in which the prior pattern of ethnic voting preference continued, Burnham had the support almost only from his own communal group. Indians and other non-

Africans (mainly Europeans, Chinese, Amerindians, Portuguese, and part of the Mixed Races population constituting about 10 to 15 per cent of the population) lost the franchise and became alienated. By declaring Guyana a republic, Burnham thwarted legal challenges to the election results that would have led to adjudication by the Privy Council in England. A predominantly African army and police ensured that the election results were not forcibly overturned by riots and demonstrations. From mid-1968 onwards, Burnham would preside over a minority government kept in office by repeated electoral fraudulence and a politicised and ethnically sanitised army and police. Needless to point out, democracy was now dead; its crucial vehicle of representation through fair elections had been tampered with. Legitimacy was lost; the state coercive machinery was the main guardian of the illegal PNC regime. A minority party had seized power. No colonial or external power had aided the PNC in rigging the 1968 elections. The colonial precedents of manipulating democratic devices to serve imperial interests had been well learnt by the Burnham government. Guyana had come full circle from colonial domination, to freedom and back to domination, this time by one non-white group over another.

C.   The Consolidation of Ethnic Domination

The 'seizure of power' in 1968 was a watershed in ethnic relations in Guyana. In a multi-ethnic society, the PNC representing a minority African group (32 per cent), grabbed the government. To avert internal disruption, the PNC government embarked on a purge of the critical pillars of its power – the coercive forces and the civil service – of most of its non-African elements. Where communal malcontents did not strike and demonstrate, many migrated to Europe and North America. This especially became the case of the Europeans, Chinese and Portuguese. The massive migration of this group from Guyana left a society which was predominantly polarised between Africans and Indians.

When Burnham seized power in 1968, he realised that the economy was essentially controlled by his communal opponents. He therefore embarked on a programme to alter the country's economic structure, which had favoured big businessmen, large property owners, and foreign companies. In part, the membership of these privileged groups coincided with many of the more powerful of his communal supporters' bases of existence. To the PNC, the economic structure did not favour most of its own communal supporters, who were mainly urban-based, underprivileged, and poor. Burnham's own survival depended on an altered economic order that addressed the needs of his communal constituents. Several critical events prompted the PNC to drastic action. First, U.S. aid to Guyana had been substantially reduced since Jagan's PPP, the 'Communist menace', had been ousted from power. Second, foreign investments decreased from about G$60 million in 1968 to G$17.3 million in 1971. Third, rice production plummeted from 5.7 per cent of the GNP in 1966 to 2.9 per cent in 1971. Finally, the sugar industry, which was not only the country's principal source of foreign exchange, but also substantially dominated by the PPP's communal segment, was frequently crippled by politically-inspired PPP opposition strikes. Economic conditions as well as political interests prompted Burnham to radical action.

Towards the end of 1969, the PNC regime proclaimed a socialist framework for Guyana's reconstruction. In 1970, Guyana was declared a 'Co-operative Republic' (Burnham, 1969). From private enterprise, the economy was to be founded on co-operatives as the main instrument of production, distribution, and consumption. But crises continued to bedevil the regime. The government ran a gauntlet besieged by high unemployment (30 per cent), under-employment (36-40 per cent), double-digit inflation, demonstrations, boycotts, strikes, and later on, as a result of the Arab-Israeli war, prohibitive fuel costs. A vicious cycle of poverty was created by a pattern of polarised and unstable ethnic politics inter-mixed with the salve of socialist rhetoric and programmatic justifications.

Between 1971 and 1976, the government nationalised nearly all foreign firms, bringing 80 per cent of the economy under state control. This unwieldy public sector supplied the job opportunities necessary to quell the increasing demands of PNC supporters for equitable participation in the economy. State corporations proliferated, but most were placed under an umbrella state agency called GUYSTAC, which controlled twenty-nine corporations and several companies valued at G$500 million. Government ministries increased from 12 in 1968 to 21 in 1977. The government also ran five banks, three bauxite companies, and a gigantic sugar corporation which at one time dominated the country's entire economy. These public agencies were overwhelmingly staffed by the regime's communal supporters.

Prime Minister Burnham himself admitted that 'we don't believe in the neutrality of the Civil Service' (Narine, 1974:1). He pointed out that the neutrality concept was a colonial relic irrelevant to Guyana's socialist revolution. But the bulging public bureaucracy was not transformed into socialist organisations. Commented Marxist scholar Jay Mandle:

Evidence that bourgeois rule persists in Guyana is found most abundantly in the nationalised sector. In all state-owned enterprises, traditional hierarchical methods of decision-making remained firmly in place. In none of the nationalised industries has meaningful workers' participation in decision-making been institutionalised (Mandle, 1976:11).

There is no question, however, that the country's economy had been radically altered. Professor Mandle pointed out that in the new set-up, the rulers were not socialist but racialist in composition:

The older colonial ruling class and its business firms have been banished and decision-making power rests with a local elite of state and co-operative-based managers. In the Guyanese context, this assumes the form of the emergence of an urban Afro-Guyanese leadership under the auspices of the People's National Congress (Ibid:11).

The police, security and armed forces, in particular, were expanded to protect the besieged PNC government. In 1964, the police and auxiliary armed forces numbered about 3,770; by 1977, they were estimated to be 21,751. In 1964, there was one military person to 234 civilians; in 1976, it was one for every 37 citizens. The budgetary allocation for the military rose from 0.21 per cent in 1965 to 8 per cent in 1973 to 14.2 percent in 1976. That is, an increase of over 4,000 per cent (Danns, 1980). More than any other public service department, the police and coercive forces were overwhelmed by Afro-Guyanese. Burnham named himself Chairman of the Defense Board, where he took personal control over promotions and appointments. The main assignment of the armed forces was to supplement the police constabulary in maintaining law and order.

For a regime to maintain and extend Guyana's economic development, it would require programmes that encouraged agricultural production. Guyana lacked even a minor industrial capacity and its mining sector was small. It is upon agricultural production that the country's capability to feed itself depended. Sugar production was the backbone of the economic system as a whole and sugar workers were mainly Indians. In the mid-1970s the sugar companies, all foreign-owned, were nationalised. The next more significant agricultural industry was rice and this was almost wholly under Indian peasant production. When Jagan was in power, he provided several programmes such as credits, subsidies, marketing, technical assistance and drainage and irrigation to the rice industry. Hence, the PNC labelled the Jagan regime as a 'Rice Government' partisan to Indian communal interests. When the PNC acceded to power, the rice growers were victimised with most state subsidies eliminated. Rice production plummeted to half its original size. The Government's Rice Marketing Board, which has a monopoly in purchasing the farmers' rice, was re-organised and staffed with PNC personnel. Rice farmers, under Jagan's instruction, boycotted rice production, creating grave shortages in the country.

Like the sugar industry, rice became a political and ethnic football. The PNC government wanted to eliminate its dependency on Indian agriculturalists for much of the country's food. In 1970, then, under its announced policy of 'Co-operative Socialism' the PNC attempted to locate land-less Afro-Guyanese on state lands previously leased to Indian farmers. The Indian stranglehold on peasant agriculture provided Jagan's PPP with a powerful base of support. The strategy of African agriculture involving re-distribution of land and subsidies failed, for rice cultivation required years of experience for success. Despite victimising them, Burnham's party continued to appeal to Indian farmers to produce. But co-operation was not forthcoming. As Mandle explained:

> ... at issue here is the nature of the PNC government; it is a regime which is manager-dominated, urban and predominantly Afro-Guyanese. As a result, it is poorly equipped either to mobilise the rural labour force or to call upon its good-will in attempting to transform agriculture (Mandle, 1976).

The judiciary also came under the PNC regime's direct influence (DeCaries, 1979). The appointment of judges and magistrates was routinely based on party loyalty. Thus, the use of the courts to challenge the legality and constitutionality of regime decisions was futile. The overall policy output of the PNC regime, even if it were to be interpreted in foremost socialist terms, pointed indisputably to ethnic favouritism and preference. The polarisation of the two main ethnic races was probably attributable as much to ethnic chauvinism among PNC activists as to PPP boycotts and strikes against the government. The economic situation had deteriorated so badly that towards the end of the 1970s, the impact reverberated adversely on everyone alike, regardless of ethnic membership. Strikes and demonstrations and other challenges to Burnham's power came increasingly from all ethnic segments, including Africans. The arsenal of coercive powers previously used against Indians was now used against African dissidents also. We will turn to this paradoxical aspect of the ethnic domination issue in the next chapter.

VIII From Ethnic Domination to Elite Cross-Communal Domination

Ethnic domination oftentimes backfires on both the manipulators of ethnic appeals and their communal constituents. Ethnic domination does not necessarily yield a larger bounty from the treasury to be disbursed to supporters. Acts of sabotage and non-co-operation, strikes as well as movements mounted by alienated ethnic sections in the form of organised resistance, secession and mass migration often accompany the enthronement of communalist regimes. In the end, the toll as attested to by such cases as Sri Lanka, Malaysia, Cyprus, Fiji, Surinam, Sudan and many others, points to national impoverishment and a smaller national product for distribution. Because of acts of resistance and sabotage by the discriminated and excluded communal sections, a greater part of the governing regime's revenues must be deployed to purchase security. If the excluded communal sections control significant aspects of the private productive sector, then acts of non-co-operation may witness more capital flight, a fall in investment, unemployment and a fall in production and government revenues. Turned into a battle field, the state cannot attract foreign investors and tourists. An increasingly beleaguered government therefore, possesses less to allocate to its communal adherents, and even less is available because of the establishment of the apparatus of a national security state. Inevitably, communal supporters suffer as much as the sections excluded from power. Progressively, the electorates are transformed from ethnically structured populations into groupings built around those who suffer from deprivation, unemployment, and poverty on the one hand, and those who are lucky to live an ample life on the other.

New acts of protest and non-co-operation may become multi-ethnic and cross-communal. Under siege, the governing regime may not only assume an elitist form, but is likely to unleash its security apparatus on all foes, communal and non-communal alike. To remain in power, the ruling elite may resort to rigged elections with the aid of heavily subsidised and pampered security forces. Or, the security forces may seize power. The quagmire of communal politics creates a universal condition of suffering and degradation. It is as if the spiral of inter-ethnic politics is constructed upon suction steps that paradoxically pull all of its participants into a shared, non-communal purgatory.

This pattern and its variations have become paradigmatic in many multi-communal Third World states. Invariably, the pattern includes a body blow to the economy, the erection of a repressive system with its attendant human rights violations, and mass migration to other countries or refugee camps. The payoff for loyalty to ethnic parties in power is almost indisputably the initial deepening of sectional divisions, followed by an economic, social and political penalty paid for, in large part, by the communal members of the ruling regime. For a number of countries such as Guyana and Sri Lanka, the penalty has amounted to the practical destruction of the state and the instalment of a security apparatus that consumes most of whatever remains of national production. The psyche of the population is disfigured.

That a new multi-ethnic electorate will emerge chastened by the lessons of irrational communalist commitment is not, however, guaranteed. Even though the evidence may abundantly show that the security state dispenses its preoccupation with power on all opponents, this can sometimes have an inter-sectional prejudice. More often, a cynical electorate involves deeply distrusting all power holders. The crippling of the society, economy and polity tends to leave the problem of ethnic politics unresolved. Fears of ethnic domination linger, even in the midst of the communalist rubble. The human creature is ambivalently tempted by an urge to reject ethnic politics and the primordial powers of community.

How Guyana evolved after its fall into the trap of inter-ethnic politics and the establishment of a communalist regime is the subject of this chapter. Guyana enacted most of the script of the foregoing paradigmatic pattern of the politics of ethnic domination, with the added peculiarity in which communalist politics were concealed by ideological Marxist rhetoric. We shall look especially at the process of rigged elections, human rights violations, and the creation of a broad national constituency with critical, if not cynical, political orientations. The consequences of communalist politics led to the negation of this constituency, and a search for inter-ethnic sharing.

A.   Nationalisation and an Opportunity at Reconciliation

The descent into tightening tiers of ethnic segmentation marked by the capture of the state by one of the ethnic groups was temporarily interrupted by the nationalisation of the major foreign firms in the Guyana economy. With both

Jagan's PPP and Burnham's PNC claiming Marxist-Leninist labels, the nationalisation of the dominant multi-national corporations and the concerted opposition this policy evoked from the Western powers provided a basis for the sectional leaders to close rank over a commonly shared platform of anti-imperialism. Hence, the trajectory of tightening ethnic confrontation was detoured from the inevitable destination in the destruction of the state. Jagan and Burnham would come close to reconciliation, but then paradoxically, they would discover the difficulties within their own parties of re-directing the energies of the ethnic monster which was nurtured and embedded in their party organisational structures.

For a number of years, the PNC's *New Nation* carried articles in praise of socialism, but no one believed them because the government continued its dependency on the United States and the United Kingdom for its markets and aid. Further, no attempt was made to challenge or restructure the capitalist economy inherited from the days of colonialism. But by 1971, the government was beset by grave economic difficulties and needed revenues to stay in power. It needed revenues to service its over staffed bureaucracy which could not be retrenched; to pay interests on overseas loans from public and private creditors to preserve the country's credit worthiness; to pay for food imports to avert large scale food shortages; and to pay the police and military whose loyalty ensured the regime's survival. The image of a poor, dependent Guyana, run by a dictatorship that pitted one non-white group against another, was inconsistent with Burnham's ambition for international recognition as a progressive leader.

Any development of the Guyanese economy that seeks to eliminate dependency on imports and maximise domestic self-sufficiency must entail the support of rural dwellers. Significantly, even though Burnham controlled the government, Jagan remained the most powerful rural figure. In essence, if Burnham's anti-imperialist rhetoric against dependency was to be realised, Indian support was indispensable. The PNC tried unsuccessfully to wean away segments of the Indian population from Jagan. Those who crossed the ethnic line were well rewarded, but had to live socially ostracised from their community. Those who did not co-operate, that is, practically the entire Indian community, suffered from undisguised discrimination. Among the punitive measures used were the loss of fertiliser and fuel subsidies for rice production, the bypassing of the farmer-controlled Rice Producers' Association in decision-making affecting the grading and pricing of rice over which the government had sole monopoly rights to purchase, and the refusal of the government to recognise the Guyana Agricultural Workers' Union (GAWU) which represented sugar workers. Added to this was the fact that Indians were routinely intimidated and harassed by an African-dominated constabulary, and a picture emerged in which the repression of Indians, partly intended to destroy the PPP's base of support, was pervasive and undisputed. The PPP initiated a boycott against the government's self-sufficiency programme charging that surplus profits were extracted to finance the civil service.

Indian alienation and animosity then, was the primary obstacle that frustrated Burnham's plan to mobilise the entire population to fulfil socialist principles which had begin to play not merely an *ex-post facto* justifying function, but had assumed a guiding, determinative role in the PNC government. Consequently, Jagan became indispensable to Burnham's designs. However, it would be inaccurate to assert that Jagan had nothing to gain from Burnham's new socialist image. Indeed, Jagan had many incentives to discontinue or modify his total opposition to the PNC regime. Burnham's socialism may be fraudulent when measured for consistency against his domestic policies and past performance, but his international reputation now rivalled Jagan's as a Marxist. Visits by Castro, Nyerere, Bandaranaike, and the like challenged Jagan's exclusive claims to the socialist, anti-imperialist ideology in Guyana. Further, he could not continue his unqualified criticism of Burnham when the latter was implementing the very policies the PPP had advocated for 25 years. In effect, while Burnham needed Jagan's co-operation, Jagan in turn had sufficient selfish reasons of his own to reciprocate.

The critical watershed in the nationalisations occurred with the acquisition of Reynolds Bauxite Co., which was a wholly-owned subsidiary of the United States-owned Reynolds Metal Co. Unlike the previous nationalisations which had involved Canadian and British firms, Reynolds was symbolic of the hovering omnipresence of Burnham's metropolitan sponsor, the United States, to which an undertaking was given that private investment in Guyana would be protected and promoted. At a rally held after the nationalisation, Burnham warned: 'There is reason to believe that all American aid to Guyana will be cut off ...' (*The Graphic,* 1974:1). That did eventuate, but from that point onward, Burnham turned heavily to Cuba and the People's Republic of China for help. Cuba granted him its highest award, the Jose Marti award, and Mao Tse-tung hosted him.

The presence of any socialist republic in the Western Hemisphere challenges U.S. traditional hegemony in this area. Events in Allende's Chile served as a reminder that even democratically-elected socialist republics in the Americas faced formidable obstacles to their survival. Burnham himself was a prime beneficiary of this policy policed by the U.S. In a curious twist of events, he found himself making explicit charges that external attempts had been made to destabilise his government. The Angolan incident illustrated the point best. During early 1976, when Cuban troops intervened in Angola to assist MPLA, the Guyana government was charged with allowing its airport to be used by Cuban troops on the way to Guinea, Africa (Omag, 1976). Rumours were also spread by a Brazilian newspaper, *O Estado De Sao Paulo,* and a Venezuelan newsmagazine, *Resumen,* which several thousand Cuban and Chinese troops were training paramilitary forces in Guyana. Burnham attributed the false rumours to 'some elements that see our relationship with Cuba as too close . . . who don't want to see a little country on the road to socialism succeed' (Latin America Bureau, 1976:1).

Guyana's foreign minister, Fred Wills, elaborated the charge of destabilisation at the Non-Aligned Conference in Algiers in 1976:

> There is a concerted attempt to destabilise the governments of non-aligned countries in Latin America. More particularly, in the Caribbean – Guyana, Jamaica and Barbados - have been subjected to the full fury of insidious techniques aimed at procuring their alignment .... (*Chronicle,* 1976:20).

The solutions to Guyana's economic problems as perceived by the Burnham regime created its own difficulties. To the deteriorating economic situation were applied acts of nationalisation to procure more revenue for the government and to halt the alienation of its supporters. However, the adoption of a socialist platform, with its concomitant foreign policy orientation to countries which were the traditional adversary of the U.S., created U.S. disenchantment. Burnham then realised that his survival would depend largely on the measure of national unity he could mobilise to deter acts of external intervention. National disunity in 1962 and 1963 provided the wedge for the manipulation of local interests that ousted Jagan from power. Burnham recognised that the continuation of African-Indian conflict would expose his regime to external destabilisation. All of this entailed only one thing – reconciliation with Jagan, who commanded the allegiance of over 50 per cent of the population.

Jagan announced his change of position in August 1975. Addressing the PPP's annual convention, he said, 'Our political line should be changed from non-co-operation and civil resistance to critical support' (*Sunday Mirror,* 1975:9). He gave as his reason the acts of nationalisation: 'If we are to arrive at our goal of socialism, imperialism must first be destroyed. And whoever helps must be praised' (Ibid.). Jagan's support, however, was not unequivocal; he called it 'critical support.'

> Critical support does not mean unconditional support. It means just what it says – giving support for any progressive measure, opposing any reactionary moves and criticising all shortcomings (Hamaludin, 1976:11).

Burnham's *quid pro quo* related to the sugar industry, which was dominated by Booker McConnell of Britain. The company's operations predated British acquisition of the colony. It was represented in Guyana by 22 companies and directly employed 23,000 persons who provided a livelihood for about 150,000 people. Thousands of others indirectly depended on the company. Bookers produced about 85 per cent of Guyana's sugar and occupied the best irrigated lands on the 5 to 10 mile coastal strip on which most Guyanese lived (*Caribbean Contact*, 1976). In addition, it provided 40 per cent of Guyana's exports, 30 per cent of the G.N.P., 35 per cent of the foreign exchange, but was 90 per cent owned by Booker McConnell (Litvak and Maule, 1975). For as long as Jagan had been in Guyanese politics beginning in 1946, he had advocated the nationalisation of Bookers. In 1976, Burnham nationalised Bookers and placed it under the management of several state corporations.

Jagan, in turn, immediately made two concessions. First, he pledged support to the government against external intervention, particularly the possibility of a military invasion by Brazil. Said Jagan, 'The PPP has a patriotic duty to defend Guyana's sovereignty, independence, and integrity' (Hamaludin, 1976:11). Second, Jagan agreed to return with his party to parliament which he had boycotted after the 1973 elections. The exchange of *quid pro quos* stopped short of a coalition government because of the internal ethnic support structures in both the PNC and PPP.

For Burnham to become truly socialist and join Jagan in a coalition arrangement, his very power base had to be abandoned in the process. Specifically, the pillars of PNC power, namely the civil service, police and military, would have had to be reorganised. When Burnham acceded to power, he refused to implement the recommendations of the International Commission of Jurists that had investigated the problem of racial imbalance in the civil service. Instead, especially after the 1968 elections, this Commission was purged of nearly all high-ranking Indian personnel. This pattern was repeated more decisively in the Police Force and especially the Guyana Defense Force.

The government's socialist philosophy required an ethnically-balanced civil service, not only to increase legitimacy, but also to mobilise all available talents to successfully run public corporations, which now had the responsibility for over 80 per cent of the economy. Jagan continued to pressure the PNC, demanding that the government draw up and implement socialist programmes 'before talking about having a socialist state' (*The Weekly Gleaner*, 1976:27). He noted that despite the nationalisations 'the same basic structures remain in these industries' (Ibid.). Turning to the procedures by which the PNC acquired power, he said, 'it is impossible to build socialism until the whole social life of the country is democratised' (Ibid.). But he got to the crux of the ethnic recruitment policy when he observed that the PNC had 'a rightist base' which did 'not want to take positive steps that will result in socialism' (Ibid.). Specifically, he pointed to the 'corrupt bureaucratic system that had developed in Guyana and that some people who were enmeshed in this corruption were opposed to any further changes' (Ibid.). The problem could have been stated differently. In a coalition government, the national pie had to be so divided that Jagan's supporters became full beneficiaries. In stark power terms, the problem concerned the sharing of strategic positions and material benefits and jobs with the previously excluded group. Should socialist principles be implemented in a coalition, Burnham might witness not only a dilution of his power base, but could conceivably encounter acts of sabotage and rebellion from his own party people, who had risen to prominence by skilfully manipulating ethnic symbols in the past. The PNC remembered well the days when it had accused the PPP of precisely the same sorts of flagrant discriminatory practices with which it was now being charged. The PPP government (1957-1964) was called a 'coolie or rice government', which allegedly tilted its annual budgets and development plans in favour of rural residents. Should the PNC risk the loss of power by inviting Indians to share command of the strategic levels of government? Should the African section, in the name of elusive socialist principles, jeopardise its security and welfare by sharing power with Indians whose superior numbers could one day catapult them into the government? These were the most crucial constraints which Burnham faced as he sought to explore the prospect of a coalition government with the PPP.

Jagan was not immune to similar pressures emanating from his own community of support. Since their arrival as indentured labourers, Indians had maintained living patterns different from those of the African and other communities. The suspicions that separated Africans and Indians were exacerbated during the period of nationalist politics, particularly as of 1955, when Jagan and Burnham parted company. It was upon this structure of inter-communal fear, distrust, and hostility that socialism had to be erected. But for the Indian community, another dimension had to be added. A majority were small property holders, had accumulated more physical property than Africans, and many owned small businesses. They considered themselves economically more industrious than Africans. It would be an unenviable task for Jagan to mobilise this peasant and property-based Indian population, which was very acquisitive and individualistic in economic habits, bound by fear of Africans and contemptuous of their economic performance, to join an experiment in inter-communal co-operation and solidarity.

Jagan had also come under pressure from middle-class Indians who could be regarded as his 'rightist' base. They considered his 'critical support' as a 'sell-out' to which he replied:

'Critical support' does not mean unconditional support. It means national unity and struggle – unity in defense of the nation and struggle against wrong-doings and shortcomings and for the well-being, rights, and liberties of the working people (Hamaludin 1976:11).

Fortunately for Jagan, a substantial number of the more wealthy and militant Indian middle-class had emigrated. But, nevertheless, forging a coalition socialist system into existence would mean such a monumental task of inducing the Indian community to work with the African, that it could well require coercion. Hence, for these reasons the period of limited PNC-PPP collaboration floundered on the rocks of the communalist interests and dispositions which were implanted in each party. Soon thereafter, the politics of repression and ethnic domination resumed.

B.   Cross-Communal Opposition against the PNC Regime

The ethnic polarisation in Guyana maintained a bi-polar party system that practically excluded any other contender from power apart from the PNC and PPP. This pattern was further entrenched by the virtual disappearance of the UF, representing Europeans and many Portuguese and Chinese. In the interstices left by the PPP and PNC domination of Guyana's politics however, there have always existed small splinter groups spanning a range from the extreme left to the extreme right. Notable among these groups in the recent past were Ratoon, the Movement Against Oppression (MAO), the Working People's Vanguard Party, ASCRIA, the Working Peoples Alliance (WPA), the Justice Party, the Liberator Party, the New World Group, etc. Many of the persons who held official positions in these organisations had been members at one time or another of either the PPP or PNC. They organised their own splinter groups, or joined pre-existing ones from which they criticised both the PPP and PNC. Ideologically, these groups had variously espoused capitalist and socialist philosophies, while ethnically, such groups as ASCRIA and Liberator, catered almost exclusively to African or Indian interests. Finally, these organisations never succeeded in establishing a comprehensive country-wide system of grassroot groups similar to networks established by the PPP or the PNC. They tended to be urban-based, composed of educated middle-class persons, and produced sporadic news sheets or pamphlets. Their popularity varied but was generally confined to small special-interest audiences. Nevertheless, their verbal and vitriolic attacks tended to penetrate the armour of the PPP and PNC.

Antagonisms among the small splinter groups limited their general effectiveness against the government. However, in the mid-1970's when the

130

PNC regime was encountering severe economic difficulties, several of the groups informally began to co-ordinate their attack against the PNC. Led by prominent Afro-Guyanese radical, Walter Rodney, who had returned from Africa several years earlier, a group of left-leaning splinter groups collectively called 'The Working Peoples Alliance' (WPA), not only criticised the Burnham regime for rigging elections and failing to internalise socialist practises in its administration, but more importantly organised anti-government rallies, demonstrations, and strikes from among supporters of traditionally PNC strong-holds.

The nationalisation notwithstanding, the WPA, other left-wing splinter groups and the PPP, repeatedly stung the PNC regime for its 'bureaucratic state capitalist' system. Compounding the PNC's difficulties was increasing inflation, persistent unemployment, widespread shortages of essential items, and breakdowns in public utilities which together, came to characterise life in Guyana. Not only Jagan's ethnic supporters, but everyone else as well, including the pivotal middle class professionals who manned the senior positions in the immense state bureaucracy, were the victims. The latter group was accustomed to the privileges of Guyanese society. While the left wing groups assaulted the PNC government for not being socialist enough, the middle-class ethnic professionals in the public service (which came to be called the 'COMPASS' group) criticised the failings of the regime for its flirtation with socialism.

Erosion of the PNC traditional grassroots support became evident. Unlike opposition from the PPP, which was perceived as ethnically inspired, the new sources of defiance and criticism came from within the PNC traditional support base. The internal institutional power structures (the Public Service Unions, the Army, and the Police) became disenchanted with the performance of the government. In the past, their loyalty to the PNC regime was maintained by the reminder of 'the Indian majority menace.' This appeal, however, displayed its limits when the everyday needs of the urban groups faced chronic shortages of essential items in their accustomed life style.

The PNC regime, especially since 1977, had become embattled. It was attacked by Rodney's WPA and the other left-wing groups; threatened by the withdrawal of support from the middle class professional group which managed the day to day operations of the government; and bewildered by the demonstrations and strikes mounted by its own supporters in its traditional strongholds such as the bauxite city, Linden. By 1978, economic and political crises had reached their pinnacle for the Guyana government. At this time, Rodney declared that: 'The PNC must go. And they must go by any means necessary' (Rodney, 1980:1). Significantly, the year 1978 was also the year when the Guyana received a significant loan from the International Monetary Fund.

Changes in U.S. – Guyana relations became identifiable when the U.S. extended a sum of US$24.7 million to Guyana in 1978. In the same year, the IMF agreed to provide the PNC government with a standby loan of US$135 million (Leroux, 1980). This was complemented by a World Bank Loan of US$15 million for a hydro-electric project in Guyana. The loans from the IMF were necessary because the Guyana national debt had grown by 700 per cent from US$267 million in 1970 to US$2 billion in 1978. About 37 per cent of the annual budget was utilised to service the country's foreign debt. It was noted that 'the confluence of US and IMF policies is not coincidence. Guyana joins South Korea and Turkey in being the only countries this year to be granted IMF loans in excess of their designated allocations' (Munroe, 1980:16). From practically losing all U.S. aid by 1975, Guyana, according to U.S. Ambassador George Roberts, was receiving the highest per capita aid from the United States during 1978-1979 (Ibid.). The *Washington Post* noted that the sudden massive aid to the Burnham regime as of 1978-1979 onwards, was part of 'U.S. efforts to check the spread of leftist influences in the Caribbean' (Ibid.).

The 'socialist' Guyana government decided to co-operate. In 1979, as part of its drift back from the left, the PNC government announced a New Investment Code inviting foreign capital to Guyana. Burnham himself promised foreign investors that 'nationalisation of new investment is not foreseeable in my time and generation' (*Financial Times*, 1978:1). Certain U.S., French and West German firms entered Guyana in the areas of oil and uranium exploration. The Guyana government was expected to retain exclusive control of 'strategic activities' in the economy. Other areas were opened for foreign and local investment. All of these were, however, merely exploratory activities which brought no structural change to Guyana.

By 1979, the PNC was tottering at the brink of disaster. The WPA was formally launched as a party in July 1979. Its ideology was inspired by Marxism-Leninism; it found fault with the PNC's 'state capitalism'. It was critical of imperialism, which it associated with the West generally, and the US in particular. The PPP decided to join the bandwagon and expressed sympathy with the WPA and coordinated several of its own boycotts, strikes and demonstrations with the WPA groups (Latin America Bureau, 1979; Race and Class, 1979). Burnham's action to alter the country's constitution (which was done by yet another rigged referendum) to introduce a presidential executive form of government was viewed by the combined PPP-WPA forces as an unconcealed preliminary manoeuvre to install a Presidential dictatorship in Guyana.

On July 11, 1979, several fires were set to two buildings in Georgetown. They included the National Development Ministry and headquarters of the PNC. The huge holocaust was attributed to WPA activists, several of whom were promptly arrested including Rodney. Prime Minister Burnham promised to retaliate against 'the counter-revolutionaries' insinuating that the WPA was led by the 'enemy of the people' (Burnham, 1979:19-20). Within a year thereafter, the PNC fought back, using its control of the coercive machinery of state to support its actions and reconsolidate power (*Caribbean Contact*, 1980:26). While the WPA had gained popularity in Georgetown and its environs, its activists were vulnerable, visible, and for the most part unarmed or poorly armed to confront the PNC coercive apparatus. In a contest for power, the PNC became desperate. A systematic campaign involving the arrests and murders of WPA officials was launched to eliminate WPA activists. The culmination of this campaign was the assassination of Rodney on June 13, 1980.

Burnham's retention of power was accompanied by a subtle change in the foreign policy orientation of his government. The challenge by the combined WPA-PPP opposition was ideologically based on claims to authentic socialist credentials. The PNC's co-operative socialism was discredited not only by the failure of the co-operative movement to bring Guyana economic equality and prosperity, but by the insistence of the PNC middle class that the state public apparatus remain overwhelmingly under Afro-Guyanese control. When the struggle ensued between the PNC and PPP-WPA groupings in the late 1970's, Burnham's most formidable threat came from persons of African descent. The combined PPP and WPA supporters had successfully breached the communal political divisions. It was because the PNC's political life was so totally threatened by both cross-communal and ideological opponents that Rodney had to be destroyed. In the struggle between the PNC and its political opponents, the ruling party not only shifted its foreign policy towards the U.S., but internally, it became wed to the middle class pro-West COMPASS group (Premdas, 1982). The COMPASS, made up of senior civil servants, wanted a return to a mixed economy and pro-western policy so that economic stability could be restored. The COMPASS group, in addition, had support from the Army. In the end, Burnham chose to ally with the COMPASS-cum Army power groups in 1978. It is important for us to examine this transition to what became essentially African elite domination (Premdas and Hintzen, 1982).

Initially, communal domination rested upon the promise of the regime to transfer enough resources to its ethnic constituents to maintain superior socio-economic status vis-à-vis the other groups. When this policy failed, the PNC began to lose communal support, causing it to shift to reliance upon an increasingly centralised machinery of control under a tighter circle of trusted elites. Inevitably, the regime had to employ its coercive machinery against its own communal group. This transition, in effect, constituted an essential aspect of elite domination. When 'co-operative socialism' in Guyana failed to alter the relative well-being of the African section, especially its lower class, regime survival gradually shifted to a strong alliance between the ruling party and the African middle class, who ran the civil administration and the security forces. Along with Western economic pressures following the nationalisation of the foreign firms, the OPEC oil crisis wreaked havoc on the Guyanese economy, especially at a time when state penetration of the private sector was getting underway. By 1978, the government was forced to make deep cuts in its current expenditure, retrenching many African public service workers in the process. Spiralling balance of payment deficits produced food and drug shortages, and shortages of other consumer goods. Electricity and water services to PNC-dominated urban areas became sporadic. By 1979, foreign reserves plummeted to minus G$175 million from a high of plus G$250 million in 1975, while the national debt increased from G$267 million in 1970 to G$1.8 billion. Unemployment soared to 30 per cent.

The effect of the economic crisis was so deep and extensive that its toll was registered beyond the African urban lower classes, extending its ravages to the privileged life style of the once loyal middle class PNC adherents. It was at that time that the Working People's Alliance (WPA), along with several other opposition groups including Jagan's PPP, revived organised strikes and rallies against the troubled PNC regime. In particular, the WPA was successful in mobilising large and growing demonstrations in major PNC strongholds, signalling the collapse of monolithic communal support for the regime. Throughout the deepening crisis, Burnham fell back on a central core of loyalists who commanded control of the public service particularly the armed forces. The situation became very unstable; no one could safely predict the outcome, given the precariousness of the embattled regime.

Repressive retaliation, including the assassination of the WPA's leader, Dr. Walter Rodney in June 1980, physically decimated the WPA's leadership. Scores of opposition party activists were arrested, victimised or placed under surveillance. The regime also dealt severely with striking workers, including its own communal supporters. For example, bauxite workers, traditionally hard core PNC supporters, were beaten, arrested and tear gassed when they responded to WPA strike calls. Sugar workers, also normally loyal to the PPP, struck for an unprecedented 135 days. Civil servants who participated in strikes were either dismissed, demoted or transferred.

The system of oligarchic control entailed a transfer of dependence from monolithic communal support to reliance on a small group in charge of the armed forces and civil administration. In return for their loyalty, this core enjoyed a privileged economic status. In 1978, the top leaders in the country earned about G$25,000 annually, senior bureaucrats from G$12,000 to G$15,000, while unskilled and semi-skilled full-time workers in the state sector earned G$3,000. In the same year, 75 per cent of the work force held lower class occupations and unemployment had soared to 30 per cent. The government devalued the dollar in 1981 and, to offset the higher costs that followed, increased the salaries of the military and senior bureaucrats but denied similar increases to all other employees of the state.

C.   The Rigging of Elections, the Abridgement of Rights and Rule by Terror and Thuggery

It was important to the style of the Burnham regime that it project an international image of maintaining democratic practices however compromised or tarnished. Hence, through rigged elections held in 1973, it provided itself with a two-third majority in Parliament which was in turn used to alter the country's constitution. In the 1973 elections, the army openly seized the ballot boxes and the PNC increased its parliamentary strength to two-thirds of the seats (Singh, 1973; C. Jagan, 1973). Elections scheduled for 1978 were postponed because the regime wanted to hold a national referendum to alter the country's constitution and introduce a presidential form of government. Like the elections, the referendum was also rigged but its fraudulence was widely publicised and exposed (Latin American Bureau, 1984). Elections in 1980 were again rigged but exposed by an international team of observers. Headed by Lord Avebury, Chairman of the United Kingdom Parliamentary Human Rights Group, and invited by the Guyanese Human Rights Association, the international team of observers concluded its report on the 1980 elections as follows:

> ... on the basis of abundant and clear evidence, the election was rigged massively and flagrantly ... the scale of the fraud made it impossible to conceal either from the Guyanese public or the outside world ... the events we witnessed confirm all the fears of the state of democracy in that country (Report, 1980:1).

This sort of costly subterfuge was enacted again and again for both elections and referendums, which were ritualistically held with their results proclaimed to the world as valid. When opposition elements complained, they were dismissed as expected cases of sour grapes. Hence, the elections conducted in 1980 under the new presidential-style constitution were rigged again; Burnham became executive President of an office that was described by a former British Attorney-General as 'virtually imperial' (Leroux, 1980:510). The President could legally suspend or dissolve parliament to which he was not accountable. He also had the power to unilaterally make laws by decree in the interest of 'national security'. At his pleasure, he could appoint or dismiss the heads of any branch or agency of the state. Finally, he retained his position of

Commander-in-Chief of the armed forces. The personalisation of control in the President and a small coterie of political and bureaucratic elites was nationalised under a PNC policy whereby the party assumed 'unapologetically its paramountcy over the government' (*Newsletter*, 1984:1).

While the Guyana constitution guaranteed freedom of expression as a basic right of citizens, under the regime of President Forbes Burnham, however, freedom of expression was practically extinguished, especially as evinced by the mass media. Writing in the *Human Rights Quarterly*, Professor John A. Lent, a specialist on communications issues said:

> In the 1970s, the government of Forbes Burnham virtually took over the Guyanese mass media, purchasing newspapers, nationalising broadcasting and harassing the opposition with legislative, economic, and physical sanctions (Lent, 1982:376)

The Inter-Church Committee on Human Rights in Latin America agreed saying: 'Generally, freedom of expression and the right of opposition groups to dissent are suppressed in Guyana' (WCC, 1982:51). In some ways, this was something of a paradox since it was Forbes Burnham along with Cheddi Jagan who, as leaders of the independence movement after World War II, became the victims of the 'Undesirable Publications Ordinance' (1947) aimed at curbing the propaganda efforts of the nationalists. When the jointly-led PPP came to power in 1953, one of its first acts was to strike down the 'Undesirable Publications Ordinance' in the name of socialist justice. Years later, the self-styled socialist regime of President Burnham brought colonial repression to a full circle, this time with a vengeance, making the 'Undesirable Publications Ordinance' seem innocuous by comparison to contemporary practices. As a lawyer, Forbes Burnham attempted to institute controls over his political opponents by using state legalism. Hence, control over the mass media was never committed by fragrant violation of the law. Rather, by controlling the Parliament through fraudulent elections, the law-making powers of the state were re-written to suppress political opposition. Much of this opposition consisted of its communal enemy as represented by Jagan's PPP and its mass media arms, but was not confined to it. While in a communally divided state, the ethnic implications of mass media suppression were inescapable and the laws were used against all opponents of the PNC.

The attack on the mass media initially began by the purchase by the government of two (*Guyana Chronicle* and *The Graphic*) of the four daily newspapers, between 1971 and 1973. The third of the dailies, The *Evening Post,* disappeared for financial reasons, and the fourth daily, *The Mirror*, the organ of Jagan's PPP, was the remaining opposition paper to be dealt with. In the meanwhile, the government established its own daily called *The Guyana*

Chronicle which combined the facilities and resources of the defunct *The Guyana Chronicle* and *The Graphic* (Lent, 1982). The remaining opposition mass media newspapers included one daily, *The Mirror*, a weekly, *The Catholic Standard*, and several periodic sheets such as *Dayclean*. The government, fearful of incurring censure by the international mass media, embarked on a set of policies intended to squeeze the activities of the opposition papers so that they might seem to choke to death of their own accord. The main device to achieve this end was a new law requiring a license to import news print and printing equipment. The impact of this legislation was devastating. *The Mirror* was reduced to a weekly and *The Catholic Standard* to a short irregular stencil sheet. Both papers found that their applications for the required license for importing newsprint were treated with maximum neglect and delay by the government bureaucracy. *The Mirror* was periodically forced to close, and even equipment sent to it by the Soviet Union was refused entry into Guyana. By the end of the 1970's, *The Mirror* which at one time had published 17,000 copies on weekdays and 32,000 on Sundays, was down to only 12,000 copies of a four-page Sunday edition printed on expensive bond paper. The *Catholic Standard*, a paper very critical of the government's human rights violations, 'was reduced to a ghost of its former self' (WCC, 1982:51). Even gifts of newsprint to *The Mirror* and *Catholic Standard* were denied entry into Guyana.

Apart from the licensing of newsprint and printing equipment importation, the government resorted to two additional measures to suppress the mass media. In 1972, a Publications and Newspaper Act required newspapers to deposit G$5,000 with the government Registrar and to provide two sureties guaranteeing similar amounts (Lent, 1982). This was justified on the basis that, in the event of a successful libel suit, fines would be paid. The first victim of this legislation was *Dayclean,* which continued publishing but refused to comply with the law. Throughout the 1970s to the present, the government would persistently sue the opposition newspapers, dragging them before the politicised courts where they would repeatedly be fined exorbitant sums. On October 4, 1974, the second measure that the government enacted to stifle opposition dissent banned any literature that was deemed 'prejudicial to the defence of Guyana, public safety, or to public order' (Ibid.).

To complete its virtual control of the mass media, in 1979 the government nationalised the only radio stations, Radio Demerara and the Guyana Broadcasting Service. Overall justifications of the stringent controls and ownership of the mass media were two-fold: national development and scarce foreign exchange. The PNC argued that national development in a socialist state required that the mass media be directed so as to mobilise the people for development purposes. The excuse of scarce foreign exchange, while available to the government's own media outlets, was used to suffocate the opposition papers into impotence.

Repression tends to breed the conditions of its creation; original factors become compounded as the opposition resists impelling the state to increase the measures of repression. Soon, repression and counter-violence reduce the state to one marked by anarchy, dictation, suffering, and almost hopeless poverty and misery. The Guyana case captures the dynamics of this re-enforcing system of self-fulfilling prophesies. Not only did the screws of repression multiply and tighten as in South Africa in response to the need for more and more security, but as the screws were applied, the victims became more numerous and included erstwhile innocent, undecided and uninvolved persons who then become embroiled and alienated in the quagmire of government terror.

Clive Thomas used the term 'fascistisation of the state' to describe events in Guyana: 'In this stage, political assassination, direct repression of all popular manifestations, and a rapid growth of the security apparatuses of the state take place. These developments are propagandised with the familiar claims of law and order, the necessities of development of a poor country and we cannot afford the luxuries of democracy" (Thomas, 1983:40). The use of formal and informal state-sponsored thuggery, harassment, inhuman treatment, assassination, terror, and violence had become part of the repertoire of repression liberally applied to maintain the power of the PNC. Once the elections were rigged and parliament brought under control, all else followed including purging of the Public Service of communal and ideological enemies; purification of the armed forces and police of potentially disloyal personnel; politicisation of the courts; the break down of the legal system as a constraint on arbitrary state action; public corruption and rape of public treasury; the rise of PNC party paramountcy and the personalistic powers of President Burnham; the breakdown of the economy and the impoverishment of the society with malnutrition and hunger widespread; and finally, the mass migration of a third of the population overseas. To catalogue all that happened from the day in 1968, when the PNC seized power through electoral fraud, to the present, would require an enormous effort filling many tomes with human rights violations.

In the 1970s, the PNC would be faced with a paradox of power: as it consolidated its control of the parliament, and courts, the coercive forces, the public service, and the mass media, it would become more insecure and become vulnerable to opposition attack. In the mid-1970s the WPA would organise and mobilise the entire spectrum of opposition forces, including Jagan's PPP, and unleashed a fierce assault on the government. If Burnham was able to maintain the loyalty of his communal segment and to cope with Cheddi Jagan by invoking the fear of Indian domination, he had no answer for

Walter Rodney. Apart from being an African like Burnham, Rodney was also a socialist with a growing reputation among Third World intellectuals for his anti-capitalist radicalism. Up to the time of Rodney's entry into Guyana's politics in 1974, the PNC had used open physical violence against its opposition sparingly, depending more on manipulating the law and on the courts. But after Rodney's WPA came on the scene, especially after 1976 as the WPA gained strength, the PNC employed a variety of informal and violent methods against the opposition, including the assassination of Rodney and several of his colleagues.

To harass and intimidate the opposition, the government employed the 'muscular' sections of the PNC as well as the police, militia, state security, and army personnel, especially where the WPA and its supporters held meetings. But this would be complemented by The House of Israel, a new organisation headed by Rabbi Washington, an Afro-American refugee from U.S. justice. The House of Israel gained the reputation as the thuggery and assassination arm of the government, for its open activities of intimidation and violence were never questioned by the police. Fr. Bernard Darke, a Jesuit priest who was a photographer for the *Catholic Standard*, was stabbed to death by a member of the House of Israel on the street outside the courts.

> His (Fr. Darke's) death was the most serious event in a pattern of violence which the government directed mainly against members of the WPA. Two activists were shot dead and others imprisoned on spurious charges, while many lost their jobs in the state sector on the grounds that they constituted security risks (WCC, 1982:50).

In using state violence against its opponents, the government appropriated the term 'terrorist' to describe the opposition. The Inter-Church Committee on Latin America gave a few recent examples:

> Twenty-two members of the PPP are currently charged with 'public terror' following the break-up of a PPP political meeting held prior to the 1980 elections. Nine members of the WPA were charged with causing 'public terror' after they had distributed leaflets from house to house on the eve of the December 1980 elections (Ibid.).

Father Mike James, writing in *The Catholic Standard*, noted how arbitrary arrest and intimidation had become a norm: 'In recent years, security forces have felt free to arrest persons without explanation because they happened to sympathise with an opposition party, criticise the regime or merely attend an opposition public meeting' (*Catholic Standard*, 1982:1). The Bar Association Review of Guyana had called for an investigation of the brutality and terror that persons who were arrested experienced in custody (*Guyana Update*, 1984:3). The politicised courts were enlisted in aid of the state's activities:

> ... in the magistrates' courts particularly, allegations of assault and, more seriously, of torture, have been made against the police by prisoners in custody ... and even in cases where prisoners have exhibited on their faces and bodies conspicuous signs of violence, reaction from the bench has been contemptuous .... (Ibid.).

The Guyana Bar Association confirmed this pattern of action:

> A statement issued in August 1981 by the Guyana Bar Association alleged that over 800 people had been arrested since August 20th for unspecified reasons and detained without being given adequate food or without any right to receive meals from the relatives and friends (WCC, 1982:51).

Walter Rodney was assassinated in 1980, but prior to and after his death, 'Guyana had become a land or horrors. Democracy was no longer on trial here. The question was whether it would survive this (Rodney's) official crucifixion' (Latin America Bureau, 1984:80). State terror had become entrenched and pervasive as a mode of maintaining the PNC in power. In the urban areas, especially Georgetown, the repression became cross-communal, but in the rural areas where Indians predominated, it assumed a decidedly racist form. Rape, burglary and arbitrary arrests by the security forces had become so prevalent that Indian villages became places of terror. The police were viewed not as a solution, but as the source of the problem. Indian homes in particular became a target of official search and seizure exercises, because as the economy deteriorated and inflation reduced the real salaries of the police and security forces, the need for public plunder as a source of revenue became compelling. Indian homes became the main target of booty, and the police knew that theft and torture committed against the Indian community were likely to go uninvestigated or ignored by the courts. In effect, while it could be argued that the persistent pattern of theft and terror committed against the regime's communal enemies (and this meant mainly Indians since nearly all of the Portuguese and Europeans had migrated from Guyana) was committed on the initiative of police and security personnel without formal approval of the PNC leadership, the fact remained that everyone knew what was happening and nothing was done to stop the plunder and terror. It could even be argued that once started for a specific purpose against only clearly identified political opponents, state terror lost control of its personnel, who privately perpetrated criminal acts against the Indian community. There is much plausibility to this argument, but it does not alter the source of ultimate responsibility, namely the ruling party, for setting a generally violent tone to Guyanese politics.

Finally, due to acts of repression, partly by diverting scarce resources to pay for an inordinately expanded coercive apparatus and partly because of persistent boycotts and strikes, the country became increasingly impoverished. Malnutrition, lack of elementary medical care, disrepair of public roads, schools, and other facilities, and the frequent interruption of water and electricity supplies cast the tenor of society as one in deep crisis. Reported the Inter-Church Committee on Human Rights in Latin America:

> ... the economic situation deteriorated rapidly causing great hardship to the poorer members of the society and the right to life itself. Malnutrition is now widespread and is causing an increasing number of deaths in children according to doctors at the Georgetown Public Hospital. There has been a rapid deterioration in social and public services (WCC, 1982:72).

Hence, the price paid for the perpetuation of illegitimate power was not only the denial of human rights to citizens but the virtual destruction of a viable economic life that had previously existed:

> The most alarming symptom of this alienation is a disastrous fall in productivity. The Guyanese economy has been contracting since 1975. Since 1978, the government has been unable to meet production targets in the 80 per cent of the economy with the current international recession, has brought the country to the verge of bankruptcy (Ibid.).

Along with personal security, the basic rights to employment and material necessities also became a casualty of the PNC regime. The government passed legislation restricting the right to strike and, without notice or compensation, retrenched civil servants in response to IMF behests. In these areas, the government made its own communal section the primary victim of its arbitrary actions.

IX Post-Script: The Elections of 1992 and a Change of Regime

After three decades of struggle by an array of forces, the ruling PNC government was forced to hold free and fair elections in 1992. The Atlanta Carter Centre For Democratic elections was mainly responsible for persuading the PNC regime to submit itself to the voice of the electorate. In previous elections, the ruling regime was virtually permitted to rig elections since this assured the West of a loyal ally in the Cold War context. With the advent of Gorbachev and *peristroïka* however, and the subsequent disintegration of the USSR, the PNC government was shorn of its Cold War shield of protection. In a new international order of human rights and democracy, the United States and the West abandoned their support of authoritarian anti-Communist regimes and actively promoted governments based on free and fair elections. The PNC was coerced by its Western backers to convene free and fair elections. On October 5, 1992, after two postponements that prolonged the constitutional life of the PNC government by two years, the elections were finally held. The outcome was dramatic. The PPP, in coalition with a minor party, defeated the PNC, bringing nearly three decades of illegitimate rule in Guyana to a close.

The 1992 elections were about the elections – their authenticity and their honesty. President Hoyte argued that previous elections in which the PNC had declared itself the victor had been fair and honest, and he therefore had no doubt of the PNC being returned to power in new elections. It was this claim that the PNC had always acquired power legitimately that stood at the centre of the elections. The opposition parties however, equated free and fair elections with the defeat of the PNC and argued for the role of an external adjudicator to oversee new elections in Guyana. In a series of prolonged challenges to the machinery that the PNC had utilised to retain power in the past, ranging from the control of the Electoral Commission to the printing of ballot boxes and the counting of the votes at centralised locations, the PNC grudgingly made concessions and lost control of the election machinery. Shred by shred , integrity was restored to the electoral process. In the struggle for procedures to ensure free elections, the issue of free elections, transparently conducted under the scrutiny of international observers, became prominently internationalised. Hoyte was cornered by his boast that the PNC was not afraid of free and fair elections. Eventually, it was too late and even though an attempt was made to disrupt the elections at the very last minute, free elections were conducted and the outcome was the that defeat of the PNC.

The October 5, 1992 elections attracted eleven contesting parties of which the three most significant were the PNC, the PPP, and the Working Peoples' Alliance (WPA). The Guyanese electorate consisted of 385,000 voters. The voters were organised into ten regions, and on election day they cast their ballots for both the national parliament and the ten regional councils. The two elections were entwined because the 65-member unicameral national legislature was constituted of 53 seats elected nationally and the remainder elected by the regional councils. Voting was conducted along a system of proportional representation.

As the campaign unfurled, ethnic polarisation of voter preference became evident. The results of the elections confirmed the pattern of communal voter choice. Given another opportunity, the Guyanese electorate decided to allow their choice of parties to be dictated by race and ethnicity. The WPA, which was a descendant of the cross-communal coalition that Walter Rodney had mobilised in the 1970s to oppose the PNC dictatorship, was literally decimated at the polls in the reassertion of ethnic voter preference on October 5. It obtained only one seat from the national poll and another from the regional councils, for a total of two seats in parliament. The victorious PPP-Civic coalition garnered 36 seats in parliament. The defeated PNC obtained 26 seats. One seat was held by the United Force.

When the Jagan-led government moved into office, everyone expected it to share power with the other opposition parties such as the WPA. This, however, did not happen, in part because the PPP, in command of an absolute majority of seats in parliament, did not see fit to distribute a significant ministerial portfolio to anyone. It preferred to keep control over its cabinet and the direction of the government. In the end, the WPA, which had done so much to remove the PNC from power, was itself entirely excluded. This meant that the PPP, which represented nearly the entire Indian electorate, virtually represented only one section of the multi-ethnic fabric of Guyana upon acceding to office. In a very real sense, the elections of 1992 did not succeed in structurally altering the proclivity for ethnic politics in Guyana. In the victory of the PPP, cross-communal legitimacy was not achieved. A broken, ethnically fractured public will entails a dark future for the PPP regime. Had the PPP sought to recruit the WPA to its fold, it would have conferred on itself a

143

measure of cross-communal legitimacy. The Jagan-led PPP stands unmistakably as an Indian party with Africans, effectively excluded just as the Indians were under PNC rule. It will be only a matter of time until the African-based PNC submits the PPP to the same sort of acts of non-co-operation that the PNC endured at the hands of the PPP in the past. Guyana can rescue itself from the ravages of ethnic instability only by altering the zero-sum exclusionary features of its political system. On this subject, much will be said in the concluding chapter.

Part II
ETHNICITY AND DEVELOPMENT

X The Political, Socio-Cultural and Psychological Dimensions

A. The Political Dimension

An analysis and evaluation of the impact of ethnic conflict on political development in multi-ethnic states requires a definition of terms. Is there an accepted body of criteria by which to measure political development? If these criteria exist only as a part of an ideological system and are accompanied with their own built-in strategies of change, can these criteria on political ends be gathered, aggregated and reconciled from the different ideological systems into a single acceptable package? In particular, our concern is not merely with criteria and strategies of political change and development in any context, but with such orientations in an environment of cultural pluralism. Have these various ideologies and strategies addressed this aspect of the environment in seeking to attain their aims? It will be useful to offer a very brief overview of the more important of these ideologies and strategies of development in relation to the issue of ethnic conflict before proceeding to establish our own criteria for analysis and evaluation.

One of the most widely used applied approaches to political development can be collectively designated as the 'modernisation' and 'developmental' school often associated with the names Samuel Huntington, Lucian Pye, and Gabriel Almond. Sometimes also daubed the 'systems' or 'structural-functional' school, this approach stresses the need for certain systemic performances to be attained in the transformation process for the condition of modernisation to occur. Samuel Huntington best expressed these as social consensus and community, legitimacy, organisation, effectiveness and stability. In this complex of interrelated factors, it is argued that politically developed states are those that are institutionalised around the function of establishing legitimate political authority in which citizens share a common vision of the public interest. Specific modern institutions should be established around a political

147

culture of widespread citizen participation, so that conflicting demands are well organised and articulated in an orderly fashion through a system of voluntary interest associations and political parties; a representative civilian body must be in place to dutifully receive and respond through appropriate policies to these demands; implementation of decisions should be routine and effected around de-personalised bureaucracies; political conflict must be adjudicated through recognised courts; and political succession and changes in government must be built around predictable procedures. All of this constitutes a complex of political means and ends which are to be attained in an environment of rapid political change and mobilisation, in which urbanisation redefines the demography of the state from the dominance of a rural traditional ethos to one marked by universal achievement norms.

The stress in the modernisation strategy of development is on maintaining order through evolving new norms and institutions which are called upon to perform the fixed functions of a stable society. The modernisation approach encapsulates its goals in processes which have often been stated as a set of interlocking and sequential steps to be overcome, namely participation, legitimacy, identity, integration, penetration and distribution. Order takes precedence over the creation of a just society; this is not, however, seen to be dependent on an economic system that is free from property disparities. Above all, in the process of transformation, the political modernisation school, while acknowledging the environment of internal cultural pluralism, has tended to see this as a barrier that would be submerged and eradicated as institutionalisation takes root and a new society is born. There are many sophisticated nuances which are omitted in this attempt to represent the fundamental factors of the modernisation approach to development, such as the evolution of institutional differentiation and autonomy, the role of socialisation and acculturation, etc., but generally, in terms of our analysis, it is critical to note that the integration and assimilationist perspectives built into this approach have tended to underestimate the arousal of ethnic group formation and the durability of ethnic identities and boundaries. These, as experience will show, are critical variables which tend to subvert the aims of development in the model. The ethnic factor is resilient and cannot be swept away in the tidal wave of technological, economic, institutional and value change as the modernisation school would have it.

In diametrical contention against the modernisation approach are the dependency and Marxist perspectives, even though these two orientations are not the same. Essentially, while the modernisation school tends to stress the role of internal cultural and economic factors in accounting for the condition of Third World 'backwardness', the dependency-cum-Marxist approaches point to the role of imperialism and capitalism in causing underdevelopment. Here,

148

the emphasis is placed on centre-periphery exploitation, class criteria and economic and property relations.

Between the modernisation and the Marxist-cum-dependency approaches a number of issues and aims of political development are shared. It is these which we shall utilise for our own analyses, giving them particular interpretations in the context of Guyana's multi-ethnic environment. In a definitional paper prepared by Rudolfo Stavenhagen, presented at a conference convened by the United Nations Research Institute for Social Development in Geneva in March, 1990, these development issues were crystallised for use in examining individual case histories such as Guyana. From all these sources then – the modernisation school, the dependency-Marxist perspective, and Stavenhagen's inventory of questions – a list of inter-related political problems serve as the criteria for measuring political development in multi-ethnic states bedevilled with persistent communal strife. Much in this configuration of inter-related political issues has already been analysed in the preceding chapters on Guyana's experience. In this chapter, we step back with our analytic categories and criteria to comment more theoretically and generally on the political developmental impact of ethnic conflict in Guyana. The categories and criteria pertain to legitimacy, unity, order, minority and human rights, as well as institutions and various mechanisms of ethnic conflict resolution. Much of the meaning of these variables can be demonstrated in a discussion of the political costs of ethnic conflict.

The political costs of the ethnic conflict in Guyana have been extensive, including the loss of regime legitimacy, the destruction of democracy, pervasive human rights violations, the fracturing of the society into polarised parts, and persistent instability. Once ethnic consciousness became the animating force that defined competition for the values and resources of the state, all political institutions – parties, voluntary associations, the electoral system, parliament, civil service, judiciary, diplomatic services, and the army and police – became infected by it. It is as if the twisted contours of ethnic preference, antagonistically expressed against other similar solidarity groups, possessed such irresistible power, that every political structure derived its form and practice from its governing principles. Ethnic hate was not confined to a few select practices and separated from others; allowed to grow on the crucible of continuing electoral competition, it slowly extended its tentacles to all institutions. The entire imported parliamentary apparatus was subverted and transformed into structures of ethnicity, dividing one citizen from the other by claims to narrow communal interests, failing to offer any form of unity to the state.

The first major casualty stemming from the ethnicisation of political competition in the allocation of values is the loss of regime legitimacy. Democratic governments are erected on the intangible factor of moral consent.

The term 'legitimacy' embodies this idea; it simply suggests that governments derive their right to rule and can expect citizens' compliance and co-operation, when and only when, the accepted rules of establishing and administering government are followed. Legitimacy refers then, not only to the propriety in the acquisition of power, but also to the practices of administering the state consonant with prevailing procedures and concepts of equity. Clearly, legitimacy is wrapped in the cultural and moral values of the society. In the end, the test of legitimacy consists of an intangible sense of rightness that citizens entertain about rule by a regime. Legitimacy is not a sporadic event that is fulfilled by a single act such as an election alone. It is a marriage between those who rule and those who are ruled; it must be affirmed everyday, in everything done.

As a phenomenon locked into the cultural system of society, legitimacy is easily established in those polities that are under girded and integrated by a body of shared institutions and customs. But this does not necessarily mean that legitimacy is equivalent to homogeneous values. These unifying values facilitate, but do not guarantee consent and acceptance of a government and its right to rule. It is quite conceivable that in a state with a diversity of cultural systems, legitimacy can be forged through a commonly agreed upon political regime. In such culturally fragmented situations, it is more difficult to establish legitimate governments, but not impossible. If the cultural cleavages are constrained by systems of inter-communal co-operation at the level of the polity, then a stable and legitimate political order can be enthroned. If these culturally diverse states, on the other hand, are permitted to evolve so that they are marked by internal ethnically-infused antagonistic relationships, then legitimacy is bound to be lost in the attempt to erect governmental order. The Guyana case illustrates all of this.

The single most important factor that induces the condition of inter-cultural antagonism is pervasive ethnic consciousness in the state. Ethnic consciousness means at once group solidarity as well as inter-group antagonism and conflict. Ethnic consciousness is a relational phenomenon built on the premise of the presence of contenders for limited territory, privileges, power, etc. In itself, ethnic consciousness is not a divisive force. Once aroused, it can nevertheless be diverted into peaceful inter-group routines and exchanges without seriously destroying the state. However, if it is actively encouraged and protracted without much restraint, such as occurs in zero-sum electoral systems in which communally-organised mass parties compete for power and privileges, then ethnic consciousness tends to become a destructive monster. Fed and reinforced by fear of domination, ethnic group activities lose all objectivity and rationality.

The theory advanced here then, postulates that at any early stage, group consciousness can actually be restrained and made into a positive force of identity formation and group solidarity. But, if nurtured and systematically sustained by personal ambition, elite interests and institutional practices, a momentum in its evolution then occurs, spreads over a widening array of institutions, and a threshold of virtual uncontrollable inter-group mass behaviour is achieved. This 'critical mass' is what imparts its first political casualty on the legitimacy of the ruling regime. The spiral of deepening ethnic conflict is not always sustained in its momentum by internal group factors. In a number of cases, including Guyana, external actors with an agenda of their own may add fuel to the fire of ethnic strife.

In Guyana, the polarisation of the state into an ethnically bifurcated structure laid the foundation for the loss of regime legitimacy. When it eventuated that neither Indians nor Africans trusted each other, the enthronement of a government preponderantly based on one or the other communally-based parties invited immediate non-recognition by the 'conquered' out groups. This in turn led to acts of non-co-operation and persistent challenges to the authority of the governing regime. In Guyana, acts of non-co-operation involved industrial strikes and mass communal demonstrations which destabilised the government. This happened in the case of both the Indian-based PPP and the African-based PNC. The fact that the economy was characterised by specialised parts, each dominated by a particular ethnic group, meant that each ethnic community could sabotage the entire production effort as well as the political order. The loss of legitimacy was followed, therefore, by endemic instability and violence which in turn required the ruling regime to recruit new police and coercive forces which created an environment in which systematic human rights infringement occurred. A major political cost of the modern post-World War II ethnic conflict in Guyana has been the exacerbation of national unity in the creation of a deeply divided bifurcated state. In a sense, this divisive factor, laid at the outset of the founding of the Guyanese state, institutionalised ethnic strife that adversely affected all subsequent effort at development. Post-colonial politics perpetuated the fragmented ethnic structure of the state and made development doubly difficult.

Several factors sustained the communal divisions in the state after the multi-ethnic mosaic was founded. Among these was the role of the colonial state in promoting these divisions as a mode of governing. From the inception of the colonial state in Guyana, its operations were converted into an instrument in the service of alien planter and imperial interests. The state that was created was neither neutral nor representative. It became imbued with the proclivities of the colour-class system of stratification and was plainly ethno-centric as well as racist. It presided over an order that was unequal and unjust, but more significantly, it institutionalised practices which laid the cornerstone of communal conflict.

Several policies of the state founded a society that was unintegrated and conflictual. Four main insights on the role of the state should be highlighted. First, the conquest of the territory was by force; this gave those who ruled an order that did not seek consent for its legitimacy or survival. Second, the colonial state deliberately imported a multi-communal population and settled them in a manner that pitched each against the other. Third, the state anchored its routines and stability on a colour-based stratification system that ignored the interests of most of the population. Finally, the state was rendered into a dependent appendage of the European metropolitan centre for its survival and prosperity. In sum, the state utilised its monopoly of violence to bring into being a multi-ethnic society to promote the needs of the minority planter interests. The colonial authorities had no interest in establishing or encouraging cross-communal understandings or institutions. On the contrary, it deliberately instigated inter-sectional suspicion and fear as a mode of governing. Yet, it would not be accurate to place the entire onus for the ensuing ethnic strife on the colonial authorities. The truth points to the role of the sectional charismatic leaders who destroyed the cohesion of the jointly-led independence movement in pursuit of private ambition. We recapitulate both of these factors in the making of the ethnic conflict in Guyana.

When slavery was abolished in 1838, the sugar companies owners required an alternative source of cheap and abundant labour to sustain the profitability of their plantations. The emancipated Africans demanded higher wages; the plantocracy refused. Indentured labours, mainly from other parts of the British Empire, were then imported. From 1838 to 1917, over a quarter million Indians from India were recruited for plantation labour in Guyana. This was the first important act of colonial and planter manipulation, approximately encapsulated in the doctrine of divide and rule, which laid the foundation of greater cultural diversity as well as antagonism between Africans and Indians. To the African, the Indians were the cause of depressing their claim to the value of their labour. They quickly came to despise the Indian 'coolies' for voluntarily enslaving themselves for a pittance. The Indian saw the African through the prism of Indian internal caste values as not only culturally, if not racially, inferior, but lacking in understanding of the plight of Indian indentureship.

Kept apart occupationally and residentially, each with its own residual values and traditions, the Indians and Africans soon accepted the definitions of themselves through the British values which became dominant. Thus, to the policy that fuelled Indian-African antipathy was added a second layer of self-definitions forged on the Anglo-centric colour-class system of stratification. The English colonist saw the Indians as industrious, compliant and culturally superior to the Africans. They saw the Africans as lazy, rebellious, and imitating of English ways. These stereotypes were compounded by perceptions and evaluations which Indians and Africans developed on their own, from their own values and from experiences with each other. Cumulatively then, these antipathies sustained the malaise between Africans and Indians.

A century of time between 1800 and 1900 witnessed the slow and compounding acculturation of the results of colonial manipulation, residential and occupational divisions, value differences, and stereotyping. It was during this time that the foundations of the ethnic boundaries firmed up around the formation of communally-based voluntary associations and distinctively different cultural practices. Not only Africans and Indians were demarcated and compartmentalised by the reinforcing multiple cleavages of residence, occupation, values and stereotypes; this fragmented structure applied equally to the Chinese, the Portuguese, the Amerindians, and the English colonists. Segmentation became total and pervasive. To be sure, a few shared practices were emerging to facilitate the economic exploitation of the colony. These included a 'Creole' pidgin language, assigned a lower value than the English language and spoken mainly by Africans and Indians; and an incipient educational system which would become more significant after World War I. The countervailing centrifugal forces of division, however, prevailed for nearly a century without much modification.

The introduction of suffrage by stages to enfranchise the non-white sector of the population in the colonial decision-making process provided the new context that promoted ethnic conflict. The 'democratisation process' can be conceived as occurring in two stages, each with a separate ethnic effect. In the first stage, as the colonial government lowered the property and other requirements to obtain the right to vote, a small group of middle class Africans and Mixed Races gained the franchise.

It was not be until after World War II that dramatic changes inaugurated the period of full-fledged mass democratic politics. Universal adult suffrage was introduced in 1950 so that the non-white middle class leaders required a new type of politics to maintain their privileges. This was not easy since two kinds of political mobilisation had occurred simultaneously, one class oriented and the other ethnically inspired. At the class level, Indian and African workers were organised into unions for industrial action against the managers and owners of plantations and factories, but because of the occupational differentiation that had developed in the colonial structure, the emergent trade unions were preponderantly uni-ethnic in composition. Almost invariably, the leadership of these unions was in the hands of the middle class.

The problem that this posed for analysis pertains to the prospect of ethnic workers unifying their efforts across the communal divide so as to establish wider collective efforts against employers. It was clear that while communal dispositions were structurally embedded in the colonial order, an opportunity was now available to modify and recast allegiances so as to transform the society away from its ethnic moorings.

Ethnically-oriented, organised life could at least be modified so as to submit communal claims to cross pressures from functional class interests. The opportunity for a radical shift came with the formation of the colony's first mass-based multi-racial party in quest of self-determination. In Guyana, in the immediate post-World War II period, an independence movement which caught the popular imagination across ethnic lines was successfully launched. It was socialist in orientation so that its appeals addressed the economic interests of workers as well as other strata; its mobilisation was cross-communal, successful in part because of the multi-ethnic leadership and in particular, the leadership by Indians and Africans. The Peoples' Progressive Party (PPP), formed in 1950 and led by Indian Cheddi Jagan and African Forbes Burnham, and also composed of a number of Chinese, Europeans, and Mixed Races leaders, successfully won the 1953 general elections, the first under universal adult suffrage. Examination of the election results showed a distinct pattern of Indian-African co-operation in all electorates giving the PPP victory in 18 out of the 24 constituencies.

In the 1953 PPP victory, the trajectory of tightly compartmentalised ethnic politics was temporarily arrested. It was a moment of opportunity to redefine, at least at the political level, the dominant role of ethnicity in giving shape to political organisation and mobilisation. Once the political levers were wrestled away from the colonial power, it was possible to re-cast institutions and practices so as to encourage cross-communal co-operation and co-existence. The direction of public policy under a cross-communal party could move away from ethnically-inspired employment and resource allocation practices which the colonial power had utilised to maintain control over the Guyanese people. Much of this, however, could only be achieved by a unified leadership in a popular mass-party committed to alternative paths of development. The task would be gargantuan, flying in the face of old communal habits and structural dispositions at every point. It was the purpose of the PPP to do this even though its vision was to establish a class society in place of one bounded by ethnic allegiances.

The 1953 however, the PPP would squander this opportunity at nation-building and the imperial colonial power would seize the occasion presented by the internally-divided PPP leadership to destroy the multi-ethnic basis of the independence movement. Dr Jagan and Mr. Burnham, serving symbolically as the dual-headed integrated leadership of the independence movement, were ambitious persons, each with his own vision of socialism. The independence struggle temporarily submerged their differences which, however, resurfaced after the momentous elections of 1953 were won. Jockeying for the pre-eminence while at the same time challenging the colonial power with radical policies meant that a divided party attempted to confront a very resourceful and still powerful colonial enemy. After 133 days in power, the British evicted the PPP from office by military force and suggested that the extreme communist views of Jagan invited such action. It played on internal division of the PPP suggesting that a more moderate position such as espoused by Forbes Burnham would be acceptable to the British.

Evicted from office, the PPP was split right down the middle between Jaganite and Burnhamite factions. Each faction sought to assign blame on the other for the British intervention. Jagan and Burnham formed their own parties each seeking to capture the mantle of cross-communal support and legitimacy that the old, unified PPP had enjoyed. Instead, the separate parties, each headed by its own ethnic leader, succeeded in obtaining the support of only its respective ethnic community. With this, Guyana was launched into a period of ethnic mass politics that exacerbated and institutionalised communal divisions. The communalised politics that ensued destroyed national unity and cross-sectional support, essential for establishing regime legitimacy. The rivalry between the two communal leaders persisted in the context of zero-sum competition for control of the state. In the end, to protect itself from domination, one section seized power in fraudulent elections, initiated a comprehensive system of repression against its communal enemies, and effectively launched the state in a tailspin of self-destruction. Failing to re-establish inter-ethnic reconciliation, the ruling regime faced persistent boycotts, strikes, and outright sabotage from the communal section that was excluded from power. All of its well-thought strategies of economic development practically collapsed because of sectional disunity and the consequent illegitimacy of the state. Without first attending to the political requisite of establishing legitimate political authority through cross-communal reconciliation and power sharing, all other efforts at social and economic transformation are doomed to fail in multi-ethnic states, as amply demonstrated by the Guyana case. This is a an essential part of the meaning of political development in multi-communal states. We shall take up this theme of reconciliation in the concluding chapter.

B.   The Socio-Cultural and Psychological Dimensions

Ultimately, development devolves on the well-being of the individual in society. Social well-being is the micro-dimension of development change; it orients and measures the impact and effects of political and economic structures and strategies on the welfare of the very subject of all directed development activities. Social development is multi-faceted, but in the last analysis, when derived from economic, political, and cultural aggregate sources, it holistically addresses the dignity, welfare, and personal development of the human creature. This however, is not always easy to specify without reference to the norms and customs of a society, for the cultural system defines the meaning of such critical categories of development as dignity, self-hood, material, spiritual and ethical values. Despite this, we cannot relativise the fundamental needs of the human person, entangling it in a thicket of ideological and cultural debate and jargon. We can proceed *de negativa* to a fruitful discovery of what features are not involved in social, ethical, psychological, and spiritual development. We know at a minimum what is not acceptable: torture, starvation, domination, isolation, dependence, discrimination, etc. That is a useful starting point for a programme of action, as well as an evaluation of the meaning of social development. Having specified what cannot be accepted, we can then proceed to establish minimal levels and optimising ideals on a critical list that defines human need. In this chapter, both the negative and positive approaches to social development will be used inter-lockingly to examine and evaluate the impact of ethnic conflict on development.

The materials are largely drawn from the earlier chapters with some new data added to them. Some of the data are not precise, for as Professor Dharam Ghai and his associates noted 'distributional data on social indicators are rare for developing countries' (Ghai, 1988:9). Evaluation is substantially subjective since 'social indicators have no common quantitative medium like money and are more indirect that economic indicators' (Ibid.). The quest for reliable and accurate social indicators over the years has led to a proliferation of methodologies which have spawned considerable confusion, as was well summarised by Professor Jan Drenowski:

> What has been created so far is an incoherent maze of variables, the definitions of which are muddled, quantification procedures questionable and practical uses, if any, externally doubtful. There is no doubt that many of them may prove quite useful, but they are lost among others which are useless. What is badly needed is the establishment of some ordering principles which would make possible a selection of useful indicators, and rejection of the ill-conceived and inapplicable ones (Drewnowski, 1972:75).

It is my contention that individual researchers must evolve appropriate categories of social indicator analysis in contemplation of the peculiarities of substantive case histories. The following categories will be examined in relation to Guyana: a) Violence, terror and personal security; b) participation; c) subsistence.

156

a) Violence, Terror, and Personal Security

It is essential to the normal survival of the human creature that its security is not threatened. That is, on an elementary day to day basis, it is a necessary condition for wholesome survival that physical life not be threatened, especially for collective irrational reasons. A reasonable measure of predictability about one's continued safety and survival is essential and a pre-requisite to all of the remaining basic needs of life. Physical insecurity disrupts and destabilises all aspects of life, and distorts every province and pursuit of behaviour, especially social and psychological existence. Terror and anxiety tend to overwhelm all behavioural dispositions, breeding their own pathologies. The omnipresent hovering threat of personal injury or even death often paralyses the will to function, especially in contexts of helplessness and open vulnerability.

In Guyana, especially between the 1975 and 1985, a reign of ethnically-oriented terror engulfed half of the population. As the crisis deepened, the terror spread beyond its original ethnic targets, becoming politically inter-ethnic. The immediate cause of this state of affairs, as the preceding chapters have showed, was the protracted ethnic rivalry that became a total engagement of practically all citizens in the communal sections of the population. In the tightening vice of the conflict between the two ethnicised political parties, a rigid, sectionally compartmentalised society evolved, breeding a spiral of tensions that periodically broke out into violence, and civil war in one notable instance. The logic of confrontation between government and opposition, fought on ethnic themes, over every conceivable policy problem, unleashed forces of sabotage and strikes by the opposition, countered by state repression and violence by the government. In the prolonged pressure exerted by these dynamics, inter-ethnic tolerance was destroyed with only a few persons and groups capable of standing outside the conflict as mediating influences. Collective ethnic conflict suffused the society comprehensively, producing an incendiary situation that could quickly become inflammable at the least provocation.

In the protracted exchanges between government and opposition, each bolstered its own violence capabilities. The PNC government, feeling threatened by the frequent massive marches and strikes by the PPP, diverted scarce resources to build a terrifying military arsenal for self-protection. Because the opposition Jagan-led PPP was perceived by the ruling regime's external sponsors as Marxist-Leninist, the PNC obtained sophisticated and plentiful supplies of security equipment and training from the West for counter-revolutionary programmes. That this weaponry would be put in the hands of an ethnicised army, police and secret service to indiscriminately terrorise and repress mainly an entire communal adversary did not inhibit the supply of arms from the West. By the time the PNC regime proclaimed itself inspired by Marxism-Leninism, it had already acquired a vast arsenal of ammunition and security devices from its Western cold war sponsors to continue its practices of ethnic repression.

Actions by the opposition Indian-based PPP to counter state terror included not only the legal methods of boycotts, marches and strikes, but also surreptitious plans to obtain its own weaponry. In many other parts of the world, this sort of ethnic conflict, which fosters state discrimination and terror, tends to engender the formation of an underground guerrilla opposition. Inclinations to do this in Guyana floundered on the sheer logistical difficulties of mounting secretive organised action in the thinly populated coastal villages. But the failure of the political opposition did not prevent the ethnicised state forces from seeing a plot to overthrow the government everywhere. This in turn fed into a system of security operations that extensively violated the sanctity of homes, communities and voluntary organisations.

What compounded the generalised violation of human rights for ostensible security purposes was the growing economic bankruptcy of the government and its inability to pay the wages and salaries of its coercive forces. The result was that the homes of the many members of the communal enemy were routinely broken into by security personnel, who for years carried out this sort of plunder unchecked by anyone. The doors and walls of the homes of the ethnic enemies who were seen to possess some material goods, cash, and jewellery were often entered, day or night, with material possessions confiscated and the occupants violated. It was indiscriminate ethnic terror that was pervasively perpetrated on numerous helpless victims. When cross ethnic friends interceded, and many in fact did, they themselves were subjected to terror. To bolster its hold on power, the ruling regime permitted various ethnically-recruited, semi-religious cults such as the infamous House of Israel (discussed in an earlier chapter) to operate freely. The House of Israel gained the reputation of being the maximum thuggery and violence arm of the ruling regime. Among Indians, it gained a reputation for ruthlessness and immunity from prosecution.

It was in the social and psychological well-being of the victim community that the semi-militarised ethnic violence reverberated directly. Unable to protect themselves, rural families feared to produce lest this invited the intruders to enter and acquire the produce of their labour. This meant, in practice, that rural residents feared planting even their gardens or raising livestock. Ethnic plunder was as petty as it was pervasive. All motivation to work having been crippled, the entire social structure was engulfed in a crisis. Anxiety about personal survival became the normal state of life. Families that seemed to have better-looking houses and had young females were the first targets. The response was to flee. Massive movements of people flowed to neighbouring Surinam (Dutch Guyana) and even to Venezuela and Brazil. Families pooled funds and sent members off to Canada and the U.S., many overstaying illegally in new Guyanese émigré ghettos. They carried their ethnic fears and prejudices with them into exile.

It should not be imagined that the initial ethic brunt, directed mainly at Indians, was welcomed by all Africans, Mixed Races, Portuguese and Chinese. Ethnically directed terror produced a generalised atmosphere of terror for all. Even though many ethnic supporters of the ruling regime benefited form Indian repression, several who were bold enough to speak out were silenced by fear and also sought refuge overseas. But in the programme of what was clearly a variant of genocidal repression, Indians as a whole lost sight of the many cross-communal sympathies that existed among them, assigning the entire blame of their plight to all of their communal adversaries. This blanket animosity did not help, and actually added to the tense ethnic crisis.

Interviews carried out by this researcher during the 1975-1985 period showed that all Guyanese people had become fearful of the state repression. To ethnic enemies, it was more acute; ordinary day to day security and survival neurotically became the single most important personal preoccupation. What had in fact happened was that state-employed security personnel, acting in collaboration with a similar gang of private persons had capitalised on the licence of the government to engage in ethnically-inspired plunder for their own material gain. The state had lost control over its security apparatus in regard to ethnic terror. In some ways, the state had become captive to this group of ethnic bandits on whose continued support the regime's own survival depended.

Ethnic, state-sponsored violence practically destroyed an entire community, striking at family life and destroying social and inter-communal relationships. The state practice of punitively dealing with one ethnic group to the immediate advantage of the other deeply divided the communities which, in turn, reinforced the basis of ethnic rule. Practically every village and town today has a large number of its members living overseas. The debris of broken families, the disrupted communities, uprooted persons, all impacted savagely on social existence. Social institutional decay was the long term casualty, the very *sine qua non* of any development efforts. Contemporary attempts to restore inter-communal co-existence often runs into the typical holocaust syndrome of alternating blame with self-pity compounded by a lack of confidence in the helping hand of a neighbour. The soul is scarred by an ethnically inscribed print that projects the deformity into future generations.

b) Participation

In its most general sense, participation refers to membership of a person in all aspects of a society. It both eliminates isolation and confers identity. It attests to the idea that the human personality is formed relationally in the ways of social interaction, which mould the mind and confer value on existence. Participation then, is not just about political rights to vote and involvement in collective decision-making, but about social self-definition and community identity. Furthermore, it refers not just to being a part of anything, however negative in its structure, but to being a member of a wholesome system of relations that does not distort human dignity and promote personality deformation.

In Guyana, as in most unintegrated multi-ethnic societies, personal identity is fragmented, derived from the norms supplied by the separate communities. In itself, this is a positive fact since it confers belonging and identity on the human person providing essential cultural anchorage and a point of collective reference. Membership confirms religion, custom, and role. It provides a structure of meaning, eliminating existential isolation. All of these advantages of social participation are, however, conditional on the existence of peaceful relations with other similar communal sections which share the same territorial state.

In Guyana, which is a small state where inter-communal and cross-sectional interactions are inevitable and frequent, a condition of inter-communal malaise that deteriorates into open and prolonged conflict can distort all the advantages of group participation. Each communal section can become a virtual military garrison, suffusing all activities with social self-assertions built on the dehumanisation of ethnic opponents Persistent ethnic struggle tends to sharpen the negative stereotypes which communal groups hold of each other. In Guyana, Indian views of their African compatriots became overladen by collective hate. Africans as a whole were portrayed in terms that made them into objects of selfishness and ruthlessness. Africans reciprocated, deeming Indians uncivilised and selfish as well. The stereotypes extended to derogations that bordered on outright racism.

In time, one factor above all – the ethnic enemy – assumed the centre stage of intense group assertion. It occupied the very centre of the soul with an obsessive preoccupation, assigning to it all manners of causes of every conceivable social problem. Apart from shaping attitudes of intense collective hate, the basis of any future inter-communal co-existence was crippled. At the level of voluntary associations, a new uni-ethnic membership and militancy developed. Water-tight ethnic compartments were created through which all normal emotions had now to be expressed.

At one level, it can be persuasively argued that being free to join social groupings such as clubs, cultural associations, and unions is important to social participation as an end in itself. It offers an intermediate arena between the state and the individual for autonomous action. It is also a form of empowerment, a form through which to express convictions and interests alike. However, when a collective spirit restricts membership only to certain uni-ethnic associations and penalises persons who dare to join groups that are cross-communal, the personal autonomy essential to individual development is lost. It would seem that a new form of social pathology sets in. In Guyana, a comprehensive set of voluntary associations evolved, and in the crucible of the ethnic strife, the ones that were mixed became purged of cross-communal membership. Cross-communal friends and sharing were lost and inter-communal hate fostered. If development means liberation and freedom to grow in healthy relationship with others, then ethnic conflict hampers, if not eliminates, this avenue of personal growth.

In effect, in the tightening claims of group loyalty, the social participation of a particular pathological type became prominent. Extremist and militant behaviour aimed at belittling the ethnic enemy was rewarded. In many schools throughout Guyana, many cross-communal friendships were formed and forced into denial by communal pressure and ostracism. All of this, of course, occurred at the same time that political participation was being extinguished in Guyana. When the PNC regime rigged the first elections after independence in 1968 (and every election thereafter), it was at first celebrated by its own communal group as it was denounced by others. It did not occur to the 'winners' that the rigging of the elections, as attested to in the subsequent electoral fraudulence, in fact disenfranchised everyone. When the ruling regime manufactured its own victories, clearly it needed the vote of no one in the electorate to remain in power and was accountable to no one. The power of participation and self-determination was negated. This fact came home with force when, as the ruling PNC presided over an increasingly impoverished population and became unpopular, a cross-communal attempt under Walter Rodney to remove the government was brutally frustrated by violent assassinations. A mighty state apparatus was fashioned from the communal cleavage in the service of an elite. It imposed obedience on all quarters and eliminated the right to dissent, rebellion and privacy.

Having obtained the right to self-determination in the struggle against the colonial power, the loss of suffrage moved the state back in a complete circle to a new form of domination. The loss of the right to elect one's government and to decide freely one's own political destiny was but one aspect of the impact on the creation of powerlessness, especially on the part of the particular communal section which constituted a majority of the population. It tended to engender its own pathologies in support of ethnic entrepreneurs and cultural chauvinists. Moderate leaders with pluralist visions of inter-communal exchanges and co-operation were jettisoned. A state of war existed and the totalising impact of communal strife permitted only one form of participation expressed in uncritical collective hate.

The organisation of ethnic solidarity had another important effect on participation. It blinded the eye to internal structures of inequality and oppression both within African and Indian sections. To participate equally requires the elimination of the more concentrated and oppressive forms of wealth and power in society. When the colonial power was forced to leave Guyana, this eliminated the more obvious form of institutional oppression marked by disparities in the distribution of wealth and privileges. In the new order that came into being, a tiny middle class emerged in both the African and Indian communities, with a hold over the values and privileges in its section. The ethnic conflict tended to divert attention away from reforming or eliminating those institutional structures which were causes of inequity and inequality. There is a convincing school of thought that views the ethnic conflict not only in Guyana but in similar places, as manipulated by intra-ethnic elites to prevent cross-communal organisation of lower income interests. While this is not altogether true, since such rational calculations soon become a casualty of the totalising effects of ethnic strife, it does suggest that individual participation and empowerment had been diverted to inter-communal strife and not towards eliminating internal sources of injustice. The continuing communal strife provided a convenient cover for the survival of internal forms of communal oppression.

In sum, the seizure of power by one of the ethnically-based parties, and the ensuing implementation of a regime of ethnically-oriented discrimination and repression, eliminated political participation as a legitimate form of social behaviour. It created a new hierarchy in inter-ethnic relations. It marginalised one communal section without benefiting the other in Guyana's bi-polar state. The thoroughgoing nature of the oppression destroyed self- reliance and people's ability to influence their environment. It destroyed the freedom to choose one's friends. It created powerless people in all the ethnic sections. It encouraged invidious forms of inter-ethnic rivalry that could only distort the friendships and love that people are capable of. It placed a premium on hate and dehumanised inter-communal perception on communications. An entire generation of Guyanese was nurtured in this environment. The social personality that evolved was suspicious, narrow and hasty; it created ingrained social dispositions that were incapable of trust and fellowship. In those situations where inter-ethnic contact persists, it has bred forms of social hypocrisy that parade as peaceful inter-ethnic co-existence. Under the veneer of civil order, a socially deformed population enacts a script of inter-ethnic antipathy that continues the ethnic war by other means in the dark recesses of the soul.

c) Subsistence

The progressive deterioration of the economy caused widespread poverty in Guyana, which replaced Haiti in the Western hemisphere as the most impoverished country. The intensifying ethnic conflict engulfed the entire society as the economic and industrial action executed by the opposition forces reduced the economy to shambles. The neglect and decay of the infrastructure of basic services created the first major social casualties. The supply of clean water became unreliable. Without clean water in a country notable for its many rivers, an important threat to health occurred. The electricity supply was marked by frequent blackouts and power shortages. Roads fell into disrepair, telephones no longer worked, and the sea defences, which protected the population from floods and were necessary because the coast on which Guyana lies is below sea level, were neglected. It was a calamity of massive proportions at the personal and community level.

A picture of degradation was filled in by the emergent parallel economy of high-priced goods and an unstable currency. Basic foodstuffs were excessively expensive as shortages stemming from the political boycotts took their toll. Rice and sugar, which were basic materials, produced in abundance at one stage in the recent history of the country, became unavailable at fair prices. The shortages were remedied by smuggling and donations of remissions from friends overseas.

All of this reverberated adversely on social life,. Unable to make ends meet, those who could not migrate faced personal and family degradation. Family life for all communal sections was thrown into turmoil as a new neurotic modality of 'hustle' developed. It marginalised many, but above all, it led to the fall in self-esteem. Personal ambitions and career structures for improvement were no longer entertained. The loss of hope, compounded by a sense of powerlessness, bred a population of cynics who could not change their government. In this ocean of despair, ethnic antipathies did not die.

Some of the costs in this environment were expressed in the loss of dignity. Many Guyanese were ashamed to tell strangers overseas that they were from Guyana. Among themselves, new forms of behaviour associated with 'hustle' included crime, excess selfishness, prostitution, drug abuse, and fear. When the curtain of economic deprivation descended, all communal sections suffered, but this did not dissolve ethnic fanaticism. The old structures and the new crises adapted to each other, resulting in the persistence of ethnic solidarity patterns. Tolerance for ethnic diversity did not emerge. Mutual appreciation across the ethnic divide did not develop. Generosity and sharing in all communities suffered from a psyche crippled by ethnic strife.

d) The Psychological Dimension

The Guyanese who were subjected to the intensifying tensions of ethnic compartmentalisation became a twisted, paranoid people. A stressful environment had been created, unconducive to healthy human development. It was not marked by ordinary struggle, but by hate, jealousy, and single-minded obsession with subjugating and destroying the ethnic enemy. The stereotypes each Guyanese carried embodied traits which dehumanised entire communities. Distrust and deceit, cordiality underlaid by hypocrisy, became operational norms of life.

Ethnic identity had, to be sure, been affirmed. This raises the fundamental question about how much ethnic or communal identity is enough to impart a sense of psychological belonging. Is there a threshold of too much ethnic solidarity when it becomes pathological and suffocating? I think protracted ethnic conflicts can engender a level of solidarity that over-saturates the need for belongingness. It brings into play, after a certain threshold of solidarity intensity is attained, a new set of adverse effects which negate the initial value of group cohesion. That threshold to which I refer can be called 'the collective insanity threshold.' When group consciousness attains a certain critical mass, it thereafter destroys the carriers themselves.

Ethnically-inspired collective insanity destroys the human perceptual apparatus, distorts all messages, and breeds a system of behaviour that destroys adaptation for a healthy, fulfilling survival. In Guyana, human creatures who were capable of love and spiritual sharing have been turned into mass instruments of hate. From this comes pervasive high blood pressure in the population, short tempers and widespread emotionally-related illnesses, which together make life not only difficult between communal groups, but within the groups themselves. From this environment have arisen several apocalyptic personalities and spiritual groups which have exploited the weak personalities that have come to typify the Guyanese citizen. The communal parties are not just political aggregates of citizen interests; they are truly cultural institutions and psychiatric clinics. They are centralised around the personalities of their leaders who offer psychological redemption.

What kind of personality is best suited for development? It is clear that the crippled personality that is born of protracted ethnic conflict is not in any way appropriate for bringing into being a wholesome society. Integral human development is therefore denied in societies caught in the vice of ethnic strife, as illustrated by the Guyana case.

XI The Economic Dimension

As for the political arena, the criteria used to measure the impact of economic development tend to be fixed around the particular ideology and strategy adopted for economic transformation. The two principal ideological systems of the post-World War II period – capitalism and socialism – have emphasised the critical role of the market and planning respectively, as the optimal mechanism with which to mobilise limited resources for production and distribution. The strategies are distinct but their aims are broadly similar in many ways. Evaluating the performance of each strategy in terms of its own ideological claims cannot be done in a vacuum however, without reference to the peculiarities of the implementation environment. It is specifically with reference to the environment of cultural pluralism that we are concerned. We argue that this environment drastically redefines the substance of the claims of each ideological system adding a level of complexity that is notoriously incapable of clear-cut solutions. For instance, it is practically impossible to unequivocally render the notion of equality espoused by both capitalism and socialism in cultural situations with radically different views of justice. The environment of ethnic and cultural pluralism recasts the issue of evaluating ideologically-inspired strategies and their ends. Inevitably, economic performance becomes entangled in a maze of both divergent values and customs. Put differently, each strategy must be seen separately in the context of its ideological value preferences and its ethnicised environment. The theoretical aspects of a strategy are, in practice, rendered into ethno-cultural constructs. The strategies of economic change may well be sold as neutral instruments impregnated with value-free technical features, but in the hands of a sectionally-based ruling party, they are inevitably inspired by communal preferences reflecting ongoing inter-ethnic struggles in the environment. Even where a ruling party is sincere about its neutrality in implementing a particular strategy, this may not occur in practice. In an environment of persistent ethnic strife from which the rulers obtained their mandate, grassroots mass supporters would not allow implementation free from sectional expectations and interests. In practice, economic strategies are ethnically adapted to fit ethno-cultural interests in the distribution of scarce resources. Ruling parties in places like Guyana, Fiji, Trinidad, etc., (even where they espouse socialist ideologies) are erected on communal support for their survival. They are trapped by the sectional proclivities of the environment, as well as by a politics of personal ambition. In the following parts of the chapter, economic strategies are evaluated in terms of the ethnic rivalry that defines the environment of implementation in Guyana.

A.   The Economic Environment Through an Ethnic Prism

Perhaps, the most crucial part of the economic environment in the typical multi-ethnic society that has been created by colonisation is its ethnic specialisation and complementarity. The specialised parts of the economy have emerged as areas of ethnic concentration so that over time, each economic sector becomes the *de facto* preserve or territory of one or another ethnic group. This was exemplified by the Guyana case. The major productive and distributive components of the economy are dominated by one or another ethnic group. To be sure, there are inter-ethnic overlaps. For instance, among sugar-field workers are African and Indian work 'gangs' that cut the cane, even though few of these groups are themselves mixed. Similarly, in many factories in urban areas and in many government offices, ethnic mixes occur. What is, however, significant is that preponderant ethnic concentrations occur in different economic sectors and that this is re-enforced by ethnically-oriented residential and occupational patterns and preferences.

While on the one hand this system of ethnic separation tended, during most of the colonial period, to maintain a substantial level of political order and stability in Guyana, it contained the seeds of self-destruction because of the imperative need for co-ordination and co-operation in and among the sectors, for smooth uninterrupted production. Put differently, each ethnic section, because of its preponderance in one essential sector of the economy, can by that fact disrupt the entire system by withdrawing its role. In the post-independence period when ethnically-based parties were formed, this was done repeatedly to sabotage and destabilise the government in power.

The creation of an economy of ethnic enclaves and economic spheres of influence also resulted in important communal disparities in the distribution of material benefits. The owners of capital were mainly Europeans; in the later evolution of Guyana, intermediate size businesses were mainly controlled by the Portuguese, Chinese, and a number of Indians. Most wealth was controlled by Europeans in combination with a handful of Portuguese, Chinese and Indians. The Africans as a whole were excluded, but in the 20th century, many of them, including a mixed-race category, occupied strategic positions in the public service. Nevertheless, the greatest degrees of poverty, unemployment and economic deprivation were generally found among Africans. Although there were many poor Indians, generally most Indians emerged as better-off than Africans. The colonial heritage, then, bequeathed an economic order of inequality that was preponderantly ethnicised.

Another aspect of uneven development left by the colonial imprint pertained to the comparatively well-developed system of roads, drainage and irrigation facilities, and sea defences which tended to favour rural residents who were Indians. This eventuated as a consequence of the colony having developed as a economy based on the plantation production of sugar. An infrastructure of well-maintained roads and other facilities serviced the plantations. Further, over time, the sugar estates provided a variety of housing and health services to their workers, most of whom were Indians. In the urban areas, however, there was a general neglect of housing and community services even though a body of exclusive schools and private hospitals and housing settlements were developed. Generally, there was a rural bias in the expenditure of government resources to facilitate the extraction of sugar and profits for overseas markets. This benefited many Indians. The same sort of skewed infrastructural benefits were bestowed on the towns of Linden and Kwakwani where bauxite workers, mainly Africans, were employed by the Canadian and American mining companies.

Finally, an important, ethnically-related aspect of the economic environment that was forged into being by the colonial power pertained to the foreign-owned financial and managerial structure of the main industries. The economy of the colony was based mainly on sugar, and to a lesser extent on bauxite. The producers of sugar and bauxite were multi-national corporations which imported European executive officers to manage the operation of the companies. They lived like a superior caste in separate residential areas in relative wealth. The importance of this form of ownership control meant that should socialist parties supported by either/or Indians and Africans seek to radically restructure the economy, they would at once create an ethnic issue and confront international sabotage. In effect, to confront the structures of economic dominance literally meant conflict between whites and non-whites.

B.   Economic Strategies and their Ethnic Impact

a) *The Colonial Capitalist Strategy*

During Guyana's colonial period, European settlers implanted a variant of the
market capitalist model for the exploitation of the country's resources. In a real
sense, the colony was but a regional outpost of the British economy, all
features architecturally re-cast into an export producer of primary products.
Only a few companies were engaged in producing sugar so that a strict
competitive system did not emerge. Most food and equipment were imported.
The colony produced what it did not consume and consumed what it did not
produce. Few ancillary support industries constituting backward linkages into
the economy were developed. No attempt was made to develop manufacturing.

What endowed the colonial market strategy with a peculiarity of its own
was the close association that the factors of production bore to the ethnic
groups and status system in the society. The owners of capital were Europeans
and the labourers were Africans and Indians. Later, as the governmental
administrative system evolved, Africans would come to dominate the public
bureaucracy, thereby fully articulating the relationship between productive
sectors and the diverse ethnic groups.

The impact of this ethno-capitalist colonial model was disastrous for the
colony in the long run. Clearly, the economic ascriptive caste system did not
rely on the maximum utilisation of human resources. It relied on race and
ethnicity as variables in the assignment of labour in the productive process.
The best investors and the finest workers were not market determined. Nor
were the sources for the disposal of the final product. A distorted capitalist
market system institutionalised ethnicity around productive activities and the
distribution of benefits. It laid the foundation for future ethnic conflict built
around the allocation of resources as the colony moved towards a more
achievement-oriented order at a later date.

Ethnic differentiation was therefore built into the economic system and, as
was pointed out in the earlier chapters, a deliberate policy of instigating inter-
communal rivalry and jealousy in the labour recruitment of immigrants was
initiated at the founding of the multi-ethnic fabric of the society. The ethnic
conflict that ensued in subsequent years derived in part from the communally
differentiated economy, and the conflict in turn reinforced those cleavages.
This clearly contributed to economic waste since the ethnic order failed to
efficiently utilise all its talents. Even the security forces were deliberately
ethnically recruited in favour of Africans. Ethnic discrimination became built
into the colonial system at all levels so that each section in control of its own
territorial preserves sought to exclude others.

b) Strategy under the First Jagan-led PPP Government

The unified independence movement under the joint bi-ethnic leadership of Dr. Jagan and Mr Burnham was socialist in commitment but lasted barely six months before it was evicted from office by British troops. An ethnically unified independence movement using a socialist ideology could have re-directed the use of resources for development, but instead the movement was destroyed. In the immediate aftermath, two ethnically polarised parties evolved which would each take its turn governing a state whose ethnic seams were severely inflamed. The environmental context of implementing any sort of economic strategy had altered radically from the pre-1955 colonial period in the respect that ethnic consciousness had been aroused, and with the impending departure of the British presence, Africans and Indians confronted each other in a deeply divided state.

The Indian-based Jagan-led PPP government won two successive elections (1957 and 1961) and had the opportunity to design an economic strategy consonant with its ideological premises for the transformation of the society. The Jagan government had professed to be a socialist party and was committed to transforming Guyana into a socialist society. This it would have to not only in an environment marked by deep ethnic bifurcation and fraught with ethnic animosity, but also while Guyana was still a colony. The colonial status would soon thereafter feature as a critical factor when Castro brought into being the first socialist system in the Western Hemisphere with a clear threat that the revolution could spread throughout Latin America and the Caribbean.

The new Jagan PPP government, smarting from its eviction from office in 1953 because of the charge that it was communist-inspired, decided on an orthodox, mixed capitalist market strategy of development. It emphasised the role of private capital, utilised much of its budget to improve the infrastructure of roads and other public facilities to attract foreign investment, and continued quietly to work within the terms of the foreign owned plantation mono-crop, export-oriented economy. In all these respects, the Jagan strategy bore the unmistakable stamp of structural economic continuity with the antecedent colonial strategy of development. What it did, however, do differently was to offer stronger budgetary support for rural development, arguing that it needed to emphasise and diversify agricultural production. It embarked upon an extensive programme to reclaim vacant lands for production of crops, to improve drainage and irrigation schemes, and to offer a variety of subsidies to farmers who were willing to diversify production away from reliance on sugar.

The choice by Jagan of an economic strategy that emphasised agricultural production and diversification and rural development, although it could be vindicated by economic arguments, entailed the emphasis of budgetary expenditures on Indians who were mainly rural residents. A highly ethnicised society sees everything through an ethnic prism. Even when it is not so, it becomes so by prophetic fulfilment as the alleged discriminated group withdraws its co-operation, leaving a particular policy and its benefits in the hands of the other ethnic group.

As traced out in the earlier chapters, the Jagan economic strategy and its alleged tilt in favour of Indians, compounded by Jagan's support for Castro's revolution, provoked extensive and decisive acts of destabilisation against the governing regime. Between 1962 and 1964, strikes and boycotts by ethnic adversaries, aided and abetted by external actors, led to virtual civil war. Ethnic violence became widespread and persistent. Severe damages were done to public properties and immense losses stemming from strikes and boycotts were incurred. The damage was done not only to human life and limb, physical assets and other material losses, but also to the fragile ethnic fabric of the state. The violence and counter-violence cannot be explained by reference to the technical features of the economic strategy adopted by the PPP government. Rather, it was the perception that these strategies of development were ethnically-oriented that offered the basis for the demonstrations and riots. Given the ethnic specialisation and compartmentalisation of the economy, it was easy for the outgroup to sabotage the entire economy. The public bureaucracy and the urban unions, which were both predominantly African in composition, came out against the Jagan government. The struggle over what could be regarded as legitimate economic differences became entangle in ethnically mobilised sentiments. Ethnic contests are irrational and intense events. In Guyana, when this occurred, it practically levelled the economic landscape into a virtual wasteland of desolation. Above all, the last residual spirit of inter-ethnic respect was lost.

c)   *The Strategy of 'Co-operative Socialism' under Burnham*

The fall of the Indian-based PPP regime under Jagan was followed by a coalition formation which obtained strong support from the United States. The Burnham-D'aguiar coalition therefore, proceeded to implement a policy direction that was unequivocally committed to the market mechanism with heavy emphasis on private, and especially foreign, investment. Loans and grants that were generously supplied by the U.S. were largely allocated to building an infrastructure of roads, communications, security, etc. to attract investors. This aspect of the economic strategy was a concession to the U.S. and to D'aguiar, the Portuguese businessman-politician who was Burnham's coalition partner. It impacted favourably to the benefit of the old plantocracy and the multinationals. But there was another aspect to this strategy, which was a grudging concession to Burnham's ethnic interest. This consisted of building the coercive and security forces out of mainly African recruits, and of the allocation of expenditures to provide jobs in the public service for urban residents. Generally, this latter ethnic bias emerged quite slowly because of the restraints imposed by the coalition structure of the government. All of this elicited strong opposition response from the Jagan forces which mounted strike after strike in the sugar industry to destabilise the government. Opposition action did cripple the economy at various times and many of Jagan's activists were jailed without trial under the 'Emergency and Security Regulations', which were promulgated by the ruling regime.

The full articulation of an ethno-economic strategy and its devastating counter responses however, not come until after Burnham's PNC virtually seized power in the fraudulent elections of 1968. This was discussed in detail in an earlier chapter. In sole control of the government, having jettisoned its coalition partner, the PNC proceeded to enunciate and implement a strategy of economic development consonant with its own views of socialism. This was set forth in its doctrine of 'Co-operative Socialism'. In 1970, Guyana officially was declared a 'Co-operative Socialist Republic.'

In 'Co-operative Socialism', the Burnham government decided to disassociate itself from the stigma of its prior attachment to a 'mixed capitalist economy', which had brought its supporters only few benefits.

Socialism in the context of Guyana envisages a re-arrangement of our economic and social relations which give the worker that substantial and preponderant control on the economic structure which he now holds in the political structure. Its strategy was built around the Co-operative (Burnham, 1970:153).

Continued Burnham:

The Co-operative is the means through which the small man can participate fully in the economic life of the nation and the means through which the small man can play a predominant part in the workings of the economy (Ibid.:153).

Through a series of nationalisations, some 80 per cent of the economy was placed under this vision of co-operative socialism. In practice, most of the nationalised companies simply became state enterprises. The strategy not only nationalised the main private corporations involved in sugar, bauxite, and banking, but also extended this policy to the vital import and export firms and to wholesale and retail businesses. Both European and Indian businessmen were the losers, since these economic activities under a massive governmental bureaucracy were placed largely under African control. However valid in theory the economic and ideological aspects of the nationalisation exercise was, it was nevertheless again interpreted through ethnic lens. 'Co-operative Socialism' was cynically seen as an ideological device to neutralise the government's economic and political opponents who also happened to be its ethnic adversaries.

As recounted in the earlier chapters, the upshot was a series of boycotts and strikes by the Jagan forces which literally frustrated the experiment in co-operative socialism. Indians saw the government's policies as masterminded by ethnic jealousies. Farmers lost their previous government supports and subsidies and their political leaders were frequently harassed and jailed. Rice production plummeted. The sugar industry, the backbone of the economy, was reduced to a cripple. In control of an integral aspect of the economy, the Indians practically paralysed the economy in the same manner as Africans did when Jagan was in power. Burnham's regime also found its difficulties compounded through the role of external actors, in the same way Jagan did. In Burnham's case, his new socialist radicalism, expressed in terms of the nationalisation of Western multinationals and the extension of diplomatic friendship with the Socialist bloc of countries, invited external boycotts. Western foreign aid dried up and Guyana's familiar source of investments and markets were nearly all eliminated. As in Jagan's case, internal ethnic divisions and external ideological interests combined to reduce the economy to virtual shambles.

Burnham retained power through continued fraudulent elections as well as through expanded and ethnicised army and security forces. The threat of perceived ethnic domination by Indians was averted through the seizure of power but the state now fell into the hands of a African bourgeoisie with a small sprinkling of support from Portuguese, Indians and Chinese businessmen. This occurred in a state which would now suffer from a recurrent cycle of economic calamities brought on by ethnic opposition boycotts and compounded by external sabotage as well as by massive increases in fuel prices. The mounting opposition strikes and boycotts broke the main agricultural production features of the economy in the sugar and rice sectors. The government spent most of its already reduced revenues on an expanded security apparatus and a bloated public bureaucracy consisting mainly of its own ethnic supporters. In an earlier chapter we pointed to the dramatic 1000 per cent increase in the size of the security forces. The damage done was not only in the productive areas, but in the distorted expenditure patterns which witnessed the neglect of roads, telephones, and sea defences, maintenance of health services, and schools. Guyana's infrastructure of electricity and water supply, its roads telephones and health systems virtually all collapsed. The persistence of ethnic conflict with its economic effects saw Guyana tumble from a prosperous country in the 1950s to the lowest rung in the Western Hemisphere in 1990. To maintain an ethnically dominant regime, the economic costs were considered secondary to that of poverty. In due course, the adverse economic effects reverberated to the loss and degradation of all ethnic sections. About a third of the population, consisting of its best trained and educated persons, migrated overseas. How far and deeply the economic effects were felt was readily identifiable by observing their impact on human welfare in the satisfaction of basic needs. To that we turn next, but before we undertake this aspect of the analysis, it will be useful to review the aggregate economic statistics which demonstrate the magnitude of the economic decline in the wake of persistent ethnic strife.

It will first be useful to examine the production statistics related to Guyana's chief commodities, sugar, rice, and bauxite-alumina. This is given in Tables 11.1 and 11.2.

Sugar, the mainstay of Guyana's economy, clearly suffered a steady decline. Whereas the industry's capacity in the early-seventies had been estimated at about 450,000 tons and had actually reached a peak performance of 374,000 tons in 1971, as the ethnic conflict intensified, and especially after the nationalisation of the industry occurred in 1975, the decline in production plummeted to nearly half its capacity during the second half of the 1980s. At the end of 1989, sugar production was 47.4 per cent of its 1978 level. At one point, having striven desperately to meet its lucrative EEC-ACP protocol quota, Guyana was forced to import sugar for local consumption.

Rice production, which had emerged as not only a source of national self-sufficiency but also a major export crop to the Caribbean, suffered boycotts by the PPP's rural supporters. Its estimated capacity of about 250,000 tons annually, which reached a peak level of 212,000 tons in 1977, declined to about half of its capacity thereafter. In 1989, rice production was 53.3 per cent of its 1977 level. At one point under the Jagan regime, rice had been exported to Cuba at high prices. That export market was terminated with the removal of the PPP from power. In 1964, about 316,000 acres were put under rice; by 1989, only 168,000 acres were planted. In 1964, about 100,000 tons of rice were exported but by 1989, only 40,000 tons were exported. A variety of agricultural subsidies such as low fuel and fertiliser prices were also eliminated. High costs of production and low prices paid for farmers' produce contributed to the decline in rice production. Rice lands fell into disrepair as farmers migrated in droves to New York and Toronto.

Table 11.1:   Guyana: Real Growth of GDP (Compound % per Annum)

	1970-1975	1975-1980	1981	1982	1983	1984	1985	1986	Total GDP
	3.9	-0.7	-0.3	-10.4	-9.6	2.5	1.0	0.3	0.9
Sugar	....	-1.3	10.9	-3.8	12.6	-3.6	...	...	
Rice	2.4	0.9	-2.2	15.6	-19.2	23.8	...	...	
Mining	-2.3	-5.3	-11.4	-31.5	-22.4	47.0	...	...	
Government	10.5	1.9	1.0	-7.7	-1.9	0.0	...	...	

Source: Commonwealth Advisory Group, *Guyana: The Economic Recovery Programme and Beyond*, Commonwealth Secretariat, London, August 1989.

Table 11.2: **Guyana: Population and Physical Output – Major Sectors 1970-86**

Year	Population* (in thousands)	Sugar	Output (in thousands of tons) Rice	Dried-Bauxite	Calcined-Bauxite	Alumina
1970	699	311	142	2290	699	312
1971	704	369	120	2108	700	365
1972	710	315	94	1652	690	305
1973	716	266	110	1665	637	234
1974	721	341	153	1383	726	311
1975	727	300	175	1350	778	194
1976	733	333	110	969	729	265
1977	739	242	212	879	709	273
1978	745	325	182	1021	590	276
1979	750	298	142	1059	589	171
1980	751	270	166	1005	598	215
1981	763	301	163	982	513	170
1982	769	287	182	958	392	73
1983	777	252	149	761	315	nil
1984	782	238	181	823	517	nil
1985	788	243	154	1096	478	nil
1986	793	245	180	1036	441	nil

Source: Commonwealth Advisory Group, *Guyana: The Economic Recovery Programme and Beyond*, Commonwealth Secretariat, London, August 1989.

The bauxite and alumina industry from which Guyana's high-grade calcined ore brought a bountiful market (90 per cent of the world market) also suffered grave decline after nationalisation in the mid-1970s. This industry was dominated by African and Mixed races so that for a while, its decline was not due to strikes and boycotts. Rather, it was traceable to the fall in world prices causing a decline in revenues. An increasingly impoverished Guyana which utilised its scarce resources to maintain a bloated security and bureaucratic system found it increasingly difficult to maintain the physical facilities of the bauxite plants and to manage them efficiently. By the 1980s, the industry's production fell to about 55 per cent of its annual capacity of 441,000 tons. Because its supply to external markets became unreliable, world demand for Guyana's superior calcined ore fell from 90 per cent to about 50 per cent and was replaced by an inferior Chinese variant.

Economist D. Pantin summarised all these declines in production extending his categories to include gold, electricity and merchandised exports. This is given in Table 11.3 below.

Table 11.3: **1989 Production of Sugar, Rice, Bauxite, Gold, Electricity and Merchandise Exports Relative to Three Benchmark Production Levels**

	As % of 1975 Production	As % of Average Annual Production[1]	As % of Peak Production[2]
Sugar	56	57	54 (1970)
Rice	81	85	78 (1983)
Dried Bauxite	72	74	43 (1970)
Calcined Bauxite	45	58	45 (1970)
Alumina	0	0	0
Gold	n.a	190	89 (1981)
Merchandise Exports	n.a.	62 (80-82)	52 (1980)
Electricity	46	52	42 (1981)

1   Average for 1970, 1975 and 1980-82
2   Peak annual production during 1970-1982
Source : Derived from Tables 11.1 and 11.2

In Table 11.3, Pantin, citing data from the Guyana Manufacture's Association, provided the more recently updated declines until 1990 as 15 per cent of utilisation capacity. Much of this astounding decline came from the breakdown of electricity and water supply systems. Electricity supply in 1989 represented 46 per cent of 1975 production levels.

The net impact of these critical productive industries reverberated adversely to every area of the economy. Real growth progressively declined from plus 3.9 per cent between 1970 and 1975, to 0.7 per cent between 1975 and 1980, to negative growth averages in the 1980s. The reduction in the physical production of sugar, rice, and bauxite also registered adversely on the balance of payments account (merchandise export continued to decline by 46 per cent from 1980 to 1988; balance of payments deficit exceeded 25 per cent of GDP for 1976-1984) foreign-exchange availability. Table 11.4 portrays a scene of economic devastation in these areas.

Table 11.4: Guyana: Monetary Indicators 1975-1986

Year	Net International Reserves US$ Million	National Debt External US$ Million Disbursed (end of year)	Internal G$ Million (end of year)	External Arrears US$ Million	Balance Payment Current Account G$	Government Finance (G$ million)			Money Supply G$ Million	Consumer Price Index (Urban) 1970=100 (Average)
						Total Revenue	Total Expenditure	Deficit		
1975	+77.4	295.5	399.2	n.a.	-35.2	497.7	638.8	-141.1	449.3	145
1976	-12.3	363.8	657.9	n.a.	-350.8	389.9	803.0	-413.0	491.5	158
1977	-39.3	404.3	853.9	n.a.	-251.1	355.1	543.6	-188.5	603.0	171
1978	-42.9	438.8	1035.2	n.a.	-72.3	365.8	542.2	-176.4	667.2	197
1979	-98.5	507.0	1312.5	n.a.	-208.1	412.2	690.7	-278.5	713.3	231
1980	-206.5	566.3	1650.8	45.4	-300.4	455.1	935.2	-480.1	850.4	264
1981	-267.4	660.0	1089.1	136.4	-475.8	578.9	1205.7	-626.8	997.1	323
1982	-362.2	681.3	2775.7	249.5	-426.0	550.6	1570.9	-1020.3	1269.3	390
1983	-552.4	692.6	3820.8	450.6	-468.0	568.2	1291.0	-722.8	1533.7	449
1984	-663.4	682.5	4544.0	595.5	-434.0	651.4	1830.2	-1178.8	1814.9	562
1985	-526.9	691.0	5425.7	771.9	-426.0	1200.2	1562.8	-362.6	2169.7	646
1986	-553.5	707.0	5399.3	897.5	-497.0	1618.1	2858.4	-1240.3	2691.7	n.a.

Source: Commonwealth Advisory Group, Guyana: The Economic Recovery Programme and Beyond, Commonwealth Secretariat, London, August 1989.

Per capita real income declined by about 33 per cent between 1975 and 1986. Recurrent deficits in the import-export accounts reverberated on the country's public and foreign debt. Guyana's external debt of about US$1.9 billion by 1988 was probably the highest in the world on a per capita basis. In 1989, it was 540 per cent of the current GNP. As a percentage of export goods and services, the debt in 1989 was 734 per cent. The internal public debt also grew dramatically as the government resorted to indiscriminate printing of money to meets its bills. Money supply increased by 1198.9 per cent between 1978 and 1989. Cash flow problems were created by the excess of debt repayments over revenue collections. Both internal and external debts had to be rescheduled. There was no foreign exchange available during the 1980s. Seeking IMF-World Bank help, the Guyana government was unable to meet its required targets; the result was the suspension of all agreements. This reverberated on the government's inability to borrow from abroad.

All of this reverberated in the inflationary rate accompanied by repeated devaluations of the Guyana currency. From 1980 to 1989, the inflationary index moved from 68 to 375. The urban consumer price index grew by a factor of nine from 1980 to 1989. Minimum wages, on the other hand, grew only by a factor of three from 1980 to 1989. Practically all of these negative effects in Guyana stemmed directly from the ethno-political crisis in the society.

B.   Basic Needs as Indicators of Economic Decline

Aggregate economic data in an environment of steeply skewed inequality can distort the real picture of deprivation in a population. A more reliable approach may entail the use of basic needs criteria built around data on health, housing, calorie intake, education, water and transportation supply, etc., especially as these relate to the broad masses of people. Gathering these data in ample and accurate form is a nightmare.

A variety of standard methods have been designed and widely utilised to generate basic needs data. A review of these methodologies for countries like Guyana depicts a picture of gross inaccuracy in data reliability. Apart from accuracy and methodology, universal cross-cultural standards are difficult to establish. Use of the quantifiable income approach, for instance, assumes that income and well-being are measurably correlated. A number of other informal and cultural practices apart from quantifiable income are usually at play and these are difficult to measure. In Third World countries, statistical services are notoriously poor apart from the problems created by suspicion, illiteracy, secrecy, etc. In the end, a seasoned field researcher must make qualitative evaluations based on prolonged observation and participation in a country.

In Guyana, all the constraints on assembling ample and accurate data on basic needs are present. This especially became the case after the economy practically collapsed and a striving informal 'parallel' black-market effectively replaced the official economy described by government statistics. The Guyana dollar has been repeatedly devalued so that its instability has resulted in its *de facto* replacement by hard foreign currencies. Until very recently, this has meant that many financial transactions are conducted in secrecy. A good deal of the supply of certain basic goods comes through smuggling and gifts in 'barrels' making official figures totally unreliable. Wage and income rates are highly dependent on external remissions from the Guyanese population resident overseas. The production and distribution of good and services now occurs through informal and subterranean channels. A 'parallel' economy has been effectively engrafted onto the traditional economic structure requiring new methodologies to measure economic well-being. Despite the lack of accurate data, a general picture of the condition of basic needs distribution can be pulled from the reports of church and human rights organisations, from surveys by news reporters and researchers, and by personal observation. Here we offer a general qualitative picture of the basic need situation from all these sources.

On social services related to health, education, housing, postal services, electricity supply, transport, safe water availability, police service etc., one researcher connected with the Guyana Institute of Development concluded, after a survey and through direct observation, that by the late 1980s 'the entire economy was reduced to pitiable conditions comparable only to what obtained in slavery' (Canterbury, 1990:4). Looking at these items specifically, it is important to first note that real wage levels and per capita generally decreased by at least a third between 1975 and 1986. This meant that workers and rural residents had to obtain food, clothing, shelter, and other basic needs from this reduced income level. Many standard services such as health, education and water supply were actually provided by the government at an earlier date. However, after 1975, the deterioration of the economy, stemming primarily from the persistent ethnic conflict and its attendant boycotts and strikes, substantially reduced the government revenues. In turn, all these services fell into neglect, disrepair and disarray.

The overall impact has been disastrous in terms of inflation, estimated at over 50 per cent annually in the 1980s. One University of Guyana researcher estimated that, using 1970 as the base year, the urban Consumer Price Index (CPI) had increased by 2,451 points by 1989 (Ibid.). Food, including beverages and tobacco, increased by 4,372.3 points; housing, including rent, fuel and light, went up by 352.7 points; clothing by 3,283 points. These estimates were made using official prices, but in practice, nothing was sold at official prices. In the same period, the Guyana dollar went down by 2,000 per cent (Ibid.). The adjectives used to describe the extensive breakdown of basic needs have not exaggerated the real picture. The government-serviced infrastructure of sea-defences, roads, sanitation and health facilities, telecommunications, etc. can be described for the 1980s as existing in a 'perilous' condition (Thomas, 1983:283). The housing situation has been described as scandalous (Ibid.).

Water supply has become erratic and drinking water, when available, must be boiled to avoid typhoid, gastro-enteritis and hepatitis. Drainage and waste disposal facilities have deteriorated steeply. Electricity supply has been described as 'nerve racking.' Blackouts have been chronic and often extended up to two weeks resulting in the loss of equipment, spoilage of food, and loss of many hours of work. Between 1976 and 1989, the electricity supply declined by 54 per cent. Food supply and malnutrition are areas which suffered. One report suggested that a 40.5 per cent malnutrition rate existed among children 12 years-old or younger. Food prices have escalated to incredible proportions so that people on fixed incomes, such as teachers and public servants, have abandoned their jobs for part time trading, and engage in corrupt and illegal activities on the job, or have quit outright. In the health area, the health services have suffered such shortages that patients need to purchase their own drugs, bandages, plaster, lint, etc. Most medical doctors and many nurses have migrated. To obtain drugs and medical supplies, the average Guyanese relies on relatives and friend overseas. Some of these drugs are found in the 'parallel' market smuggled in from Venezuela and Brazil, but with no guarantee to their safety. It has been estimated that large numbers of people have died from inadequate medical care. The public hospitals have been compared to torture chambers.

The breakdown of the infrastructure of social services, the soaring prices and the fall in wages have registered their effects in part on the crime rate. One researcher referred to this phenomenon as the 'criminalisation of the population' (Canterbury, 1990:4). The burglary rate increased by 149.3 per cent from 1973 to 1989. In the courts, male convictions increased by 293 per cent and female convictions by 124 per cent for the period between 1973 and 1988 (Canterbury, 1990). At the same time, police services declined and bribery and corruption in the constabulary became normal. The government reinstated the death penalty for major crimes, but its own officers are often among the perpetrators of crime. The impact of these conditions was not evenly distributed. While a few persons actually prospered from the 'parallel black market' and the economic collapse, the broad base of Guyanese, all the way from the middle to the lowest classes and of all ethnic groups, suffered. Guyanese emigrated in droves. It was estimated that about 1,000 in a population of 750,000 people emigrated legally every month. Of these, about half were skilled and semi-skilled. There has been a decline in the population growth since 1975. About three-fourths of **all natural increases in births** migrate.

Accurate statistics on birth and death rates, longevity, nutrition conditions, housing, transport, education, etc. are not available. But the tale of decline and widespread suffering in the wake of the persistence ethnic struggle needs not be told in figures to exist or to be true. After a certain point, no one keeps count on who lives, dies or migrates; or on how deep the poverty and how high the prices go; or the frequency of electricity blackouts or water supply interruptions; or devaluations and corresponding wage declines; or on other vital statistics. Everything seems to get worse rather than better. Economic suffering became a leveller in material well-being for many Indians and Africans. Many inter communal strikes were called and at times. it appeared that a new class society transcending ethnic affiliation was about to be born. A closer examination shows a different picture. Ethnic biases die hard. One ethnic group holds the other accountable for their joint misery. Both, of course, are guilty. The ethnic conflict has not so much disappeared as been re-directed to new arenas of engagement and expression. With new fair and free elections promised by the PNC for Guyana in 1992, there has been a resurgence of ethnic partisan preferences once again for the PPP and PNC. In ethnic affairs, it seems that the more things change, the more they remain the same.

XII Conclusion: Diagnosis and Prescription

As traced out in this work, the features of ethno-nationalism as it emerged, asserted itself, transformed politics, and impacted adversely on development, all attest to a phenomenon that is as pervasive as it is potent in the life of the contemporary multi-ethnic state. In this final chapter, an attempt will be made to abstract the patterns of communal conflict that were generated by the Guyana case with a view towards constructing a framework of ethnic conflict regulation. As such, the effort will be both analytic and prescriptive. The observation must be made at the point of departure that not all multi-ethnic states are alike. Nevertheless, we advance the view that the ethnic phenomenon is universally the same even though its patterns of behaviour may vary in different communal settings.

In the analysis and prescriptions that follow, we will look first at the role of the state as an important actor in contemporary ethnic conflicts. We stay close to our data generated by the Guyana case to show how the colonial state created a multi-ethnic society, how the institutions and practices of the state promoted and exacerbated communal strife, and how much as of this could have been circumvented. We follow this by looking at other forces and features of the 'ethnic state' which contributed to the communal conflict in Guyana. We attempt to set forth recommendations *via de negativa* in constructing what is labelled an 'anti-model'. Put differently, apart from a list of prescriptions which decision-makers should do to regulate ethnic conflict, there is an equally powerful potion of actions emanating from the Guyana case which multi-communal states must seek to avoid at all cost. Together, the positive and negative list of recommendations do not fully comprehend and exhaust the full range in the repertoire of conflict regulation mechanisms which can be derived from studying a collection of dissimilar country cases. We have tried to stay as close as possible to the empirical evidence embodied in the Guyana case, referring only periodically to other country cases of multi-ethnic politics.

A.   The State

Essential to the analysis of Guyana's communal strife is the creation of an 'ethnic state', a concept that alludes to the dissensus in the social demographic structure created by colonialism. The multi-ethnic state in Guyana, as in many parts of the Third World, was a colonial artefact. State and nation were not co-terminous entities; rather, the colonial state deliberately spawned an ethnically segmented social and cultural fabric. The role of the state in the creation of the underlying conditions of communal conflict is therefore critical to an understanding of Guyana's difficulties. In looking at the state, attention is focused not only the policies related to the formation of a multi-ethnic society, but also on the political institutional apparatus through which state power is contested. Specifically, this refers to the competitive parliamentary system which was engrafted onto Guyana as part of the state apparatus and which engaged parties in zero-sum struggles for power.

a) A Zero-Sum Competitive Parliamentary System

When Guyana obtained independence, the state apparatus bequeathed to the local rulers was the most highly articulated and developed set of institutions in the entire society. However, it was trammelled by an institutional political apparatus that tended to accentuate the ethnic segmentation in the society. A particular variant of the imported parliamentary system fashioned on the zero-sum electoral and party system in Britain played a major role in structuring and institutionalising ethnic conflict and competition in the state. In Britain, a body of consensual values had evolved nationally, serving as a means to moderate rivalry over the values of the state. Guyana lacked such a system of settlement over basic issues. The rival parties, linked to discrete ethnic clusters, confronted each other in a manner similar to military warfare over fundamental issues in the form of the society, economy and polity. The salient issue was that the mode of conflict resolution adopted in collective decision-making tended to encourage the formation of ethnic groupings which, in turn, competed for outright control of all the values of the state. Zero-sum parliamentary contests do not encourage sharing or fixed proportions. This meant that the stakes were high in the contest for political power and victory viewed as conquest. A system of pre-arranged results with guaranteed minimum rewards would have tended to depoliticise the intensity and stakes in the contests enabling the defeated a share in the polity and society. This is particularly important in a setting where the constituent elements in the population are cultural communities which share few overarching traditions and institutions. To be sure, there is controversy over the prescription of pre-established shares as a device to regulate ethnic conflict, but this tends to occur in societies such as the United States and Canada which are already relatively integrated. The social structure of these societies bear little resemblance to the fissiporous features which characterise the plural societies in the Third World.

The zero-sum parliamentary contest takes place in the electoral process and, as demonstrated in the chapter on election campaigns in Guyana, the result is a rising crescendo of ethnic tensions over successive elections, thereby exacerbating the sectional divisions that already exist. But, this not the full extent of zero-sum competition for power. The repercussions permeate all aspects of inter-group relations in spheres of social inter-action and daily cross communal communications which were previously benign. The zero-sum electoral struggle, in effect, spills over into and permeates all areas of life, sparking communal fear, suspicion and stereotyping. To contain the competition over power by eliminating zero-sum electoral struggles is to constrain and contain the ravages of ethnic strife in a strategic area of political life.

Could not the system of zero-sum competition for exclusive control of the state be supplanted by an alternative order based on power-sharing? The post-World War II history of Guyana shows how this option availed itself and was lost. In the independence movement, the opportunity was created for a formula for sharing office. The PPP headed by Jagan and Burnham was, however, more preoccupied with winning the first general elections under universal adult suffrage than with inventing a formula for sharing power. Besides, it was not clear that the PPP would win the elections. Moreover, while the popular euphoria in political campaigning submerged all fears and anxieties between Africans and Indians, it was probably unwise to open the potentially contentious issue of power-sharing and resource allocation and invite unnecessary internal friction in the independence movement.

For all of these reasons, no attempt was made to develop a formula for the sharing of power. This is a familiar situation which was also enacted in many multi-ethnic Third World countries that mounted unified struggles for independence. In Guyana, almost immediately after virtual victory over the antecedent colonial regime, the independence party was riven by divisive squabbles over power. Because the jockeying was between the two major charismatic ethnic leaders, the rivalry assumed a communalist connotation to followers. As the internal struggle continued, the inter-ethnic mass following was corrrespondingly fractured. Inter-elite intransigence triggered a situation over which they literally lost control. The opportunity to establish a stable formula for power sharing was overcome by events. Once fed into popular emotions, the chances of a rational solution were greatly diminished.

In Guyana, the opportunity for power sharing was lost to a new order marked by open zero-sum rivalry. After this, the fear of ethnic domination became part of the vocabulary of inter-ethnic interaction. Stated in this way, the stakes in the competition became co-terminous with both the survival of an ethnic group and the state itself. Through a few fortuitous events, one section acquired power and retained it through the armed forces and fraudulent elections. Thereafter, ethnic repression and discrimination ensued and were met by collective ethnic retaliation. A spiral of violence and counter-violence created a situation in which all prosperity ceased.

b) Resource Allocation

Apart from the fact that the state was created and marked by a system of ethnic stratification from the outset, and that at independence lacked a consensus over its basic institutions, it was also in its totality the most well-equipped and endowed apparatus in the society. In many ways, the state was larger than the society. Anyone who captured it could overwhelm the society, bringing it to the service of its own particular interests. Civilian institutions were weak and fragmented and could not rival the state as a countervailing force. The ecclesiastical bodies were divided, the political parties were polarised and the voluntary associations weak and dependent. The main rival political parties, each representing one or the other of the major ethnic groups, recognised the value of capturing the government in its entirety. The strongly centralised state power was so overwhelmingly powerful that it could be used as an instrument for promoting personal ambition as well as ethnic domination, even genocide. It was this sort of predisposing situation in which basic institutional consensus was absent and in which ethnic mass parties operated that invited ethnic politics in its extreme pathological form.

The cultural pluralism, the absence of overarching values and institutions, and the implanting of zero-sum political competitive institutions can, together, be conceived as the predisposing factors which laid the foundation of ethnic conflict in the state, with its attendant destructive effects on all development efforts. The factors that triggered ethnic conflict were clearly identifiable but occurred at different times during the evolution of the problem. These factors were: (1) colonial manipulation; (2) introduction of mass democratic politics; and (3) rivalry over resource allocation. It is necessary to cumulatively conceive of the problem in which these factors at different points served as precipitating 'triggers.' At various times, a particular triggering factor deposited a layer of division which in turn provided the next step for the deposit of a new layer of forces to the accumulating crisis. However, these accumulations could have been neutralised or even entirely reversed by some form of deliberate state intervention. There was nothing inevitable or automatic about the transition from one stage to the next. To be sure, it would appear that after a number of successive reinforcing deposits of divisive forces, a critical mass in momentum had been attained so that every ethnically related issue became magnified and inflammable.

Despite this, many opportunities for change from this compartmentalised stranglehold often avail themselves. There is nothing which says that the colonially-derived communal system should be permanent. Ethnic boundaries are notoriously fluid in rapidly changing environments; ethnically communalised life can be modified so as to submit sectional claims to regulation. Deliberate state intervention can moderate the combustive properties of ethnic mobilisation on which ethno-nationalist leaders strive. One such area of planned intervention relates to the allocation of shares and benefits bestowed by the state.

It is difficult to precisely locate the time when the question of ethnic shares became an issue in the struggle among the communal sections in Guyana. In a sense, the entire colonial pyramidal ethnic structure not only embodied resource allocation, but also explained its existence. The colonial state in Guyana was constituted of a hierarchical ranking of ethnic groups, with the European section occupying the dominant position. Through a colour-class system of stratification, the skewed distribution of values and status was rationalised and regulated. As long as the European retained his pre-eminent position, African-Indian rivalry was restrained. Besides, the separate ethnic compartments provided territorial zones and a buffer against direct rivalry. Inter-ethnic suspicion and fear however, materialised from the moment of the Indians' entry into the society and their subsequent migration from rural areas to towns for government jobs. Indians were cast in the role of a late-comer who diluted the entitlement of the African. When Africans became acculturated to English ways and accepted Christianity and the English school system, this gave them prior and strategic entry into public service positions and to many urban-based jobs in the private sector. Indian acquisition of English education came relatively late, and only after Africans had already consolidated their hold on the lower-level echelon positions available to them in the public and teaching services. Indian-African conflict can therefore be explained by this competition over public jobs and public resource allocation in general.

As independence approached, it became evident that the European section would lose its pre-eminence. How Indians would relate to Africans became a source of anxiety. Already, Indians had started to acquire westernised skills and education. Some had begun to claim jobs in the public and teaching services. Intimations of inter-sectional conflict were already appearing in the immediate post World War II period. Rivalry, especially between middle class Africans and Indians, reared its head at various points in the conflict.

How power and privileges should be distributed between these two dominant groups was, in some ways, an open issue. The transfer from the British political institutional model meant open competition on merit for the allocation of public service jobs. In the long run, this was bound to challenge the African hold on the public service and, given the rapid growth and education of the Indian population, convert an unranked African-Indian ethnic system into one that was ranked, thus lending itself not to a system of regulated sharing, but to a new hierarchical system of ethnic differentiation. This eventuality was not, however, inevitable.

It is easy to overestimate the importance of the material basis of ethnic conflict by making it the single most significant factor in communal strife, as the Marxist-Leninist political economy school does. If it were true that this material basis was the main explanation of communal conflict, one would expect that with enough jobs being created, this competition and conflict would diminish and disappear. The evidence from the Guyana case suggests that in many occupational sectors where jobs were available in plentiful supply, African-Indian antagonisms persisted. Transposed overseas and no longer in competition with each other over jobs and resources, Guyanese Africans and Indians continue the ethnic feud with even greater intensity. It is therefore necessary to place this resource allocation variable in a facilitating role which is significant, but not determinant, in the outcome of communal conflict. Put differently, the regulation of resource competition can act as a significant brake on the movement of the society into polarised warring camps.

c) Need for Capability to Suppress Inter-Ethnic Violence

Ethic violence seems to have the special combustive ability to overwhelm all rationality and engulf the entire society in total war of all against all. For this reason, control of ethnic strife to non-physical disagreements is essential to the prospect of restoring harmony. Besides, open warfare tends to add a new, almost indelible encrustment of complaints and grievances that drive communities farther apart.

To be sure, there was considerable ethnic tension among Guyana's communal sections, but much of this, at least during the colonial period, was regulated by rituals of interaction that confined and concealed the strains. For all practical purposes Guyana, like many ethnically segmented societies, was quietly but perpetually at war with itself. Surrogates for physical violence suffused the system. These encompassed such forms as rivalry around the celebration of their respective religious holidays, competition in business and government, etc. Stereotypes which tended to belittle and depreciate entire communal sections nevertheless served as a defence mechanism that offered a private and quiet victory of the mind over the communal opponent. However, they also tended to dehumanise ethnic enemies, setting the stage for violence. When democratic politics and mass parties were introduced, and ethnically-based parties emerged, these underlying stereotypical antipathies were harnessed to them. The new collective forces accentuated ethnic hostilities. Competition at elections tended to provide the occasion for these antagonisms to be vented openly; often, political campaigns seemed like military engagements. All of this kept the society unstable and continuously lingering on the brink of violence.

Collective ethnic violence occurred in civil war proportions in Guyana between 1963-1964 as the two major political parties confronted each other over the control of the government. In many ethnically-mixed villages, where a preponderance of either Indians or Africans resided, ethnic violence or its threat occurred against the minority group. This sort of 'ethnic cleansing' led to the migration of these minorities from these villages, adding to the concentration of self-segregated communal residential settlements in Guyana. For many months, protracted ethnic violence convulsed the small multi-ethnic state until British troops were called into restore order.

For many Guyanese, the civil war, marked by ethnic violence, was a traumatic event that led to irreversible commitment to communal solidarity. While it was true that throughout Guyanese history, Africans and Indians had maintained tense relations marked by mutual suspicion and covert hostility, the outbreak of physical violence seemed to have crossed the psychological threshold of no return to cross-cultural cordiality.

A new level of ethnically oriented physical violence was unleashed in Guyana when in 1968, the African-based PNC government, with police and army support, rigged the elections. The legitimacy of the government was lost and opposition challenges mounted. Over the next decade, the size of the coercive forces expanded dramatically. Expenditures for them increased by over a thousand times. What emerged was a state apparatus with no legitimacy which sought to maintain its power and control by repressing its communal enemies. The Burnham regime, however, did not go about physically exterminating its ethnic enemies. Rather, a system of non-violent terror was established to control the behaviour of its opponents. State institutions such as the courts were ethnically politicised and converted into instruments of communal discrimination.

The Indians responded to state terror and the threat of violence by sabotaging the economy. Since the economic system under colonial rule had resulted in a coincidence of economic specialisation and ethnic concentration, this meant that unless all segments co-operated, the economy could fall apart. Hence, African control of the public service was utilised as the lever to destabilise the Indian-based Jagan government, while Indian control of the sugar and rice industries was used to sabotage the African-led Burnham government. Economic inter-dependence invited mutual sabotage.

The impact of persistent Indian strikes and boycotts in the economic sector accompanied by mass migration and the loss of essential skills from Guyana, reverberated adversely on all ethnic groups alike. Economic collapse imparted universal suffering. African workers, who like Indian workers under the Jagan government had supported discriminatory policies, soon felt the full brunt of the diminishing economy and a bankrupt government. When they went out on strike for more pay and for job security, the state apparatus turned its coercive arsenal against them. When the regime unleashed violence against its own communal members, it treated them as if they were misguided and had betrayed an ethnic trust. The communal members of the regime who opposed the government were made special objects of terror and violence. They were treated as traitors with the sort of passion and hate that only brothers could concoct against each other.

Under these circumstances, it is necessary for the state to become strong in order to contain dissent, especially that which comes from its ethnic adversaries. However, the capability to contain violence is clearly not enough to regulate such violence in multi-ethnic states. One additional ingredient is vital. The institution charged with administering law and order, including the police and the judiciary, must be multi-ethnic in composition. In some ways, this is almost impossible to implement because those who govern are likely to have relied on the ethnic composition of the coercive institutions in bringing them to power. To alter the composition of these institutions may be tantamount to committing political suicide. There is however, no way around this kind of police force, apart from one supplied by an external mediator such as the United Nations. In the end, this can only be a temporary device albeit one that can recruit and train a multi-ethnic force so as to detribalise it and render it neutral and formidably effective in controlling all outbreaks of ethnic violence.

B.   Will and Compromise

One of the grievous harms caused by persistent and protracted strife in a multi-ethnic society, is the loss of will and capability to reconcile. After many years of ongoing communal struggle, it appears that a feeling of fatalism enters through the backdoor of consciousness, compelling the battered psyche to accept the ethnic battle lines and the necessary adaptations to them as inevitable and permanent. A new socio-cultural architecture of human settlement and communal interaction emerges with ethnic roles and social institutions defined in neat niches of unholy compromises and concordances. Usually, while the struggle continues, an odd sort of social stability in personal and group relations emerges and persists. It is, in effect, a dual-level social structure, one marked by clever cordiality, the other more subterranean, marked by communal anger, hate, plots and silent violence.

A broken will, enfeebled and unprepared for reconciliation, emerges reinforced by countless symbols of old battles, won and lost, as well by organisations and interests which institutionalise and structure the conflict. To be sure, at any earlier time, the leaders and elites in the various ethnic communities are able to communicate and beat out compromises for inter-communal co-existence. But as the conflict continues and deepens, even this upper layer becomes a victim of inter-communal intransigence. The ethnic monster devours everyone in the end.

Compromise and co-operation are at the very heart of the developmental process. This is true of all social structures, integrated and divided alike. The democratic fabric is constituted not only of substantive give-and-take in beating out public policy, but is under girded by a culture and psychology of mutual trust in exchanges. The mortar of co-operation and compromise maintains the integrity of the edifice of society. In the multi-ethnic states of the Third World, the tension in working out mutually satisfactory exchanges is often over-strained by the fact the cleavages and differences are ethnicised. Protracted institutional ethnic conflict is the stuff out of which a culture and psychology of co-operation are undermined, rendering collective development difficult if not impossible.

Compromise and co-operation are embodied in devices for conflict resolution. In Guyana, compromise and co-operation came alive and were implemented in the first unified independence movement under the original PPP. Internal differences, accompanied by external manipulation, torpedoed the coalition of personalities and interests that held the PPP together. Thereafter, even in the midst of the ethnic division that ensued, many efforts at restoring the old compromises in unity were made, but as one party captured power and then maintained it by electoral fraudulence, the two ethnic groups drew farther apart and the periodical talk of a government of national unity assumed the air of a mechanical public relations exercise. Each group settled into its own ugly niche in an ethnically-influenced structure, and actually sustained each other in their respective camps. With the will to compromise broken, the new forms of conflict resolution assumed the form of a divorce.

C.   The Guyana Anti-Model

Theorists must be willing to examine both failed and successful cases in ethnic conflict in order to adduce evidence towards a framework of ethnic conflict resolution. In this regard, the Guyana case can be conceived as an 'anti-model.' It tells more of what not to do, since Guyana committed many of the critical false steps that catapulted the state towards a disastrous destination. As an 'anti-model,' the Guyana case points to the destructive role of leaders who put private ambition before the long term interests of citizens in a unified state. The leadership factor is clearly critical; practically alone, it was accountable for both the successful communal mobilisation of each section, making it possible to pressure the colonial power out of Guyana and, at the same time, was primarily culpable in launching the state into an irretrievable tailspin of ethnically-ignited passions that led to collective catastrophe.

If it is true that, in the actions of the main communal leaders after they won the elections of 1953, they led Guyana down the road to communal self-immolation, it is equally accurate to assert that in the immediate pre-1953 elections period they had discovered a formula for inter-ethnic unity. This was incorporated in the organisation of the independence movement itself. The lessons show that multi-ethnicity is not inevitably destructive. It can be harnessed for constructive ends. In Guyana, ethnic sentiments were mobilised during the independence movement and harnessed to a multi-ethnic mass party which promised to mobilise the collective energies of citizens from culturally diverse communities towards the development and transformation of the state. In the successful effort at cross-communal accommodation between 1950-1953 reside suggestive ingredients for a theory of consolidation. How did a broadly-based cross-communal party emerge? What factors featured in the amalgam and which ones were critical and peripheral in the process? Can the process be repeated and generalised in other multi-ethnic states? From 1950 to 1953 the Guyana case does generate some important insights, such as the role of recognising the identity and interests of the separate communities, the importance of leaders in the different communities subordinating their private ambitions to the larger goal of maintaining peace in a just distribution of values, the value of compromise and a mechanism to resolve ongoing disputes free from the immediate pressures of outbidders and mass passions, the search for a mutually agreeable formula for sharing jobs, titles, and political offices, the need to exclude external actors who tend to intervene for their own goals and the importance of evolving institutions and practices for a shared citizenship. Together, the presence of some but the absence of others of these factors caused the independence movement to disintegrate into discrete ethno-nationalist parts.

The Guyana 'anti-model' also points to the lack of understanding of the dynamics of the ethnic factor once it has been aroused and directed to promote rival communal claims for jobs, self-protection and self-assertion. It was clear that the communal leaders, while cultivating and feeding the ethnic monster

191

for practical gain, could not constrain it to rational appeal and national reconstruction thereafter. They became victim to a monster of their own creation; did they not understand that the nature of the ethnic creature was so uncontrollable and volatile that they could not be masters of it, but would in time be captured by it instead? The Guyana case describes the descent into a vertigo of self-reinforcing, ethnically-charged forces once ethnic solidarity was entertained for narrow political gain. Political leaders in multi-ethnic states can learn from the Guyana 'anti-model', as well as from similar cases, about the irrational features of the ethnic factor. Ethnic solidarity, when properly harnessed, can contribute to identity formation and energise a state towards development, but when antagonistically attached to rival communities occupying the same territory and government, as almost inevitably tends to be the case, it can wreak irreparable harm and havoc.

The Guyana 'anti-model' has its institutional lessons. While on one hand it can be argued that a participant democratic system is essential for the establishment of legitimate authority and for the mobilisation of citizens for development challenges, it is clear from the Guyana case that an institutional competition party system with its zero-sum implications for the distribution of power and privileges is inappropriate for the maintenance of elementary order and stability in multi-ethnic states. After the leadership split between the two communal leaders in 1955, successive electoral campaigns conducted in a zero-sum warlike combat, exacerbated ethnic strife in Guyana probably more than any other factor.

In the Guyana experience between 1950 and 1953, an example of consociation and accommodation was successfully experimented with. Institutional engineering can seek to depoliticise many areas of contention such as minority rights, distribution of jobs and contracts, and the protection of cultural identity, etc. In the consociational arrangement set forth by Arend Lijphart, the main ingredients of an accommodation are a coalition government and a system of proportional sharing of values (Lijphart, 1977). A coalition is clearly required and its forms and variations can be many. Its main limitation pertains to the secret diplomacy that accompanies the deliberations of sectional elites in working out the terms of a compromise package for rule. Professor Brian Barry warned against the 'elite cartel' as advocated by Lijphart, especially underlining the potential for secret inter-elite negotiations to become self-serving class coalitions (Barry, 1975). The 'proportionality principle' in the Lijphart model of consociation pertains directly to problems in the Guyana 'anti-model' (Premdas, 1986). A familiar interpretation of the ethnic conflict in Guyana coming from Marxists in the political economy school argues that the struggle for material rewards explains the struggle (Premdas and Hintzen, 1982). Put differently, if the issue of rewards can be settled or depoliticised, then the conflict will disappear. The Guyana 'anti-model' case illustrates the limitations of the 'politics of preference' or 'resource allocation' school. It aptly points to the irrational nature of ethnic conflict, showing that even where material resources ceased to be a variable, in the context of the shared poverty of both Indians and Africans, the communal strife persisted. To be sure, resource allocation served as a major instigator of ethnic conflict in Guyana, especially among the middle classes of both Indians and Africans (Horowitz, 1985). Nevertheless, when Indians and Africans migrated to overseas destinations and became well-off and were no longer in competition with each other for scarce resources, they continued their communal antipathies and animosities.

What perhaps explains the persistence of the ethnic conflict from a materialist and a resource allocation perspective even better is the idea of 'relative deprivation' and 'comparative advantage'. Donald Horowitz underscored the role of this factor, noting that even when ethnic communities identified with a particular regime have been impoverished, they continue to support 'their government' simply to keep out an alternative regime with a better potential for performance but associated with an ethnic community (Premdas, 1993). The resurgence of ethnic solidarity in Guyana, which hurt everyone after years of repression, confirms Horowitz's perception.

The Guyana 'anti-model' also contains abundant materials on the process of withdrawal and escape mainly through mass migration. Engaged in an intense struggle that was psychologically and economically damaging to the well-being of both of the ethnic communities, Guyanese sought refuge everywhere and anywhere. Some left for adjacent Suriname, Venezuela, and Brazil, while most migrated legally and illegally to North America, literally voting with their feet after having lost the franchise at home. The great loss of people only added to the impoverishment of the Guyanese people. To those who ruled and who survived as opposition politicians, the lesson was clear: population loss meant the debilitating destruction of the state in an area that defined the very viability of its existence - the loss of people in haemorrhaging proportions. The people who left, many middle class, were, however, the very people who had espoused ethnic attachment but who later found it convenient to escape from the very abode that they had lit afire. The paradox of the situation underscores the larger point that the ethnic monster consumes its own children and makes a mockery of ethno-nationalist pretences to *patria* and group loyalty. In the end, everyone wants out. The highest aspiration of the Guyanese child is not to be physician or professor but simply to escape by migration. This aspect of the 'anti-model' has created much cross-communal cynicism of politicians and the polity among Guyanese as a whole. The very 'outbidders' who appeal to ethnic sentiment and mobilise followers to hate and violate the ethnic enemy runs away from the holocaust that he/she ignites. The true believer in ethnic solidarity becomes nauseated to the extent that he/she takes flight. Ethnic loyalty and fanaticism spawn their own disloyalty and alienation.

Another feature of general use that can be derived from the Guyana 'anti-model' refers to the manner in which early initial and limited ethnic actions progressively spreads like a cancer to take over and reorganise the entire state into communal compartments. At all levels – parties, unions, associations, parliaments, the public service, private businesses, corporations, armies, churches, etc. – the entire system and all its institutions are suffused by the ethnic toxin. To be sure, in early colonial times, the seeds of division were laid so that residential, occupational, and value cleavages separated the communities. What the ethnicisation of a state entails is the release of the arsenal of latent prejudices into active hate and discrimination, erecting a garrison state of ethnic encampments and armies. Little room for tolerance and cross-communal institutions exists thereafter. The system is choked to death by its own arteries which are filled with hate. The Guyana 'anti-model' shows that the ethnic factor can be appropriately likened to the embrace of a hostile octopus. The tentacles spread everywhere and squeeze the state into paralysis. At the same time that the ethnic sectors are consolidated and fossilised by the ethno-nationalist parties and leaders, hypocritical talk of cross-communal amity increases among the very politicians who promote ethnic loyalty.

This brings us to the element of 'hypocrisy' displayed in the Guyana 'anti-model.' Both the ruling and opposition parties in Guyana's ethnically bipolar state openly professed to be Marxist with class-based interests but were, in fact, preponderantly ethnically-based groupings. They spun out an elaborate system to parade a picture of representing and promoting cross-sectional interests. They decorated their organisations with a facade of officers from the other cultural community. They sported Marxist-Leninist jargon *ad nauseum* and in public conducted their debate as if ideological issues were most significant. Overseas observers believed in this cynical circus, but the local citizens who knew what the game was about did not. The practice of deliberately camouflaging the colour of partisan politics is most probably a pattern of public denial that is found in democratic politics in other multi-ethnic Third World countries. What the Guyana 'anti-model' suggests is that leaders are often quite aware of what course of action is morally correct but cleverly seek to conceal their defiance of this moral ethic by engaging in repugnant hypocritical behaviour. The ethnic monster is seen by all as loathsome, yet it is indulged. Ethno-nationalist leaders are allowed to parade before the international community not as pariahs who pander to ethnic and racial sentiments, but as persons pretentiously in genuine pursuit of toleration and cross-communal nation-building. The Guyana 'anti-model' suggests the need for critical monitoring and international exposure of such hypocritical behaviour. That apart, the Guyana case points to a moral dilemma that ethno-nationalist leaders face, on one hand needing to cater to ethnic appeals in order to retain sectional popularity and on the other, needing cross-communal endorsement to obtain regime legitimacy and govern effectively.

Yet another perspective that can be derived from the Guyana 'anti-model' pertains to the role of international actors in exacerbating the internal divisions in a multi-ethnic state. External actors, be they other states or private groups, have their own interests to pursue. They are sometimes economic predators such as those multi-national corporations which see some benefit from taking one side or the other in the communal conflict. There are also political predators such as regional states, which may have geo-political designs in entering an ethnically-ignited internal fray. Also, and very frequently, there are diaspora communities which have spilled over from the ethnic conflict and have been created in enclaves in other countries. In North America, many Guyanese citizens have settled in ethnic ghettos and engage in support roles in sustaining the ethnic conflict at home. The Guyana case points to the internationalisation aspects of the ethnic conflict in all of its diverse dimensions. The Cold War actors found surrogate partisan support in the ethnically split Guyanese state. This was a main force in exacerbating communal tensions. The regional geo-political factor was played by Venezuela and Surinam. Even today, the diaspora Guyana communities in North America and Britain play an active part in providing funds for the persistence of ethnic strife in Guyana. In effect, the Guyana 'anti-model' draws attention to the proposition that internal ethnic conflicts tend to invite external actors which may add fuel to the ethnic division in the state. This is not to argue that the impact of external actors is always negative. Sometimes, external intervention is required to prevent genocide or even to offer third party assistance in conflict resolution. However, as the Guyana case suggests, the persistence, if not the exacerbation of the ethnic strife, is often caused by the role of external actors in the internationalisation of the conflict.

Finally, the Guyana 'anti-model' suggests an examination of the related issues of partition and secession. At one time, partition seemed to be a desirable solution and on one occasion, an Amerindian group sought secession from Guyana in order to join Venezuela. The Guyana case shows the potential, although probably not as well as other cases such as Nigeria and Yugoslavia, of ethno-nationalist movements, mutating into separatist claims. Often this is either a consequence of attempted genocide or an invitation to genocide. In either case, partition, secession and genocide all carry ethnic conflict to the brink of no-return in reaching reconciliation. Once civil war has broken out, secession has been sought and genocide committed, a new qualitative stage in the ethnic conflict has been reached.

Together, and in other ways, the Guyana 'anti-model' is rich with lessons of what not to do lest disaster in manifold economic, political, and psychological dimensions be courted. The Guyana case raises anew the familiar question of what makes a society coherent and what makes a society truly a society. Most of the multi-ethnic Third World states have been created through colonial rule, arbitrary boundary-drawing and population transfers. They face the problem of designing an appropriate political system to accommodate the rival claims of their terminal ethno-nationalist communities. The record in this regard is one replete with the wreckage of Third World states which have, instead, succumbed to communal violence and instability, ethnic domination and repression, and instances of genocide and secession. This can be avoided. First the ethno-nationalist force must be understood in its workings and dynamics, and then this knowledge can be applied towards ethnic conflict resolution and inter-communal co-existence. Without this first step, there can be no development. The Guyana case offers insights into the challenge of national-reconciliation and nation-building and national development in the Third World.

Bibliography

Adelman, M. (1964) *The Symbolic Uses of Politics*, University of Illinois Press, Urbana

Anderson, B. (1983) *Imagined Communities*, Verso, London

Armstrong, A. (1982) *Nations Before Nationalism*, University of North Carolina Press, Chapel Hill, North Carolina

ASCRIA (African Society for Cultural Relations with Independent Africa) (1968) *Teachings of the Cultural Revolution*, Bovell Printery, Georgetown

Ayearst, M. (1969) *The British West Indies: The Search For Self-Government*, New York University Press, Washington

Banton, M. (1967) *Race Relations*, Tavistock, London

Banton, M. (1983) *Ethnic and Racial Competition*, Cambridge University Press, Cambridge

Barry, B. (1975) 'The consociational model and its dangers', *European Journal of Political Research*, Vol.3, No.4, December

Barth, F. (ed) (1969) *Ethnic Groups and Boundaries*, Universitetsforlaget, Bergen

Bendix, R. (1969) *Citizenship and Nation-Building*, Doubleday, New York

Blackman, B.B. (1947) 'Introducing the labor party', *The Weekly Herald*, 5 October

Blanshard, P. (1947) *Democracy and Empire in the West Indies*, Macmillan, New York

Bradley, C.P. (1961) 'The party system in British Guyana and the General Election of 1961' *Caribbean Studies*, October

Braithwaite, L. (1953) 'Social Stratification in Trinidad', *Social and Economic Studies*, Vol. II, Nos. 2 and 3

Breuilly, J. (1982) *Nationalism and the State*, University of Manchester Press, Manchester

197

British Guyana Labour Union (BGLU) (n.d.) *Rule Book of the British Guyana Labour Union*, mimeo., Georgetown

Burnham, L.F.S. (1955) 'Our party - its Tasks', *Thunder*, Part 1, November

Burnham, L.F.S. (1968) *Address by the Hon.L.F.S. Burnham to the 11th Congress of the People's National Congress*, Daily Chronicle Press, Georgetown, 14 April

Burnham, L.F.S. (1969) *Towards a Cooperative Republic*, Chronicle Publishers, Georgetown

Burnham, L.F.S. (1970) *Destiny to Mould*, Longman Caribbean, London

Burnham, L.F.S. (1979) *Towards a People's Victory*, Guyana Printers Ltd., Georgetown

Canterbury, D.C. (1990) *Production and Social Services in Rural Guyana*, paper presented at the Caribbean Institute of Rural Development, Trinidad and Tobago, July 17-19

1960 Census (1961) Vol. 2, Government Printery, Georgetown

Caribbean Contact (1976) 'Farewell to booker's empire', March

Caribbean Contact (1980) 'The Rodney Affair: Assassination or accident?', June, p.26

Catholic Standard (Guyana) (1982) 24 October, p.1

Chase, A. (1964) *A History of Trade Unionism in Guyana, 1900-1961*, New Guyana Co., Georgetown

Chronicle (Guyana) (1947) 'Final results', 28 November, p.1

Chronicle (Guyana) (1956) 'New red move to take over B.G.', 22 December p.1

Chronicle (Guyana) (1976) 'Stand firm - evil forces at work', 2 June, p.20

Clementi, C. (1937) *A Constitutional History of British Guyana*, MacMillan, London

Commonwealth Advisory Group (1989) *Guyana: The Economic Recovery Programme and Beyond*, Commonwealth Secretariat, London, August

Commonwealth Secretariat (1980) *Report of the International Team of Observers at the Elections of Guyana in December 1980*, London

Connor, W. (1972) 'Nation-building or nation-destroying?', *World Politics*, Vol. 24, April

Connor, W. (1973) 'The politics of ethno-nationalism', *Journal of International Affairs*, Vol. 28, No. 7

Cullen, J. (1948) 'Tribes of the Guyanas', in J. Stewart (ed.), *Handbook on South American Indians*, Smithsonian Institution, Washington D.C.

Daly, V.T. (1966) *A Short History of the Guyanese People*, Daily Chronicle Press, Georgetown

Danns, G. (1980) 'Militarisation and development in Guyana', *Transition*, Vol. 2, No. 2, Guyana

DeCaries, D. (1979) 'Intense political pressures on Guyana's judicial system', *Caribbean Contact*, June

Despres, L.A. (1967) *Cultural Pluralism and Nationalist Politics in British Guyana*, Rand McNally, Chicago

Drewnowski, J. (1972) 'Social indicators and welfare measurement: Remarks on methodology', *Journal of Development Studies*, Vol. 8, No. 3, April

Emerson, R. (1966) *From Empire to Nation*, Harvard University Press, Cambridge, Massachussetts

Enloe, C. (1973) *Ethnic Conflict and Development*, Little and Brown, Boston

Esman, M. (ed.) (1977) *Ethnic Conflict in the Western World*, Cornell University Press, Ithica, New York

Farley, R. (1954) 'The rise of the peasantry in British Guyana', *Social and Economic Studies*, Vol. 2

Financial Times (London) (1978) 5 May, p.1

Fried, M. (1956) 'Some observations on the Chinese in British Guyana', *Social and Economic Studies*, Vol. 5, 9 March

Furnivall, J.S. (1939) *Netherlands India: A Study of Plural Economy*, Cambridge University Press, Cambridge

Furnivall, J.S. (1948) *Colonial Policy and Practice*, Cambridge University Press, Cambridge

Geertz, C. (ed) (1963) *Old Societies and New States*, Free Press of Glencoe, Evanston, Illinois

Gellner, E. (1983) *Nations and Nationalism*, Basil Blackwell, Oxford

Ghai, D., M. Hopkins, and D. McGranahan (1988) *Some Reflections on Human and Social Indicators*, United Nations Institute for Social Development, Geneva

Glaser, N. (1975) *Ethnicity: Theory and Experience*, Harvard University Press, Cambridge, Massachussetts

Glasgow, R.A. (1970) *Guyana: Race and Politics Among Africans and East Indians*, Martinus Nijhoff, The Hague

(*Government Information Services (GIS)* (1966) 'Economic Survey of Guyana', Georgetown

Greene, J.E. (1974) *Race versus Politics in Guyana*, University of the West Indies, Jamaica

The Graphic (Guyana) (1968) 'Guyana Trades Union Council endorses People's National Congress for workers support in December 16 elections', 14 December, p.8

The Graphic (Guyana) (1969) 'P.M. announces to people the Hinderland', 28 May, p.2

The Graphic (Guyana) (1974) 'Burnham warns U.S. aid may be cut off', Georgetown, 28 October, p.2

Guyana Institute of International Affairs (GIIA) (1968) 'End of racial pressure groups', Vol. 1, September

Guyana Update (GU) (1984) 'Lawyers call for an investigation into police brutality', London, September-October

Hamaludin, H. (1976) 'PPP's attitude today', *Sunday Chronicle*, 12 September

Hayes, C.J.H. (1948) *The Historical Evolution of the Modern State*

Hechter, M. (1985) *Internal Colonialism*, University of California Press, Berkeley

Hintzen, P. (1976) 'Civil military relations in Guyana and Trinidad', (mimeo), Berkeley, California, 6 June

Hobsbawn, E. (1992) *Nations and Nationalism*, Cambridge University Press, Cambridge

Horowitz, D. (1985) *Ethnic Groups in Conflict*, University of California Press, Berkeley

Issacs, H. (1975) *Idols of the Tribe*, Harper and Row, New York

Jagan, C. (1966) *The West on Trial*, Michael Joseph, London

Jagan, C. (1970) *Guyana's Economic Situation and Future Prospects Against the Background of World Poverty*, The New Guyana Co. Ltd., Georgetown

Jagan, J. (1973) *Army Intervention in the 1973 Election in Guyana*, New Guyana Co., Georgetown

Jagan, J. (1963) *History of the PPP*, New Guyana Co., Georgetown

Jayawardena, C. (1963) *Conflict and Solidarity on a Guyanese Plantation*, Athlone Press, London

Jayawardena, C. (1966) 'Religious belief and social change: Aspects of the development of Hinduism in British Guyana', *Comparative Studies in History and Society*, Vol. 6, January

Kedourie, E. (1960) *Nationalism*, Hutchinson, London

Keyes, C.F. (1981) *Ethnic Change*, University of Washington Press, Seattle

Kohn, H. (1944) *The Idea of Nationalism*, MacMillan, London

Lane, R. (1965) *Political Life*, The Free Press of Glencoe, Evanston, Illinois

La Palombara, J. and M. Weiner (1960) 'The origin and development of political parties', in J. La Palombara and M. Weiner (eds.), *Political Parties and Political Development*, Princeton University Press, New Jersey, p.28

Latin America Bureau (LAB) (1976) 'United we stand', in *Latin America*, London, 4 June

Latin America Bureau (LAB) (1979) 'Guyana: Burnham jolted', in *Latin America*, Vol. 13, No. 28, London, 20 July

Latin America Bureau (LAB) (1984) *Guyana: Fraudulent Revolution*, London

Lens, S. (1965) 'American Labor Abroad', *The Nation* (U.S.A.), 5 July

Lent, J.A. (1982) 'Mass media and Socialist governments in the Commonwealth Caribbean', *Human Rights Quaterly*, Vol. 4, No. 3, Fall

Leroux, P. (1980) 'Jonestown Nation', *The Nation* (U.S.A.), 15 November

Lijphart, A. (1977) *Democracy in Plural Societies*, Yale University Press, New Haven

Lipset, S.M. (1960) *Political Man*, Doubleday, New York

Litvak, J. and C. Maule (1975) 'Foreign firms: social costs and benefits in developing countries', *Public Policy*, Spring

Lustick, I. (1979) 'Stability in deeply divided societies: Consociationalism and control', *World Politics*, Vol. 31, No.3, April

Maha Sabha (n.d.) *Rules of the Sanatan Maha Sabha*, Angal Printery, Georgetown

Mandle, J. (1976) 'Continuity and change in Guyanese underdevelopment', *Monthly Review*, Vol. 21, No.2

Mark, F.X. (1964) 'Organised labor in British Guyana' in F. Andic and T.G. Mathews (eds.), *The Caribbeanin Transition*, University of Puerto Rico Press, Puerto Rico

Melson, R. and H. Wolpe (1970) 'Modernisation and communalism', *American Political Science Review*, 64

Menezes, M.N. (1973) 'The Dutch and Indian Policy of Indian subsidy', *Caribbean Studies*, Vol. 13, No.3

Milne, R.S. (1982) *Politics in Ethnically Bipolar States*, University of British Columbia Press, Vancouver

Milnor, A.J. (1969) *Elections and Political Stability*, Little and Brown, Boston

Ministry of Information (Guyana) (1980) *1980 Census*, Georgetown

Munroe, C. (1980) 'Burnham given broader powers', *Guardian*, New York, 15 October

Narine, S. (1974) 'Public servants not forced to join the PNC', *Graphic*, Guyana, 20 December

Nath, D. (1950) *A History of Indians in British Guyana*, Thomas Nelson and Sons, London

Newman, P. (1964) *British Guyana: Problems of Cohesion in an Immigrant Society*, Oxford University Press, London

Newsletter (1984) No.4, Guyana Embassy, Washington, D.C., September-December, p.1

New World (NW) (1965a) 'Independence', Vol. 1, No. 15, 28 May

New World (NW) (1965b) 'The Rice Bill', Vol. 1, No. 17, 15 June

New World (NW) (1965c) 'Independence', Vol. 1, No. 17, 15 June

New World (NW) (1965d) 'The dirty game of politics', Vol. 1, No. 18, 9 July

New World (NW) (1965e) 'The independence game', Part 3, Vol. 1, No. 20, 6 August

New World (NW) (1966a) 'Rice and politics', Vol. 1, No. 36, 18 March

New World (NW) (1966b) 'The trades union situation', Vol. 1, No. 40, 13 May

New World (NW)(1966c) 'National security', Vol. 1, No. 49, 10 October

New World (NW) (1968) 'Immigration', Vol. 1, No. 43, August

Nyerere, J. (1968) *Freedom and Development*, Oxford University Press, Dar-es-Salaam

Omag, J. (1976) 'U.S. blamed for campaign to destabilise Guyana', *Guardian*, London, 21 March

The Political Affairs Committee Bulletin (PACB) (1946a) 'The aims of the Political Affairs Committee', 6 November

The Political Affairs Committee Bulletin (PACB) (1946B) 'The cooperative way for British Guyana', 6 November

Pearson, D. (1964) 'U.S. faces line-holding decision', *Washington Post*, 31 May

People's National Congress (PNC) (1964) *The New Road*, B.G. Lithographic Co., Georgetown

People's Progressive Party (PPP) (1962) *Twelve Years of the PPP*, New Guyana Co., Georgetown

Premdas, R. (1977) 'Ethno-nationalism, copper and the secession', *Canadian Review of Studies in Nationalism*, Vol. 4, No. 2

Premdas, R. (1982) 'Guyana: Changes in ideology and foreign policy', *World Affairs*, Fall

Premdas, R. (1986) 'The politics and preference in the Caribbean', in Nevitte and C. Kennedy (eds.), *Ethnic Preference and Public Policy in Developing States*, Lynne Rienner, Colorado

Premdas, R. (ed) (1993) *The Enigma of Ethnicity: Ethnic and Race Relations in the Caribbean and the World*, School of Continuing Education, University of the West Indies, Trinidad

Premdas, R. (1994) 'Guyana: The politics of resource competition', in B. Samaroo (ed.), *Indians and Race Relations in the Caribbean*, Macmillan, London

Premdas, R. and P. Hintzen (1982) 'Guyana: coercion and control in political change', *Journal of Inter-American Studies and World Affairs*, Vol. 24, No.3

Rabushka, A. and Shepsle, K. (1972) *Politics in Plural Societies*, Merill Lynch, Ohio

Race and Class (1979) 'Repression in Guyana', Vol. 21, No. 2, Autumn

Report of the British Guyana Commission of Inquiry on Racial Problems in the Public Service (1965a) International Commission of Jurists, Geneva

Report of the British Guyana Constitutional Commission (1950) HMSO, Colonial No.280, London

Report of the British Guyana Constitution Conference (1960) HMSO, London

Report of the British Guyana Independence Conference, 1962 (1962a) HMSO, London

Report of the British Guyana Independence Conference, 1962 (1962b) MSO, London

Report of a Commission of Inquiry into Disturbances in British Guyana in February 1962 (1962b) Her Magesty's Stationery Office (HMSO), No. 354, London

Report of a Commission of Inquiry into the Sugar Industry in Guyana (1968) Government Printery, Georgetown

Report of the Demba Panel of Consultants on Community Attitudes and Their Effect on Industrial Relations, Chairman Ival Oxaal (1968) Government Printery, Georgetown

Report on the General Elections of Members of the General Assembly (1953) Government Printery, Georgetown

Report on the General Elections of Members of the Legislative Assembly, 1961 (1962c) Government Printery, Georgetown

Report on the General Elections of 1957 (1958) Government Printery, Georgetown

Report of the International Team of Observers at the Elections of Guyana in December 1980 (1980) Commonwealth Secretariat, London

Reid, P.A. (1968) *Our Rice Industry- Its Future*, Government Printery, Georgetown

Rex, J. and D. Mason (eds) (1986) *Theories of Ethnic and Race Relations*, Cambridge University Press, Cambridge

Rice Producers Association (RPA) (1968) *The Government and the Rice Industry*, Labour Advocate Press, Georgetown

Rice Review (1965) 'Industry faces crisis', Guyana Rice Producers Association, Vol. 7, No.1

Rodney, W. (1980) 'Voices of revolutions', *Guardian*, New York, 2 July

Rodway, J. (1912) *Guyana: British, Dutch and French*, T. Fisher and Unwin, London

Rothschild, J. (1981) *Ethno-Politics*,Columbia University Press, New York

Ruhomon, P. (1946) *Centenary History of the East Indians in British Guyana, 1838-1938*, The Daily Chronicle press

Saunders, A. (1969) 'Amerindian Attitudes and Integration', *New World*, Vol. 1, January

Saunders, A. (1987) *The Powerless People*, Macmillan,London

Schermerhorn, R.A.(1970) *Comparative Ethnic Relations*, University of Chicago Press, Chicago

Schlesinger, A. Jr. (1965) *A Thousand Days*, Houghton Mifflin Co., London

Sheehan, N. (1967) 'C.I.A. men aided strikes in Guyana against Dr. Jagan', *New York Times*, 22 February

Shibutani, T. and K.M. Kwan (1965) *Ethnic Stratification: A Comparative Perspective*, MacMillan, New York

Simms, P. (1966) *Trouble in Guyana*, Allen and Unwin, London

Singer, P. and E. Araneta (1967) 'Hinduisation and Creolisation in Guyana', *Social and Economic Studies*, Vol. 16, 9 September

Singh, R. (1973) 'Look at these facts and see if you can rejoice', *Sunday Graphic*, 22 July

Skinner, E.P. (1960) 'Group Dynamics and Social Stratification in British Guyana', in V. Rubin (ed.), *Social and Cultural Pluralism in the Caribbean*, Annals of the New York Academy of Sciences, New York

Smith, A.D. (1981) *Ethnic Revival in the Modern World*, Cambridge University Press, Cambridge

Smith, A.D. (1986) *The Ethnic Origins of Nations*, Basil Blackwell, Oxford

Smith, M.G. (1965) 'Institutional and political conditions of pluralism', in L. Kuper and M.G. Smith (eds.), *Pluralism in Africa*, University of California Press, Berkeley

Smith, R.T. (1956) *The Negro Family in British Guyana*, Routledge, Kegan and Paul, London

Smith, R.T. (1959) 'Some social characteristics of Indian immigrants to British Guyana', *Population Studies*, Vol. 32, July

Smith, R.T. (1962) *British Guyana*, Oxford University Press, London

Smith, R.T. (1976) 'Race, class, and political conflict in a post-colonial society', in S.G. Neumann (ed.), *Small States and Segmented Societies*, Praeger, New York

Stavenhagen, R. (1988) 'Ethnic conflict: An agenda for research' (mimeo.), paper presented at a UNRISD conference on Ethnicity and Development, Geneva

Stone, J. (1977) *Race, Ethnicity, and Social Change*, Duxbury Press, North Seituate

The Sun (1968a) 'Peter hits out', 24 August, p.1

The Sun (1968b) 'Let's vote for a change', 14 December, p.7

Sunday Argosy and Evening Post (1963) 'Il Grace', 1 December, p.3

Sunday Mirror (Georgetown, Guyana) (1969) 'PPP says 'No' to West Indian immigration', 1 June, p.1

Sunday Mirror (Georgetown, Guyana) (1975) 'Dr. Jagan's Address (PPP Annual Convention)'. 7 August, p.9

Sunday Times (London) (1968) 'Has Guyana's election been already decided', London, 15 December, p.5

Tajfel, H. (1970) 'Experiments in inter-group relations', *Scientific American*, Vol. 223, No.5

Thomas, C. (1983) 'State capitalism in Guyana', in F. Ambursely and R. Cohen (eds.), *Crisis in the Caribbean*, Monthly Review Press, New York

Thunder (1950) 'Aims and programmes of the PPP', Vol. 1, No. 4, April pp.6-7

Trades Union Council (TUC) (1964) *The Freedom Strikers: an Account of the 1963 TUC General Strike*, Georgetown

Truman, D.B. (1967) *The Governmental Process*, Alfred A. Knopf, New York

United Force Party (UFP) (1964) *The Communist Martyr-Makers*, Georgetown

van den Berghe, P. (1967) *Race and Racism: A Comparative Perspective*, Wiley and Sons, New York

van den Berghe, P. (1978) 'Race and ethnicity: A socio-biological perspective', *Ethnic and Racial Studies*, 4

Wagley, C. (1960) 'The Caribbean culture area', in V. Rubin (ed.), *The Caribbean: A Symposium*, Washington University Press, Seattle

The Weekly Gleaner (1976) 'Jagan: Guyana not yet a Socialist state', Jamaica, 19 September

Williams, E. (1964) *Capitalism and Slavery*, Andre Deutsch, London

World Council of Churches (WCC) (1982) 'Guyana: Situation report', in *Newsletter of the Inter-Church Committee on Human Rights in Latin America*, Geneva, March/April

Young, A. (1958) *The Approaches to Local Self-Government in British Guyana*, Longmans, Green and Co., London

Young, C. (1976) *The Politics of Cultural Pluralism*, University of Wisconsin Press, Madison, Wisconsin

Young, C. (1993) 'The dialectics of cultural pluralism: Concept and reality', in C. Young (ed.), *The Rising Tide of Cultural Pluralism: The Nation-State at Bay?*, University of Wisconsin Press, Madison

Research in Ethnic Relations Series

Ethnicity, Class, Gender and Migration
Greek-Cypriots in Britain
Floya Anthias

The Migration Process in Britain and West Germany
Two Demographic Studies of Migrant Populations
Heather Booth

Perceptions of Israeli Arabs: Territoriality and Identity
Izhak Schnell

Ethnic Mobilisation in a Multi-cultural Europe
Edited by John Rex and Beatrice Drury

**Post-war Caribbean Migration to Britain:
The Unfinished Cycle**
Margaret Byron

**Through Different Eyes: The Cultural Identity of
Young Chinese People in Britain**
David Parker

**Britannia's Crescent: Making a Place for Muslims
in British Society**
Danièle Joly

Religion, Class and Identity
The State, the Catholic Church and the Education
of the Irish in Britain
Mary J. Hickman

**Migration, Citizenship and Ethno-National Identities
in the European Union**
Edited by Marco Martiniello